L sson Mast rs B

UC**S**MP
SCOTTFORESMAN

✓ W9-AHH-755

THE UNIVERSITY OF CHICAGO SCHOOL MATHEMATICS PROJECT

GEOMETRY

SCOTTFORESMAN INTEGRATED MATHEMATICS

Further practice on
SPUR objectives

 ScottForesman
A Division of HarperCollinsPublishers

ScottForesman
Editorial Offices: Glenview, Illinois
Regional Offices: Sunnyvale, California • Tucker, Georgia
Glenview, Illinois • Oakland, New Jersey • Dallas, Texas

Contents

ISBN: 0-673-45789-3

1 2 3 4 5 6 - MH - 0 0 9 9 9 8 9 7 9 6

LESSON MASTER 1-1 B

Vocabulary

1. **a**. The tiny dots that make images on television
   screens, computer monitors, and calculator
   displays are called ___?___.   _____

   b. What is a *matrix*?

   _____

   _____

   c. What does it mean if computer screen A has better
   resolution than computer screen B?

   _____

   _____

   _____

Skills Objective A: Draw discrete lines.

In 2–4, match the phrase with the diagram.

2. vertical discrete line   _____   **a.** ● ● ● ● ● ●

3. oblique discrete line   _____   **b.**

4. horizontal discrete line   _____   **c.**

5. Draw two oblique discrete lines
   that intersect in a point.

6. Draw a horizontal discrete line
   and a vertical discrete line that
   cross but do not have a point
   in common.

▶ **LESSON MASTER 1-1B** *page 2*

Properties Objective F: Given a property of points and lines, tell whether it is
true in discrete geometry.

**In 7–9, tell whether the statement is *true* or *false*
in discrete geometry.**

7. A point is a dot. _____

8. A line has no thickness. _____

9. Two crossing lines intersect in a point. _____

Uses Objective J: Use discrete geometry to model real-world situations.

---

10. Use the matrices at the right
    to create your initials.

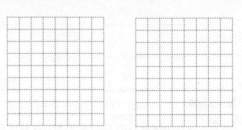

11. Use Seurat's technique
    of drawing with dots to
    draw a flower.

12. Draw a picture of a sign
    formed by light bulbs. Use
    a message that you might
    see on such a sign.

LESSON MASTER 1-2 B

Vocabulary

1. Explain what it means when a number line is *dense*.

   _____

   _____

Properties Objective F: Given a property of points and lines, tell whether it is true in synthetic geometry.

In 2–4, tell whether the statement is *true* or *false* in synthetic geometry.

2. A point is a physical dot.   _____

3. A line has no thickness.   _____

4. A line extends in two directions.   _____

5. When two points are exact locations, how
   many lines contain the two points?   _____

6. Refer to the number line at the right.

   a. Give a possible coordinate
      for point *Y*.

   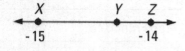

   _____

   b. How many points are there between
      points *X* and *Z*?

   _____

Uses Objective I: Apply the definition of distance to real situations.

7. Timmy placed his foot on a 12-inch ruler. It
   stretched from the $3\frac{1}{2}$-inch mark to the end of
   the ruler. How long is Timmy's foot?   _____

8. On a vacation, the Ortegas drove at an average
   speed of 51.5 miles per hour the first day and
   63 miles per hour the second day. How much
   faster was their average speed the second day? _____

9. From a roll of wax paper, Marcia tore off a piece and saw the imprinted message, "12 feet remaining." Several days later she tore off a piece that read "5 feet remaining." How much wax paper was there between messages? _____

10. According to the 1995 *Information Please Almanac,* the record high temperature on Earth was recorded at 136° F in Libya in 1922. The record low temperature is -129° F in Antarctica in 1983. How much hotter is the record high than the record low? _____

In 11–13, refer to the table of air distances in miles given below.

	Cairo	Hong Kong	London	Rio de Janeiro	San Francisco
Cairo		5061	2181	6146	7364
Hong Kong	5061		5982	11,021	6897
London	2181	5982		5766	5357
Rio de Janeiro	6146	11,021	5766		6621
San Francisco	7364	6897	5357	6621	

11. How much closer is London to Cairo than London is to San Francisco? _____

12. Which trip is shorter, London to Hong Kong to San Francisco, or London to Cairo to Rio de Janiero? _____

13. If you fly directly from Rio de Janiero to Hong Kong, how much shorter is the trip than if you fly from Rio de Janiero to San Francisco and then to Hong Kong? _____

Representations Objective K: Determine distance on a number line.

In 14 and 15, refer to the number line at the right.

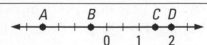

14. Find each distance.

   a. *CD* _____   **b.** *AD* _____   **c.** *BC* _____

15. **a.** If *H* is on the number line and *DH* = 10, what are two possible coordinates of *H*? _____ _____

   b. If *M* is on the number line and *CM* = 6, what are two possible coordinates of *M*? _____ _____

LESSON MASTER

Vocabulary

1. **a.** Another name for the coordinate plane is ____?____ .

   _____

   b. For whom is the answer in Part **a** named?

   _____

2. Give the standard form of an equation for a line.

   _____

Properties   Objective F: Given a property of points and lines, tell whether it is true in plane coordinate geometry.

In 3–5, tell whether the statement is *true* or *false* in coordinate geometry.

3. A point is a number.   _____

4. A line is a set of ordered pairs.   _____

5. A curve is a set of ordered pairs.   _____

6. Give coordinates for a point on the *x*-axis.   _____

7. Give coordinates for a point on the *y*-axis.   _____

Representations   Objective L: Graph points and lines in the coordinate plane.

In 8–13, graph the point on the coordinate plane. Label the point with its letter name.

8. A (4, 1)   9. B (3, -2)

10. C (-5, -5)   11. D (0, 4)

12. E (-4, 0)   13. F (-2, 2)

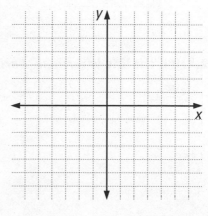

▶ **LESSON MASTER 1-3B** *page 2*

In 14–19, find two points on the line with the given
equation. Then graph the line on the coordinate plane.

14. $y = -3x$

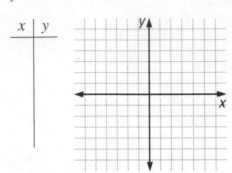

15. $y = 2x + 3$

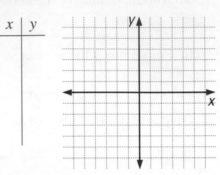

16. $2x + y = 4$

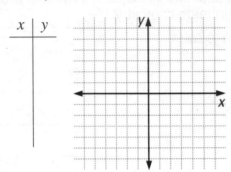

17. $x = -5$

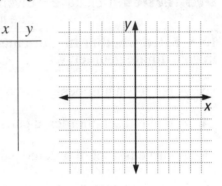

18. $y = 4$

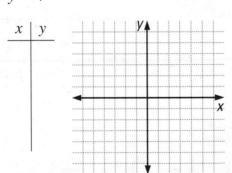

19. $x - 3y = 1$

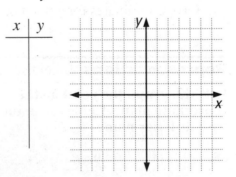

In 20–22, tell if the line is *vertical*, *horizontal*, or *oblique*.

20. $3x + 8y = 22$ _____

21. $x = 12$ _____

22. $y = 1550$ _____

LESSON MASTER 1-4 B

Skills Objective B: Analyze networks.

1. Consider the network at the right.

   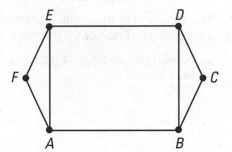

   a. How many even nodes are there? _____

   b. How many odd nodes are there? _____

   c. Is the network traversable? If so, identify a path.

   _____

2. Consider the network at the right.

   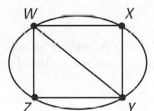

   a. How many even nodes are there? _____

   b. How many odd nodes are there? _____

   c. Is the network traversable? If so, identify a path.

   _____

3. Draw a network with 4 nodes and 6 lines.

Properties Objective F: Given a property of points and lines, tell whether it is true in graph theory.

In 4–7, tell whether the statement is *true* or *false* in graph theory.

4. A point has a size. _____

5. Two points lie on no more than one line. _____

6. A line may contain just one point. _____

7. A line is dense. _____

▶ **LESSON MASTER 1-4B** *page 2*

Uses Objective J: Use graph theory to model real-world situations.

8. The diagram at the right shows the floor plan of a drug store. The heavy lines are the aisles.

   a. Model the aisles as a network of nodes and lines.

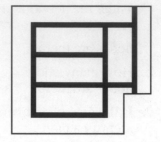

   b. Would a customer be able to walk down each aisle exactly one time? Justify your answer.

   _____

   _____

9. At the right is a diagram of World Wonders Amusement Park. The stream through the amusement park is crossed by 5 bridges.

   a. Represent the bridges and land masses as a network of nodes and lines.

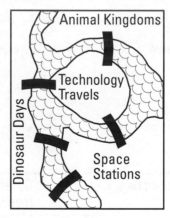

   b. Is the network traversable? Justify your answer.

   _____

   c. Suppose another bridge is to be built. Can it be built so the network of 6 bridges is traversable? If so, draw it in the diagram of the amusement park.

   _____

LESSON MASTER

1-5
B

Vocabulary

1. In a realistic perspective drawing, vanishing points lie on the ____?____ , which is also the horizon line. _____

Skills Objective C: Make and analyze perspective drawings.

In 2–5, determine whether the drawing is a perspective drawing. Write *yes* or *no*.

2. _____

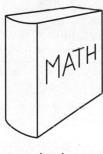

book

3. _____

chair

4. _____

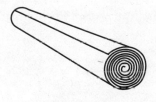

roll of carpet

5. _____

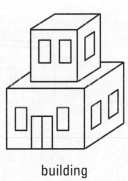

building

6. Draw the hidden lines in the cube below.

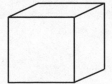

7. Draw a cube in perspective, showing the hidden lines.

▶ **LESSON MASTER 1-5B** *page 2*

8. Draw the picture below in perspective.

trees on a highway

In 9–12, locate the vanishing point(s) in the drawing.

9.

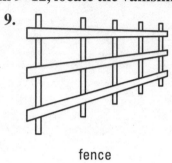

fence

10.

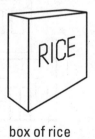

box of rice

11.

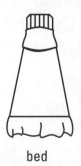

bed

12.

skyscraper

LESSON MASTER

1-6
B

Properties Objective E: Give the dimensions of figures and objects.

**In 1–6, give the number of dimensions of the figure or object.
Ignore small thicknesses.**

1. a number line

_____

2. a cube

_____

3. a point (as a location)

_____

4. a carton

_____

5. a toothpick

_____

6. a sheet of paper

_____

Properties Objective G: Recognize the use of undefined terms.

7. **a.** Explain *circularity*.

_____

_____

   b. Explain how defining the word *decay* might lead
   to circularity.

_____

_____

_____

8. Name three undefined geometric terms used in
   your textbook.

_____ _____ _____

9. Name three undefined algebraic terms or phrases
   used in your textbook.

_____ _____ _____

10. What is a *figure*?

_____

11. What is the *space* of a geometry?

_____

In 12–15, write a description of "point" for the type of geometry given.

12. discrete geometry

_____

13. graph theory

_____

14. synthetic geometry

_____

15. coordinate geometry

_____

In 16–19, label the line with the type of geometry in which it would appear.

16.

_____

17.

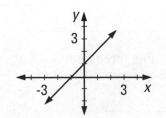

_____

18.

_____

19.

_____

LESSON MASTER   **Questions on SPUR Objectives**

Vocabulary

1. What is a *postulate*?

_____

2. What is a *theorem*?

_____

_____

3. a. Define *parallel lines*.

_____

_____

b. Use symbols to write
"line *m* is parallel to line *n*."   _____

Properties Objective G: Recognize the use of postulates.

In 4 and 5, complete the statement.

4. The postulates for ____?____ geometry fit both
synthetic geometry and coordinate geometry.   _____

5. Refer to the diagram at the right.

a. According to the ____?____ Assumption,
there is exactly one line through points
M and *N*.

_____

b. In symbols, the name of the line
is ____?____ .

_____

c. According to the ____?____ Assumption, all the points
on the line can be put in one-to-one correspondence
with the real numbers with point *M* corresponding
to zero and point *N* corresponding to 1.

_____

6. In the diagram at the right, line *t* is on plane
R. Plane R is in space. Draw two other
points on or outside of plane R. Use the
Dimension Assumption to explain where
these points are located.

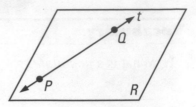

_____

_____

_____

7. Refer to the diagram at the
right. Name all the lines that
appear to be parallel to line *u*.

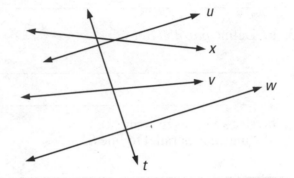

_____

**In 8–10, graph the system of two equations on the same
grid and tell if the lines are parallel.**

8. $\begin{cases} y = x - 1 \\ y = x + 3 \end{cases}$ **9.** $\begin{cases} y = 3x \\ y = 3 \end{cases}$ **10.** $\begin{cases} 2x + y = 3 \\ 4x + 2y = 6 \end{cases}$

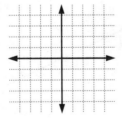   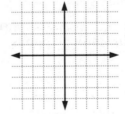   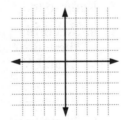

_____   _____   _____

11. Describe a property in discrete geometry that is *not*
true in Euclidean Geometry.

_____

_____

12. Describe a property in graph theory that is *not* true
in Euclidean Geometry.

_____

_____

LESSON MASTER 1-8 B

Vocabulary

1. Points *P* and *Q* are on a number line. The coordinate of point *P* is -3.4 and the coordinate of point *Q* is 7.5. Is a point on the number line with the given coordinate *between P and Q*?

   a. 9 _____   b. 5 _____   c. 0 _____

   d. -2 _____   e. -3 _____   f. 7 _____

   g. -5 _____   h. 7.2 _____   i. 7.5 _____

   j. -3.2 _____   k. 3.5 _____   l. 3.8 _____

Skills Objective D: Recognize and use notation for lines, segments, and rays.

2. Draw $\overleftrightarrow{GH}$.   3. Draw $\overrightarrow{JK}$.   4. Draw $\overline{ST}$.

In 5–11, refer to the diagram at the right.

5. Name the line in three different ways.

   _____

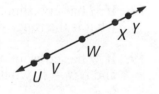

6. In three different ways, name the ray with endpoint *X* that contains point *W*.   _____

7. In two different ways, name the segment with endpoints *X* and *U*.   _____

8. Name the ray opposite to $\overrightarrow{VU}$.   _____

9. Is $\overrightarrow{XY}$ the same as $\overrightarrow{YX}$?   _____

10. Is $\overline{XY}$ the same as $\overline{YX}$?   _____

11. Is $\overline{WX}$ the same as $\overline{WX}$?   _____

12. Draw $\overrightarrow{AE}$ with B between A and E.

13. Draw $\overline{RS}$ with G between R and S and H between G and R.

Properties Objective H: Apply the Distance Postulate properties of betweenness.

In 14–19, refer to the diagram at the right.
N is between M and O.

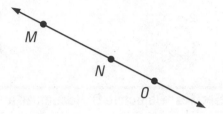

14. If $MN = 8.3$ and $NO = 4.4$, what is MO?

_____

15. If $NO = 13$ and $MO = 34$, what is MN?   _____

16. If $NO = x$, $MN = 2x$, and $MO = 42$, what is x?   _____

17. If $MO = 18$, $MN = 4y$, and $NO = 4$, what is y?   _____

18. If M has coordinate -4 and O has coordinate 3, what is the range of coordinates for N?   _____

19. If M has coordinate -2, N has coordinate 7.6 and $NO = 5$, what is the coordinate of O?   _____

In 20–23, use the number line at the right.
Write an inequality to describe the
coordinates of points on the given figure.

W	X	Y	Z
-20	-10 0 10	20	30

20. $\overrightarrow{WY}$ _____

21. $\overrightarrow{YW}$ _____

22. $\overline{XY}$ _____

23. $\overline{WZ}$ _____

LESSON MASTER **Questions on SPUR Objectives**

2-1
B

Vocabulary

1. Define *convex set*.

_____

_____

_____

Skills Objective A: Distinguish between convex and nonconvex figures.

In 2–10, tell whether the set is *convex* or *nonconvex*.

2.

3.

4.

_____

5.

6.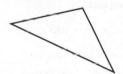

7.

_____

8.

9.

10.

_____

In 11 and 12, draw the figure.

11. a nonconvex 6-sided region

12. a convex 5-sided region

▶ **LESSON MASTER 2-1B** *page 2*

13. Draw a segment showing why the set at the right is *not* convex.

14. Explain why Figure 1 is convex, but Figure 2 is nonconvex.

Figure 1   Figure 2

_____

_____

_____

_____

Review Objective G, Lesson 1-7

In 15–17, complete each statement.

15. Consider the Point-Line-Plane Postulate.

   a. Through any two points, there is ___?___.

   _____

   _____

   b. Given a line in a plane, there is at least ___?___.

   _____

   _____

   c. Given a plane in space, there is at least ___?___.

   _____

   _____

16. According to the Line Intersection Theorem, two different lines intersect in ___?___.

   _____

   _____

17. By definition, lines *c* and *d* are parallel if and only if ___?___.

   _____

   _____

LESSON MASTER 2-2 B

Vocabulary

In 1 and 2, complete the statements.

1. An if-then statement is also called a _____ .

2. In an if-then statement,

   a. the clause following "if" is called the _____

   or the _____ .

   b. the clause following "then" is called the _____

   or the _____ .

Skills Objective C: Use and interpret the symbol ⇒.

In 3–6, write in words with u = today is Tuesday;
v = macaroni is served;
w = school lets out early;
x = we will eat at Dorsey's.

3. $u \Rightarrow w$ _____

   _____

4. $u \Rightarrow v$ _____

   _____

5. $v \Rightarrow x$ _____

6. $w \Rightarrow x$ _____

   _____

Properties Objective G: Write conditionals.

In 7 and 8, underline the antecedent once and the consequent twice.

7. If you were perfect, then you would not need an eraser.

8. Take the bus if the car won't start.

In 9 and 10, rewrite as a conditional.

9. Any dogs in the park must be on a leash.

10. Pentagons have five sides.

▶ **LESSON MASTER** 2-2B *page 2*

Properties Objective H: Evaluate conditionals.

11. Consider the BASIC program at the right.

```
10  INPUT G
20  IF G < 4 THEN PRINT "NONE"
30  END
```

   a. Give a value for G which will cause the printer to print "NONE". _____

   b. When Laura ran the program, the computer did not print anything. Explain why this might have happened.

   _____

In 12 and 13, a conjecture is given. Determine whether each example is an *instance* of the conjecture; a *counterexample* to the conjecture; or *neither* an instance nor a counterexample to the conjecture.

12. If $u > -5$, then u is positive.

   a. $u = -2$ **b.** $u = -12$ **c.** $u = 4$

   _____   _____   _____

13. If a figure is a convex set, then it is a 6-sided region.

   a.   **b.**   **c.**

   _____   _____   _____

Uses Objective K: Apply properties of conditionals in real situations.

14. An ad said "If you purchase your tickets by 6:00, you pay half." Mr. Yi bought his tickets at 5:30. What happened?

   _____

15. If you got at least 82% on the last test, your final grade will be an A. You got 89% on the last test. What will happen?

   _____

16. **a.** Rewrite as a conditional: It is always winter when it snows.

   _____

   b. Is the conditional in Part **a** true? Justify your answer.

   _____

GEOMETRY © Scott, Foresman and Company

LESSON MASTER

2-3
B

Skills Objective C: Use and interpret the symbol ⇒.

In 1 and 2, write the converse of the given statement.

1. $m \Rightarrow n$ _____

2. $h \Rightarrow g$ _____

Properties Objective E: Write the converse of a conditional.

In 3 and 4, *multiple choice*. Choose the correct phrase to complete the statement.

(a) is true   (b) is false   (c) may be true or it may be false

3. If a statement is true, its converse ___?___. _____

4. If a statement is false, its converse ___?___. _____

In 5–12, a. is the conditional true? If not, give a counterexample. b. Write the converse. c. Is the converse true? If not, give a counterexample.

5. If you are in Texas, then you are in Houston.

a. _____

b. _____

c. _____

6. If you are in Nevada, then you are in the United States.

a. _____

b. _____

c. _____

7. If it rains, then you will get wet.

a. _____

b. _____

c. _____

▶ **LESSON MASTER 2-3B** *page 2*

8. If the water boils for 3 minutes, then it boils for 180 seconds.

   a. _____

   b. _____

   c. _____

9. You have more than a dollar if you have eleven dimes.

   a. _____

   b. _____

   c. _____

10. If $x < 8$, then $x < 10$.

    a. _____

    b. _____

    c. _____

11. If $y > 2$, then $y < 14$.

    a. _____

    b. _____

    c. _____

12. A polygon is an octagon if it has eight sides.

    a. _____

    b. _____

    c. _____

Uses Objective K: Apply properties of conditionals in real situations.

13. Suppose T. R. West Bank advertises "If you bank with us you'll earn 6%." Last year Joanna's savings earned 6%. Did she bank at T. R. West Bank? Explain your answer.

    _____

    _____

    _____

GEOMETRY © Scott, Foresman and Company

LESSON MASTER 2-4 B

Vocabulary

1. Write the definition of *midpoint*.

   _____

   _____

2. Write the definition of *circle*. _____

   _____

   _____

Skills Objective C: Use and interpret the symbol ⇔.

In 3–6, write in words with e = **today is Sunday;**
f = **today is the first day of the week;**
g = **tomorrow is Monday;**
h = **yesterday was Saturday.**

3. $e \Leftrightarrow g$ _____

   _____

4. $e \Leftrightarrow f$ _____

   _____

5. $f \Leftrightarrow h$ _____

   _____

6. $g \Leftrightarrow h$ _____

   _____

Skills Objective D: Use the definition of midpoint to find lengths of segments.

In 7–9, use the number line at the right.

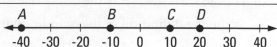

7. Give the coordinate of the midpoint of each segment.

   a. $\overline{AC}$ _____   **b.** $\overline{CD}$ _____   **c.** $\overline{AB}$ _____

   d. $\overline{BC}$ _____   **e.** $\overline{BD}$ _____   **f.** $\overline{AD}$ _____

8. Give the coordinate of E if D is the midpoint of $\overline{AE}$. _____

9. Give the coordinate of F if B is the midpoint of $\overline{CF}$. _____

▶ **LESSON MASTER** 2-4B *page 2*

In 10–12, S is the midpoint of $\overline{PQ}$.

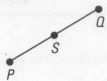

10. Suppose $PS = 3x$ and
    $SQ = 4(x - 1)$. Find PQ. _____

11. Suppose $PQ = 18 - 6e$ and $PS = 7 + e$. Find SQ. _____

12. Suppose $PQ = 5m - 3$ and $SQ = 7m - 15$. Find PS. _____

Properties Objective F: Apply the properties of a good definition.

In 13–15, write a sentence explaining which property of a good definition is violated by these "bad" definitions.

13. A triangle is a polygon that has three sides and these
    three sides form three angles.

    _____

14. A circle is a closed curved figure.

    _____

15. A line segment is the intersection of two faces of
    a polyhedron.

    _____

16. Consider this definition of concurrent lines: Three or more
    lines are concurrent if and only if they intersect in a single
    point. Name two undefined terms used in this definition.

    _____   _____

Properties Objective G: Write biconditionals.

17. Consider this definition for a secant of a circle: A line is a secant
    of a circle ⇔ it intersects the circle in exactly two points.

    a. Write the definition as two conditionals.

    _____

    _____

    _____

    _____

    b. Underline the conditional in Part **a** that goes in the direction
    characteristics ⇒ term.

LESSON MASTER

2-5
B

Vocabulary

1. Write the symbol used for each term.

   a. *union*   **b.** *intersection*   **c.** *empty set*

   _____   _____   _____ or _____

2. Another name for the empty set is the _____ .

Properties Objective I: Determine the union and intersection of sets.

In 3–9, two sets are given. a. Find $G \cup H$. b. Find $G \cap H$.

3. $G = \{-4, -2, 7, 9\}$; $H = \{-8, -2, 6, 7, 10\}$

   a. _____   **b.** _____

4. $G = \{3, 5, 9, 15\}$; $H = \{3, 5, 9, 15\}$

   a. _____   **b.** _____

5. $G = \{-11, 0, 17, 21, 30\}$; $H = \{-4, -3, 1, 19, 26\}$

   a. _____   **b.** _____

6. $G = \{-5, 0, 5, 10\}$; $H = \{-4, 0, 4\}$

   a. _____   **b.** _____

7. $G = \{\ \ \}$; $H = \{7, 77, 777\}$

   a. _____   **b.** _____

8. $G = \{0, 3, 6, 9, 12, 15, 18, \ldots\}$; $H = \{0, 6, 12, 18, 24, 30, \ldots\}$

   a. _____   **b.** _____

9. $G =$ the set of white piano keys; $H =$ the set of black piano keys

   a. _____   **b.** _____

10. Let $J =$ the set of numbers x with $x \geq 4$ and $K =$ the set of numbers x with $x \leq 10$.

   a. Graph J on a number line.   **b.** Graph K on a number line.

     $J:$  $K:$

   c. Graph $J \cup K$ on a number line. ⟵――――――――⟶

   d. Describe $J \cup K$. _____

   e. Graph $J \cap K$ on a number line. ⟵――――――⟶

   f. Describe $J \cap K$. _____

In 11–15, use the diagram at the right. Name the segments or points in each figure.

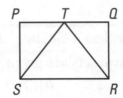

11. $\triangle PTS \cap \triangle QTR$ _____

12. $\triangle PTS \cup \triangle QTR$ _____

13. $\triangle STR \cap PQRS$ _____

14. $\triangle STR \cup PQRS$ _____

15. $\overline{PS} \cap \overline{QR}$ _____

16. Draw two segments $\overline{EF}$ and $\overline{WX}$ so $\overline{EF} \cap \overline{WX} = M$.

17. Draw two rays $\overrightarrow{NO}$ and $\overrightarrow{YZ}$ so $\overrightarrow{NO} \cup \overrightarrow{YZ} = \overleftrightarrow{OZ}$.

Review Objective A, Lesson 2-1

In 18–20, tell whether the set is *convex* or *nonconvex*.

18.

19.

20.

_____   _____   _____

LESSON MASTER

2-6 B

Vocabulary

1. Define *polygon*.

_____

_____

_____

2. Refer to the polygon at the right.

   a. Give two different names for
      the polygon.

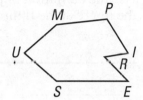

   _____ _____

   b. Name its *vertices*.   _____

   c. Name its *sides*.   _____

   d. Name two *consecutive* vertices. _____

   e. Name two consecutive sides. _____

   f. Draw a *diagonal* and identify it. _____

Skills Objective A: Distinguish between convex and nonconvex figures.

3. Draw a convex hexagon.   **4.** Draw a nonconvex nonagon.

Skills Objective B: Draw and identify polygons.

5. Identify each polygon.

a.   **b.**    **c.** 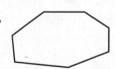   **d.**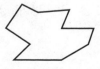

_____   _____   _____   _____

▶ **LESSON MASTER 2-6B** *page 2*

6. *Multiple choice.* Choose the most appropriate drawing.

(i)   (ii)   (iii)

a. equilateral triangle   **b.** scalene triangle   **c.** isosceles triangle

_____   _____   _____

7. Use the definition of polygon to explain why the figure at the right is *not* a polygon.

_____

_____

8. Draw a figure that is the union of five line segments but is not a pentagon.

Uses Objective L: Identify polygons used in the real world.

9. The Math Resource Room has tables shaped like Figure 1 at the right. When group discussion is needed, the tables are put together as shown in Figure 2.

Figure 1

a. Classify the polygon in Figure 1 by the number of sides.   _____

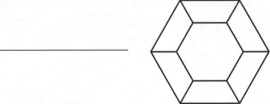
Figure 2

b. The outer edges of the tables in Figure 2 form what type of polygon?   _____

Representations Objective N: Draw hierarchies of triangles and polygons.

10. At the right, draw a hierarchy relating the following terms: polygon, figure, isosceles triangle, scalene triangle, hexagon, pentagon, triangle.

LESSON MASTER

2-7 B

Properties Objective J: Determine whether a triangle can be formed with sides of three given lengths.

In 1–10, can these numbers be the lengths of the sides of a triangle? Justify your answer.

1. 4, 5, 7 _____

2. 4, 5, 9 _____

3. 4, 5, 10 _____

4. 60, 60, 105 _____

5. 8, 16, 8 _____

6. 3, 11, 6 _____

7. 9.8, 4.1, 5.9 _____

8. .73, .98, 1.66 _____

9. $\frac{3}{4}, \frac{1}{2}, \frac{11}{8}$ _____

10. $\frac{2}{3}, \frac{2}{3}, 1$ _____

11. In $\triangle RST$ at the right, how long can $\overline{ST}$ be? _____

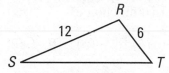

12. In $\triangle ABC$ at the right,

    a. if $AC = 25$ how long can $\overline{BC}$ be? _____

    b. if $BC = 40$ how long can $\overline{AC}$ be? _____

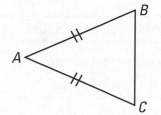

13. Two sides of a triangle are 15 ft and 22 ft. How long can the third side be? _____

14. Two sides of a triangle are 7.3 m and 14.6 m. How long can the third side be? _____

▶ **LESSON MASTER 2-7B** *page 2*

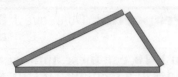

In 15–19, thin rods varying in length from 1 in.
to 24 in. are arranged to form triangles. Each
rod is cut to the nearest whole inch. Two
rod lengths are given. a. Find the minimum
length of the third rod. b. Find the
maximum length of the third rod.

15. 4 in., 6 in.   a. _____   b. _____

16. 7 in., 7 in.   a. _____   b. _____

17. 2 in., 15 in.   a. _____   b. _____

18. 1 in., 1 in.   a. _____   b. _____

19. 18 in., 5 in.   a. _____   b. _____

Uses Objective M: Apply the Triangle Inequality Postulate in real situations.

---

20. At a state park, camp headquarters are 4 km from
the store. The store is 6 km from the ranger's office.
From this information alone, how far is it from
the ranger's office to camp headquarters?   _____

21. *Multiple choice.* Kitchen designers usually plan a
kitchen triangle, the triangular path from the stove
to the refrigerator to the sink. Plans for a new kitchen
place the stove and refrigerator 10 ft apart and the
sink and the stove 6 ft apart. Between the sink and
the refrigerator, which of these distances are possible?
List all choices.   _____

(a) 4 ft   (b) 5 ft   (c) 6 ft   (d) 10 ft   (e) 12 ft   (f) 16 ft   (g) 18 ft

---

Review Objective G, Lesson 1-7

---

22. What is a *postulate*?

_____

_____

23. What is a *theorem*?

_____

_____

_____

LESSON MASTER 2-8 B

Vocabulary

1. What is a *conjecture*?

_____

_____

2. Complete each statement.

   a. A conjecture that is thought to apply to all situations of a particular type is called a _____ .

   b. A conjecture is _____ when it refers to a particular situation.

Properties Objective H: Evaluate conjectures.

In 3–6, tell if the conjecture is *specific* or a *generalization*.

3. Los Angeles has a greater population than Seattle.   _____

4. The area of quadrilateral *DEFG* is 18 square units.   _____

5. The perimeter of $\triangle ABC = AB + BC + AC$.   _____

6. Every person has eight great-grandparents.   _____

In 7–11, a conjecture is given. Determine whether each example is

  (i) an *instance* of the conjecture;

 (ii) a *counterexample* to the conjecture;

(iii) *neither* an instance nor a counterexample to the conjecture.

7. If $n < 0$, $n^3 \geq 1$.

   a. $n = -.3$ **b.** $n = 8$ **c.** $n = -2$

   _____   _____   _____

8. If $x > 0$, then $4 + x > 0$.

   a. $x = 7$ **b.** $x = 0$ **c.** $x = -5$

   _____   _____   _____

9. "i" before "e" except after "c"

   a. receive   **b.** tried   **c.** fancied

   _____   _____   _____

10. If $\overline{AB} \cap \overline{CD} = \{\ \}$, then $\overleftrightarrow{AB}\ /\!/\ \overleftrightarrow{CD}$.

a.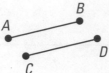

b.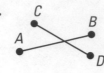

c.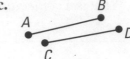

_____   _____   _____

11. If $UV = 2(UW)$, then W is the midpoint of $\overline{UV}$.

a.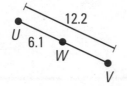

b.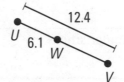

c.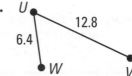

_____   _____   _____

In 12–15, a conjecture is stated. Draw pictures to help you decide whether you think the conjecture is true or false. If you believe it is false, provide a counterexample.

12. If the sides of rectangle *ABCD* are twice the lengths of the sides of rectangle *WXYZ*, then the area of rectangle *ABCD* is four times the area of rectangle *WXYZ*.

_____

13. If the four sides of a quadrilateral are equal in length, then the quadrilateral is a square.

_____

14. If $A \cup B = 8$, and set *B* has 8 elements, then set $A = \{\ \}$.

_____

15. If the vertices of a triangle are the two endpoints of the diameter of a circle and another point of the circle, then the triangle has a right angle.

_____

LESSON MASTER 3-1 B

Vocabulary

1. Define *angle*.

_____

_____

2. Define *bisector of an angle*.

_____

_____

_____

Skills Objective A: Draw and analyze drawings of angles.

3. Refer to the drawing at the right.

   a. Name the *vertex* of the angle.

   _____

   b. Name the *sides* of the angle.

   _____

   c. Give five different
   names for the angle. _____

   d. Shade the *interior* of the angle.

   e. Measure the angle with a protractor. _____

In 4 and 5, refer to the figure at the right.

4. a. Name two distinct straight angles.

   _____   _____

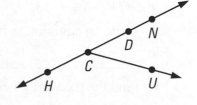

   b. Name two distinct zero angles. _____   _____

5. a. Describe two things you *may* assume from the diagram.

_____

_____

   b. Describe two things you *may not* assume from the diagram.

_____

6. Draw and label an ∠*JFD* with measure 64.

7. Draw and label ∠3 with measure 155.

8. Draw the bisector $\overrightarrow{KE}$ of ∠*K* below.

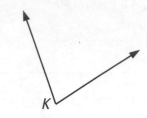

9. Refer to the figure at the right. Find the measure of each angle.

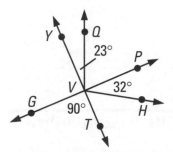

    a. ∠*TVH* _____

    b. ∠*GVH* _____

    c. ∠*GVY* _____

    d. ∠*GVQ* _____

    e. ∠*QVH* _____

    f. ∠*YVH* _____

Skills Objective B: Use algebra to represent and find measures of angles.

10. At the right, m∠*ENR* = 123, m∠*END* = 2*x* + 10, m∠*DNR* = 4*x* + 5. Find *x* and m∠*END*.

    x = _____   m∠*END* = _____

11. At the right, $\overrightarrow{CH}$ bisects ∠*JCZ*, m∠*JCH* = 4*x* + 7, m∠*JCZ* = 10(*x* − 1). Find m∠*JCZ*.

    _____

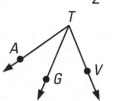

12. At the right, m∠*ATG* = 4*y*, m∠*GTV* = 5(*y* + 1), m∠*ATV* = 8*y* + 13.

    a. Write an equation to find *y*.

    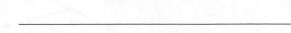
_____

    b. Find the measure of each angle.

_____

Properties Objective H: Give justifications for conclusions involving angles.

In 13 and 14, refer to Question 12.

13. What property did you use in Part **a**? _____

14. Does $\overrightarrow{TG}$ bisect m∠*ATV*? Justify your answer. _____

_____

LESSON MASTER

3-2 B

Vocabulary

1. Complete each statement for the figure at the right.

   a. ∠*SUG* is a _____ .

   b. The "thicker" arc is a _____ arc.

   c. The "thinner" arc is a _____ arc.

   d. What is the degree measure of the minor arc? _____

   e. What is the degree measure of the major arc? _____

2. What are *concentric circles*? _____

Skills Objective E: Draw rotation images and find magnitudes of rotations.

3. Rotate $\overrightarrow{AB}$ 40° about *F.*

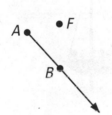

4. Rotate △*HJK* -90° about *D.*

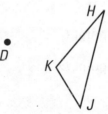

5. Rotate *EMST* 120° about *E.*

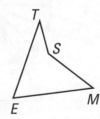

6. *X* is the image of *N* after a rotation about *Z.* What is the magnitude of the rotation?

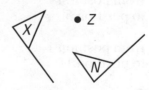

_____

Skills Objective F: Find the measures of central angles and the degree measure
of arcs.

7. Refer to ⊙*T* at the right, in which m∠*GTD* = 45 and
   m∠*WTG* = 67. Find the measure of each arc.

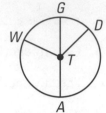

   a. $\overset{\frown}{WG}$ _____

   b. $\overset{\frown}{GD}$ _____

   c. $\overset{\frown}{WD}$ _____

   d. $\overset{\frown}{AGD}$ _____

8. Refer to the concentric circles at the right. Suppose
   m∠*UOP* = 90 and m $\overset{\frown}{RS}$ = 38°. Find each measure.

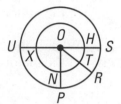

   a. m∠*ROP* _____

   b. m $\overset{\frown}{XT}$ _____

   c. m $\overset{\frown}{UP}$ _____

   d. m $\overset{\frown}{XN}$ _____

Uses Objective I: Apply angle and arc measures in real situations.

9. At the highest point of the Swinging
   Canoe ride, m∠*ABC* = 100. Find
   the measure of the arc swept as point
   A travels

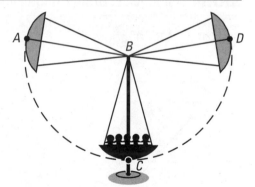

   a. to point *C*. _____

   b. to point *D*. _____

10. Find the magnitude of the given rotation
    of a seat on this Ferris wheel.

    a. from position 1
    to position 2 _____

    b. from position 1
    to position 5 _____

    c. from position 1
    to position 11 _____

    d. from position 8
    to position 16 _____

    e. from position 11
    to position 4 _____

LESSON MASTER

Questions on SPUR Objectives

Vocabulary

In 1–8, match each term with the appropriate figure.

1. *linear pair* _____
2. *obtuse angle* _____
3. *right angle* _____
4. *vertical angles* _____
5. *acute angle* _____
6. *complementary angles* _____
7. *straight angle* _____
8. *non-adjacent supplementary angles* _____

(a)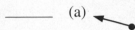

(b)

(c)

(d)  118° 62°

(e)

(f)

(g) 40° 50°

(h)

Skills Objective A: Draw and analyze drawings of angles.

9. Draw and label a pair of vertical angles ∠1 and ∠2.

10. Draw a linear pair. Label the angles ∠3 and ∠4.

11. Draw and label a pair of adjacent angles ∠5 and ∠6.

12. In the diagram at the right, m∠*WVX* = 142. Find the measure of each angle.

    a. ∠*XVY* _____   b. ∠*ZVW* _____

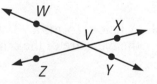

Skills Objective B: Use algebra to represent and find measures of angles.

13. At the right, m∠1 = 4*x* and m∠2 = 6*x* + 5. Find each measure.

    m∠3 _____   m∠4 _____

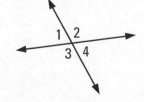

Name _____

14. At the right, $m\angle 8 = 2(3y + 4)$ and $m\angle 6 = 2(y + 34)$.

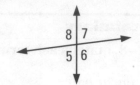

   a. Write an equation to find *y*.

   _____

   b. Explain how you found the equation in Part **a.**

   _____

   c. $y =$ _____ $m\angle 5 =$ _____ $m\angle 7 =$ _____

In 15 and 16, find the measures of both angles.

15. Two angles are complementary. The
   measure of the larger is 6 less than
   3 times the measure of the smaller.   _____ _____

16. Two angles are supplementary. The
   measure of the larger is 54 more than
   8 times the measure of the smaller.   _____ _____

Uses Objective I: Apply angle measures in real situations.

17. A plane is flying 20° north of west.

   a. At the right, draw the path of the plane.

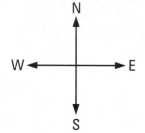

   b. How many degrees must the plane turn to
   change its course to due north?

   _____

18. A ladder forms a 73° angle with the level ground. What is
   the measure of the other angle it forms with the ground?   _____

19. Refer to the barbecue tool pictured at the right. The
   range *x* of possible measures for $\angle 1$ is $24 \le x \le 170$.
   Find the range of possible measures for each angle.

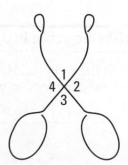

   a. $\angle 3$ _____

   b. $\angle 4$ _____

LESSON MASTER

3-4
B

Properties Objective G: Recognize and use the postulates of equality and inequality.

In 1–10, choose the statement that illustrates the given property.

1. Substitution Property _____

2. Addition Property of Equality _____

3. Addition Property of Inequality _____

4. Equation to Inequality Property _____

5. Multiplication Property of Equality _____

6. Multiplication Property of Inequality _____

7. Reflexive Property of Equality _____

8. Symmetric Property of Equality _____

9. Transitive Property of Equality _____

10. Transitive Property of Inequality _____

(a) If $AB = CD$ and $CD = XY$, then $AB = XY$.

(b) If $x = 35.2 + y$, then $7x = 7(35.2 + y)$.

(c) $m\angle 3 = m\angle 3$

(d) If $m\angle MNO = m\angle ABC$, then $m\angle MNO + 90 = m\angle ABC + 90$.

(e) If $2(UV) = 17$, then $17 = 2(UV)$.

(f) If $14 + 20 = r$, then $r > 14$ and $r > 20$.

(g) If $m\angle F < m\angle G$, then $-2(m\angle F) > -2(m\angle G)$.

(h) If $CY < EF$ and $EF < UR$, then $CY < UR$.

(i) If $m\widehat{CD} = m\widehat{MN}$, then $5(m\widehat{CD}) = 5(m\widehat{MN})$.

(j) If $m\angle P < m\angle Q$, then $m\angle P + 45 < m\angle Q + 45$.

11. **a.** If $m\angle FEG + m\angle GED = 87$ and $m\angle GED = m\angle DEH$ then what can you conclude about $m\angle FEG$ and $m\angle DEH$ using the Substitution Property?

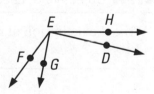

_____

b. If $m\angle FEG = m\angle GED$, and $m\angle GED = m\angle DEH$ what can you conclude using the Transitive Property?

_____

12. **a.** Use the Distance Postulate to write
an equation relating *PQ*, *QR*, and *PR*.

_____

b. Use the Equation to Inequality Property
to write a true statement about *PR* and *QR*.   _____

c. Is it possible to conclude that $QR < PQ$?   _____

13. Suppose m $\widehat{AB} = 180 - x$. Find m $\widehat{AB}$ if

a. $x = 37$.   _____

b. $x = 6d$.   _____

c. What property did you use in Parts **a** and **b**?   _____

In 14 and 15, give the properties used in solving the following.

14. $65 = 4r + 17$ Given

$48 = 4r$ _____

$12 = r$ _____

$r = 12$ _____

15. $-5m - 6 < 34$ Given

$-5m < 40$ _____

$m > -8$ _____

Review Objective D, Lesson 2-4

16. Write the definition of *midpoint*.

_____

_____

**In 17 and 18, use the number line at
the right. The coordinate of *M* is 7.**

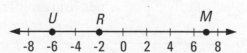

17. Give the coordinate of the midpoint of $\overline{UM}$.   _____

18. Give the coordinate of *N* if *M* is the midpoint of $\overline{RN}$.   _____

LESSON MASTER 3-5 B

Vocabulary

1. Define *proof*.

_____

_____

_____

2. What is a *justification*?

_____

_____

_____

Properties Objective H: Give justifications for conclusions involving angles and lines.

In 3–7 *multiple choice*. Choose the correct justification for the conclusion reached.

3. Given: *D* is between *A* and *G*.   _____

Conclusion: $AD + DG = AG$.

(a) definition of midpoint

(b) Distance Postulate

(c) Addition Property of Equality

4. Given: $\angle 1$ is acute.   _____

Conclusion: $m\angle 1 < 90$.

(a) definition of angle

(b) definition of acute angle

(c) definition of right angle

5. Given: $\angle D$ and $m\angle F$ are   _____
                  complementary.

Conclusion: $m\angle D + m\angle F = 90$.

(a) definition of supplementary angles

(b) definition of right angle

(c) definition of complementary angle

6. Given: ∠1 and ∠3 are vertical _____
angles.

Conclusion: m∠1 = m∠3.

(a) definition of vertical angles

(b) Vertical Angle Theorem

(c) Angle Addition Postulate

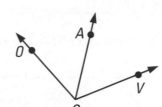

7. Given: m∠OQA = m∠AQV. _____

Conclusion: $\overrightarrow{QA}$ bisects ∠OQV.

(a) definition of angle bisector

(b) definition of adjacent angles

(c) Angle Addition Postulate

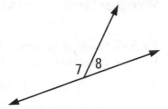

In 8–11, write a justification for each conclusion.

8. Given: ∠7 and ∠8 form a linear
pair.

Conclusion: ∠7 and ∠8 are
supplementary.

_____

9. Given: △JMH is equilateral.

Conclusion: JM = MH = JH.

_____

10. Given: ⊙C.

Conclusion: TC = ZC.

_____

11. Given: HY = YE.

Conclusion: Y is the midpoint of HE.

_____

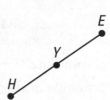

LESSON MASTER

3-6
B

Vocabulary

1. Refer to the figure at the right, in which $j \parallel k$.
   Complete each statement.

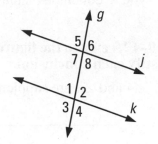

   a. _____ is a transversal for j and k.

   b. $\angle 1$ and _____ are
   corresponding angles.

   c. $\angle 6$ and _____ are corresponding angles.

   d. $\angle 4$ and _____ are corresponding angles.

Skills Objective C: Determine measures of angles formed by parallel lines and
transversals.

In 2–6, refer to the figure for Item 1 above.

2. If $m\angle 4 = 78$, find the measures of every other angle.

   _____

3. If $m\angle 7 = 105$, find the measures of every other angle.

   _____

4. If $m\angle 8 = 3u$, find the measures of every other angle.

   _____

5. If $m\angle 2 = 2(m\angle 1)$, find the measures of every other angle.

   _____

6. If $m\angle 5 = 5(x + 1)$ and $m\angle 1 = 3x + 31$,
   find the measure of $\angle 6$ and of $\angle 2$.   _____ _____

Properties Objective H: Give justifications for conclusions involving angles and
lines.

7. If $r \parallel s$, $s \parallel y$, and $y \parallel e$, what theorem
   allows you to conclude that $r \parallel e$?   _____

8. If line *m* has slope 3.5 and line *f* has slope 3.5, then what theorem allows you to conclude that *m // f*? _____

In 9–12, refer to the figure at the right. Justify each conclusion.

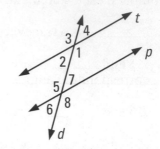

9. ∠4 and ∠1 are supplementary.

_____

10. m∠5 = m∠8.

_____

11. If *p // t*, then m∠5 = m∠3. _____

12. If m∠4 = m∠7, then *p // t*. _____

Representations Objective K: Determine the slope of a line from its equation or given two points on it.

In 13–19, find the slope of the line described.

13. the line containing (3, -5) and (6, 1) _____

14. the line containing (*u, v*) and (*a, b*), with $u \neq a$ _____

15. the line with equation $y = 3x - 1$ _____

16. the line with equation $2x + 5y = -20$ _____

17. Line *r* at the right _____

18. Line *s* at the right _____

19. Line *t* at the right _____

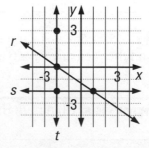

Representations Objective L: Determine the slope of a line parallel to a given line.

20. What is the slope of a line parallel to the line with equation $y = -6x + 5$? _____

21. What is the slope of a line parallel to line *r* shown in the graph for Questions 17–19? _____

LESSON MASTER **3-7 B**   **Questions on SPUR Objectives**

Vocabulary

1. Define *perpendicular.*

_____

_____

_____

2. Two symbols are used to indicate perpendicularity.
Show an example of how each is used and explain
what your examples mean.

Skills Objective C: Determine measures of angles formed by parallel lines,
perpendicular lines, and transversals.

3. At the right, $FE \perp FG$ and
$m\angle EFG = 4(x + 2)$. Solve for x. _____

4. At the right, $m\angle UVR = 54$. Give the measure
of each angle.

a. $\angle RVT$ _____   **b.** $\angle TVS$ _____

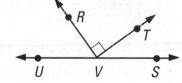

5. At the right, $m\angle 1 = 2(a + 21)$ and
$m\angle 2 = 7a + 6$. Is $QP \perp ON$?

_____

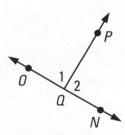

6. Given: $a \perp c$ and $m\angle 3 = m\angle 4$.

a. Is $b \perp c$? _____

b. Is $a /\!/ b$? _____

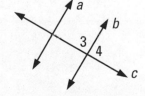

Properties Objective H: Give justifications for conclusions involving angles and lines.

In 7–10, use the diagram at the right.

Given: $\overline{WX} \,/\!/\, \overline{MN}$, $\overline{WX} \,/\!/\, \overline{ZY}$, $\overline{WX} \perp \overline{XY}$.

Multiple Choice. **Choose the correct justification for the conclusion.**

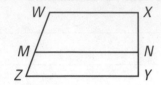

7. $\overline{MN} \,/\!/\, \overline{ZY}$. _____

8. $\overline{ZY} \perp \overline{XY}$. _____

9. $\angle WXY$ is a right angle. _____

10. m$\angle WMN$ = m$\angle MZY$. _____

(a) definition of perpendicular

(b) Corresponding Angles Postulate

(c) Two Perpendiculars Theorem

(d) Transitivity of Parallelism Theorem

(e) Perpendicular to Parallels Theorem

(f) definition of parallel lines

Representations Objective L: Determine the slope of a line perpendicular to a given line.

11. When is the product of the slope of two perpendicular lines not equal to -1? Explain.

_____

_____

In 12 and 13, refer to the graph at the right.

12. Find the slope of any line perpendicular to

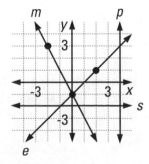

a. the *x*-axis _____   **b.** the *y*-axis _____

c. line *e.* _____   **d.** line *m.* _____

e. line *p.* _____   **f.** line *s.* _____

13. Is $m \perp e$? How can you tell without using a protractor?

_____

LESSON MASTER

3-8 B

Vocabulary

1. a. What is a *bisector* of a segment?

_____

_____

b. What is the *perpendicular bisector* of a segment?

_____

_____

2. What are the only tools that may be used in a construction?

_____

3. Complete the following statement. A(n) _____
is a sequence of steps leading to a desired end.

Skills Objective D: Draw parallel lines, perpendicular bisectors, and
perpendicular lines.

In 4–6, construct and label the required line.

4. *v*, the ⊥ bisector
of $\overline{GH}$

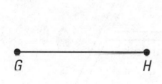

G ———————————— H

5. *e*, the ⊥ bisector
of $\overline{AB}$

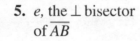
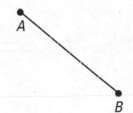

A
B

6. line *f* ⊥ to *y* at *Q*

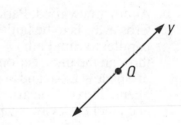

y
Q

7. Use the figure at the right. Use the tools of
your choice to draw the given line.

a. the line through *C* ⊥ to *s*, with the
intersection labeled *K*

b. the line through *C* // to *s*, with the line
labeled *r*

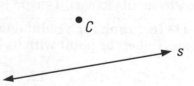

• *C*

s

8. In Question 7, state the relationship between *r* and *s*. _____

Uses Objective J: Apply parallel and perpendicular lines in real situations.

9. **a.** A bridge is to be built connecting point *A* on Highway D to Highway H. Draw the shortest bridge possible.

   b. Highway Y is to be built parallel to Highway H through point *A* on Highway D. Draw Highway Y.

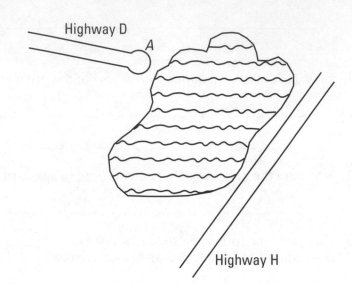

10. **a.** A new road, Shadow Lane, is to be built perpendicular to Elm Path at its midpoint. Construct and label Shadow Lane.

    b. Another new road, Park Crossway, is to be built parallel to Elm Path through the intersection of Shadow Lane and Scenic Drive. Construct and label Park Crossway.

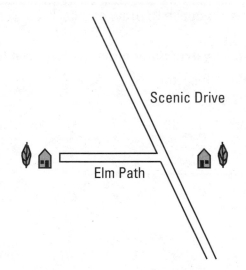

Review Objective L, Lesson 1-3

In 11–16, graph each point on the coordinate plane. Label the point with its letter name.

11. $A = (2, 1)$ 12. $B = (3, -4)$

13. $C = (-4, -4)$ 14. $D = (0, 3)$

15. $E = (-5, 0)$ 16. $F = (2, -2)$

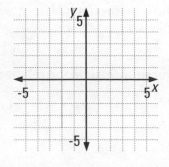

LESSON MASTER 4-1 B

Vocabulary

1. Complete the following definition.

   a. For a point P not on a line m, the *reflection image* of P over line m is the point Q if and only if

   _____ .

   b. For a point P on m, the reflection image of P over line m is

   _____ .

2. **a.** Complete this definition: A *transformation* is a correspondence between two sets of points such that

   _____

   _____

   _____ .

   b. What is another name for transformation? _____

Skills Objective A: Draw figures by applying the definition of reflection image.

3. **a.** Draw $r_e(H)$.

   b. Draw $r_e(K)$.

   c. Draw $r_e(J)$.

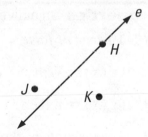

4. Refer to the figure at the right.

   a. $r_a(N) =$ _____

   b. $r_b(N) =$ _____

   c. $r_b(W) =$ _____

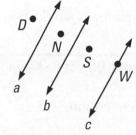

▶ **LESSON MASTER 4-1B** *page 2*

5. a. Draw line ℓ so that $r_\ell(T) = U$. Is line ℓ
unique? Explain.

_____

_____

b. Draw line *m* so that $r_m(T) = T$. Is line *m*
unique? Explain.

_____

6. Use folding and
tracing or a
reflecting tool
to find the
reflection image
of the bird over
line *d*.

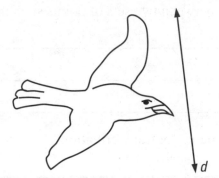

Properties Objective E: Apply the definition of reflection to make conclusions.

In 7–10, *true or false.*

7. If $r_g(X) = X$, then X is on g. _____

8. If $r_g(X) = Y$, then $r_g(Y) = X$. _____

9. If line *u* contains the midpoint of $\overline{AB}$, then $r_u(A) = B$. _____

10. Every transformation is a reflection. _____

Representations Objective K: Find coordinates of reflection images of points
over the coordinate axes.

In 11–16, give the coordinates of each image.

11. $r_{x\text{-axis}}(3, -5)$

12. $r_{y\text{-axis}}(3, -5)$

13. $r_{x\text{-axis}}(0, 6)$

_____ _____ _____

14. $r_{y\text{-axis}}(0, 0)$

15. $r_{x\text{-axis}}(a, b)$

16. $r_{y\text{-axis}}(c, d)$

_____ _____ _____

LESSON MASTER

4-2
B

Skills Objective A: Draw figures by applying the definition of reflection image.
Objective B: Draw reflection images of segments, angles, and polygons over a given line.

1. Draw $r_j(\overline{GH})$.

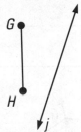

2. Draw $r_k(\Delta XYZ)$.

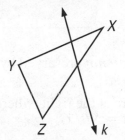

3. Draw $r_{\overleftrightarrow{AB}}(ABCDE)$.

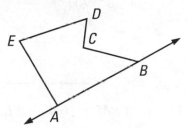

4. Draw $r_m(W)$.

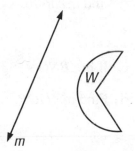

5. Draw a so $r_a(\angle RST) = \angle R'S'T'$.

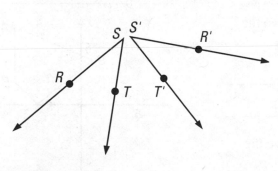

6. Draw b so $r_b(EKHG) = CKOF$.

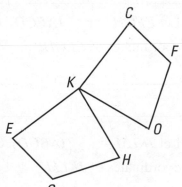

7. At the right, draw and label a
figure showing $r_c(RQTS) = RWTY$.

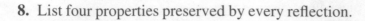

Properties Objective E: Apply properties of reflections to make conclusions.

8. List four properties preserved by every reflection.

_____

_____

9. List a property *not* preserved by reflections. _____

10. Use the figure at the right, where
    $r_{\overleftrightarrow{GN}}(\Delta RMG) = \Delta BPG$.

    a. If m∠P = 46,
       find m∠M.   _____

    b. If m∠BGN = 70,
       find m∠RGB.   _____

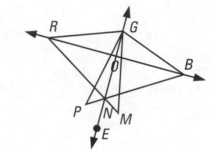

    c. If m∠BNG = 58, find m∠RNE.   _____

    d. Find m∠GOR.   e. If RB = 18, find RO.   f. If RM = 16.4, find BP.

    _____   _____   _____

Representations Objective K: Find coordinates of reflection images of points
over the coordinate axes.

11. a. Let $EFGH = r_{x\text{-axis}}(ABCD)$. Give the
       coordinates of *EFGH*.

       _____   _____

       _____   _____

    b. Let $JKLM = r_{y\text{-axis}}(ABCD)$. Give the
       coordinates of *JKLM*.

       _____   _____

       _____   _____

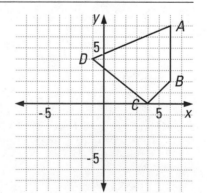

LESSON MASTER 4-3 B

Uses Objective I: Use reflections to find a path from an object to a particular point.

1. Ball *B* is rolling toward a wall without spin. Draw the rest of the path showing how the ball will bounce off the wall. Mark any congruent angles made by this path.

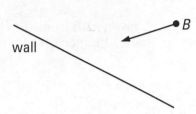

2. Draw the path to bounce ball *N* off the wall and hit ball *M*. Mark any congruent angles made by this path.

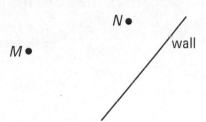

3. Refer to the miniature golf hole at the right.

   a. Is there a direct path from the golf ball *G* to the hole *H*? How do you know?

   _____

   _____

   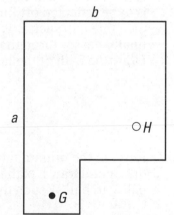

   b. Draw a path from *G* to *H* with a bounce off wall *a*.

   c. Draw a path from *G* to *H* with a bounce off wall *b*.

GEOMETRY © Scott, Foresman and Company

4. Refer to the miniature golf hole at the right.

    a. Draw a path from *G* to the hole at *H* with a bounce off one wall.

    b. Draw a path from *G* to the hole at *H* with a bounce off two walls.

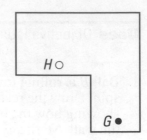

5. Refer to the miniature golf hole at the right. Draw a path from *G* to the hole at *H*.

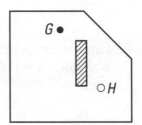

6. Refer to the diagram at the right. A laser beam sent from point *D* is to be reflected off line *m* and then line *n* in such a way that it finally passes through point *E*. Draw the path of the laser beam.

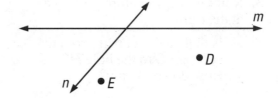

7. Refer to the billiard table at the right. Draw a path from ball *V* to ball *W* such that ball *V*

    a. bounces off wall *a*.

    b. bounces off wall *a* and then wall *b*.

    c. bounces off three walls.

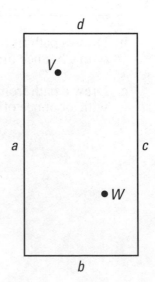

LESSON MASTER

4-4 B

Vocabulary

1. Define *composite* of two transformations S and T.

_____

_____

2. a. Define *translation.*

_____

_____

b. What is the *magnitude* of the translation?

_____

c. What is the *direction* of the translation?

_____

Skills Objective D: Draw or identify images of figures under composites of two reflections.

In 3 and 4, use reflections to draw the image of the figure under the indicated composite.

3. $r_u \circ r_v(\triangle ABC)$

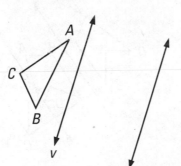

4. $r_p \circ r_q(DEFG)$

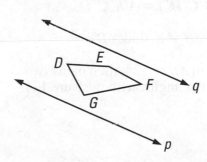

In 5 and 6, use the Two-Reflection Theorem for Translations to draw the indicated image.

5. $r_n(r_m(\triangle HJK))$

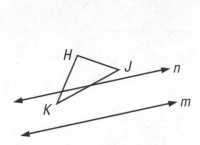

6. $r_h(r_g(RSTU))$

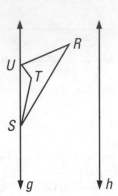

Properties Objective F: Apply properties of reflections to obtain properties of translations.

Objective G: Apply the Two-Reflection Theorem for Translations.

7. List five properties preserved by every translation.

_____

_____

In 8–12, in the figure at the right, $p \parallel q$, $r_q(ABCD) = A'B'C'D'$, **and** $r_p(A'B'C'D') = A''B''C''D''$.

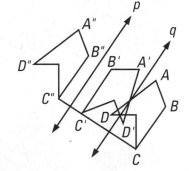

8. If $AB = 8$, find $A''B''$. _____

9. If $m\angle B = 124$, then name two other angles with measure 124. _____ _____

10. State a relationship between $\overline{CC''}$ and p. _____

11. If $DD'' = 25$, then find the distance between p and q. _____

12. If $DD'' = 25$, then give three other distances equal to 25. _____ _____ _____

LESSON MASTER 4-5 B

Vocabulary

1. a. Define *rotation*.

_____

_____

b. Where is the *center* of the rotation?

_____

Skills Objective D: Draw or identify images of figures under composites of two reflections.

In 2 and 3, draw the indicated image.

2. $r_u \circ r_k(\Delta ABC)$

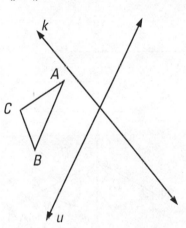

3. $r_c(r_d(WXYZ))$

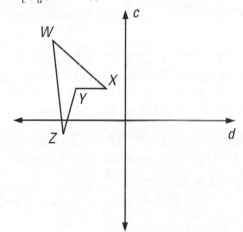

4. Draw $r_{y\text{-axis}} \circ r_{x\text{-axis}}(\Delta PQR)$. Label the image $\Delta P''Q''R''$.

a. Give the coordinates of P, Q, and R.

_____   _____

_____   _____

b. Give the coordinates of P'', Q'', and R''.

_____   _____

_____   _____

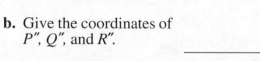

c. What is the image of (a, b) under this rotation? (Hint: Examine your answers in Parts **a** and **b**.)

_____

Properties Objective F: Apply properties of reflections to obtain properties of rotations.
Objective G: Apply the Two-Reflection Theorem for Rotations.

5. List five properties preserved by every rotation.

_____

_____

6. Refer to the diagram at the right. Is $\Delta C'D'E'$ the image of ΔCDE

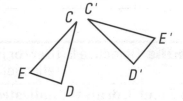

   a. under a rotation? Why or why not?

   _____

   _____

   b. under a reflection? Why or why not?

   _____

7. A figure has been rotated -77°. Give the measure of the acute angle formed by the two lines of reflection that define this rotation.   _____

8. At the right, $A''B''C''D''$ is the image of $ABCD$ under a rotation, and m$\angle NMD = 47$.

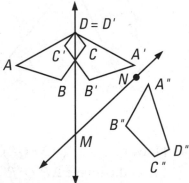

   a. Name the center of the rotation.   _____

   b. What is the direction of the rotation?   _____

   c. What is the magnitude of the rotation?   _____

   d. What is the magnitude of the rotation that maps $A''B''C''D''$ onto $ABCD$?   _____

   e. Find m$\angle CMC''$.   _____

   f. If m$\angle ABC = 110$, then find $\angle A''B''C''$.   _____

9. Can the composite of two reflections ever be both a rotation and a translation? Why or why not?

_____

_____

Name _____

LESSON MASTER 4-6 B

Vocabulary

1. Define *vector.* _____

_____

Skills Objective C: Draw translation images of figures.

In 2–5, draw and label the image of the figure under the translation described by the indicated vector.

2.

3.

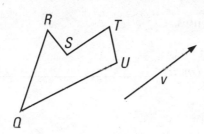

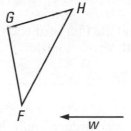

4. $\overrightarrow{AB}$

5. $\overrightarrow{MK}$

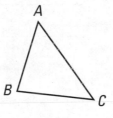

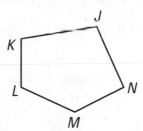

In 6 and 7, draw and name a vector for each translation.

6.

7.

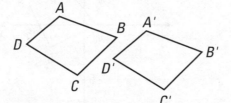

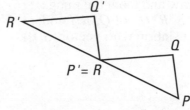

Representations Objective K: Find coordinates of translation images of points over the coordinate axes.

8. A vector has the ordered-pair description (-6, 14).

   a. Name its horizontal component.   _____

   b. Name its vertical component.   _____

   c. Describe, in words, the translation with this vector.

   _____

   _____

9. Find the image of each point under the translation with vector (3, 0).

   a. (5, -6) _____   **b.** (*m, n*) _____

10. Give an ordered-pair description for each vector.

   a. a vector to translate a point 7 units left and 5 units up   _____

   b. a vector to translate a point 6 units down and 2.4 units left   _____

   c. a vector to translate a point 12 units up   _____

   d. a vector that translates (4, 8) to (-2, 16)   _____

11. The image of point *P* under a translation by vector (20, -44) is (10, -50). What are the coordinates of *P*?   _____

12. **a.** Draw and label the image *Q'S'R'H'* of *QSRH* under the translation with vector (-6, -1).

   b. Draw and label the image *Q*S*R*H** of *QSRH* under the translation with vector (3, 0).

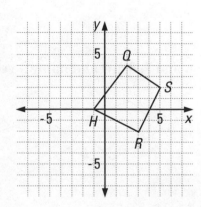

LESSON MASTER 4-7 B

Vocabulary

1. Define *isometry*.

_____

_____

2. Complete the following definition. A *glide reflection* is the composite of a reflection and a translation such that the

_____ and the

_____ are parallel.

Skills Objective C: Draw glide-reflection images of figures.

3. Draw G(ΔXYZ) where G = T $\circ$ r$_a$, and T is determined by $\vec{v}$.

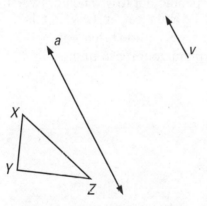

4. Draw G(S) where G = r$_m$ $\circ$ T, and T is determined by $\vec{w}$.

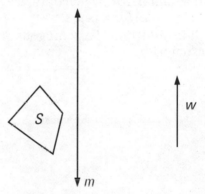

5. Draw G($PQRS$) where G = T $\circ$ r$_k$, and T is determined by $\overrightarrow{PQ}$.

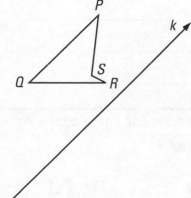

6. $\Delta D'E'F'$ is the image of ΔDEF under a glide reflection. If line n is the line of reflection, draw a translation vector.

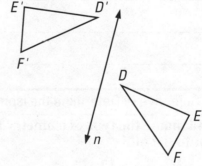

Name _____

7. Draw $H(\triangle JKL)$ where $H = T \circ r_{x\text{-axis}}$, and T is the translation with vector (5, -4).

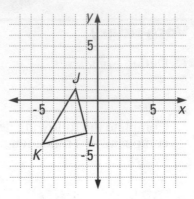

Properties Objective F: Apply properties of reflections to obtain properties of glide reflections.

8. *True or false.* The composite of an odd number of reflections reverses orientation.   _____

9. Draw three parallel lines, *u, v,* and *w,* and $\triangle ABC$. Then draw $r_u \circ r_v \circ r_w(\triangle ABC)$. Is $r_u \circ r_v \circ r_w$ a glide reflection? Explain your reasoning.

10. Draw line *a* and lines *b* and *c* each perpendicular to *a*. Then draw $\triangle XYZ$ and $r_c \circ r_b \circ r_a(\triangle XYZ)$. Is $r_c \circ r_b \circ r_a$ a glide reflection? Explain your reasoning.

_____   _____

_____   _____

_____   _____

_____   _____

Uses Objective H: Determine the isometry which maps one figure onto another.

In 11–14, name the type of isometry that maps one letter onto the other.

11. K K

12. F Ⅎ

13. P d

14. N И

_____   _____   _____   _____

LESSON MASTER

Vocabulary

1. Define *congruent figures*.

   _____

   _____

2. Complete the following statements.

   a. If two congruent figures have the same
   orientation, then they are __?__ congruent.   _____

   b. If two congruent figures have opposite
   orientation, then they are __?__ congruent.   _____

3. Complete the statement: A congruence
   transformation is another term for __?__ .   _____

Uses Objective J: Use congruence in real situations.

**In 4–9, tell whether the performed task involves the
concept of congruence. Explain why or why not.**

4. growing a tomato plant

   _____

   _____

5. transplanting a tomato plant

   _____

   _____

6. photocopying a printed sheet at 100%

   _____

   _____

7. photocopying a printed sheet at 50%

   _____

   _____

GEOMETRY © Scott, Foresman and Company

8. smashing a watch

_____

_____

9. replacing the battery in a watch

_____

_____

10. Describe a task different from those in Questions 4–9 that involves the concept of congruence.

_____

11. Describe a task different from those in Questions 4–9 that does *not* involve the concept of congruence.

_____

12. a. Before cutting, Pattern Piece A is pinned onto fabric that has been folded into two thicknesses. Explain why this is done.

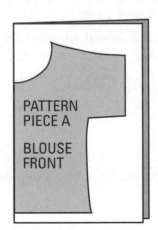

_____

_____

_____

b. What does this have to do with congruence?

_____

_____

_____

Review Objective G, Lesson 3-4

In 13–15, choose the statement that illustrates the given property.

13. Reflexive Property of Equality   _____

14. Symmetric Property of Equality   _____

15. Transitive Property of equality   _____

(a) If m∠E = m∠A, and m∠A = m∠T, then m∠E = m∠T.

(b) $RS = RS$

(c) If 4(m $\overset{\frown}{AB}$) = 180, then 180 = 4(m $\overset{\frown}{AB}$).

LESSON MASTER 5-1 B

Vocabulary

1. Below, △*FTE* = S(△*UDR*). Match the corresponding parts.

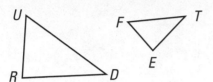

  a. $\overline{RD}$ _____   (i) ∠*TEF*

  b. ∠*T* _____   (ii) ∠*U*

  c. $\overline{UD}$ _____   (iii) $\overline{FT}$

  d. $\overline{FE}$ _____   (iv) ∠*D*

  e. ∠*DRU* _____   (v) $\overline{ET}$

  f. ∠*F* _____   (vi) $\overline{UR}$

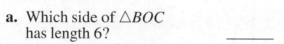

Skills Objective A: Identify and determine measures of parts of congruent figures.

2. At the right, r_h(△*BOC*) = △*VMX*, *VM* = 12, *VX* = 6, *XM* = 8, m∠*X* = 117, m∠*M* = 27, m∠*V* = 36.

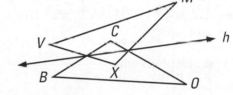

  a. Which side of △*BOC* has length 6? _____

  b. Which angle of △*BOC* has measure 36? _____

3. $r_b \circ r_a$(*TQGI*) = *EZJN*, *GI* = 43, *IT* = 33, *TQ* = 27, *QG* = 44, m∠*Q* = 71, m∠*G* = 81, m∠*I* = 68, m∠*T* = 140.

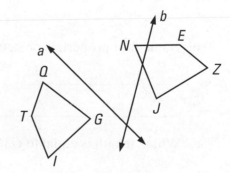

  a. Which side of *EZJN* has length 44? _____

  b. Which angle of *EZJN* has measure 71? _____

Name _____

Properties Objective E: Make and justify conclusions about congruent figures.

4. △ASK ≅ △WHY.

   a. At the right, draw a diagram
   for this situation. Mark the
   congruent parts.

   b. List six pairs of congruent parts.

   _____   _____   _____

   _____   _____   _____

5. Assume the triangles at the right are congruent.
   Write an appropriate congruence statement with
   the vertices in the correct order.

   _____

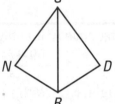

6. T(*UVWX*) = *WMNO*, and T is
   an isometry.

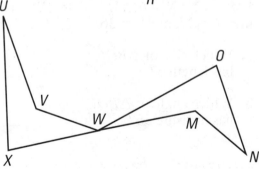

   a. Explain why
   UVWX ≅ *WMNO*.

   _____

   _____

   _____

   b. Name four properties preserved by T.

   _____

   _____

   c. Which length is equal to *OM*?   _____

7. At the right, △ABC ≅ △SEH. If BC = 9, can
   you conclude that SH = 9? Why or why not?

   _____

   _____

   _____

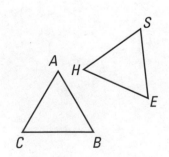

LESSON MASTER

5-2 B

Skills Objective A: Identify and determine measures of parts of congruent figures.

1. At the right, draw and label a segment $\overline{FG}$ such that $\overline{FG} \cong \overline{AB}$.

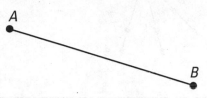

A

B

2. At the right, draw and label an angle $\angle X$ such that $\angle X \cong \angle U$.

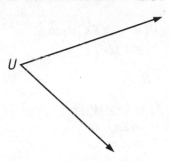

U

3. At the right, $\overline{HJ}$ and $\overline{IK}$ bisect each other, $\overline{HJ} \cong \overline{IK}$. If $HJ = 18 + 4e$, find each length.

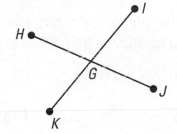

   a. IK _____

   b. HG _____

   c. GI _____

H
I
G
J
K

4. At the right, $\angle PYA \cong \angle XYM$. If m$\angle XYA = 24$, find m$\angle PYM$.

_____

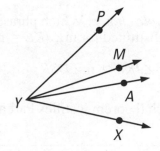

P
M
A
Y
X

▶ **LESSON MASTER 5-2B** *page 2*

5. At the right, $\overleftrightarrow{NK}$ bisects ∠*DOC* and ∠*BOT*, ∠*DOC* ≅ ∠*BOT*, and m∠*BOK* = 31. Find the measure of each angle.

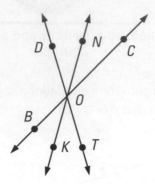

  a. ∠*NOC* _____

  b. ∠*DOC* _____

  c. ∠*DON* _____

  d. ∠*TOC* _____

Properties Objective E: Make and justify conclusions about congruent figures.

In 6–8, choose the statement that illustrates the given property.

6. Reflexive Property of Congruence _____

7. Symmetric Property of Congruence _____

8. Transitive Property of Congruence _____

(a) If ∠*PQR* ≅ ∠*XYX*, then ∠*XYZ* ≅ ∠*PQR*.

(b) $\overline{AB} ≅ \overline{AB}$

(c) If m∠*M* ≅ m∠*W*, and m∠*W* ≅ m∠*G*, then m∠*M* ≅ m∠*G*.

9. a. *Multiple choice.* Which phrase below may be substituted for $\overline{UN} ≅ \overline{TE}$. _____

  (i) $UN ≅ TE$ (ii) $\overline{UN} = \overline{TE}$ (iii) $UN = TE$

  b. Which theorem justifies Part **a**?

_____

10. a. *Multiple choice.* Which phrase below may be substituted for m∠*JKE* = m∠*DSR*? _____

  (i) m∠*JKE* ≅ m∠*DSR*   (ii) ∠*JKE* ≅ ∠*DSR*   (iii) ∠*JKE* = ∠*DSR*

  b. Which theorem justifies Part **a**?

_____

LESSON MASTER 5-3 B

Properties Objective E: Make and justify conclusions about congruent figures.

In 1–5, *multiple choice*. Choose the justification which allows you to make the given conclusion.

1. If $EFGH \cong ABCD$, then $\overline{EF} \cong \overline{AB}$.　　　　　_____
   - (a) Segment Congruence Theorem
   - (b) definition of midpoint
   - (c) CPCF Theorem
   - (d) definition of congruence

2. If $\angle X \cong \angle A$, then $m\angle X = m\angle A$.　　　　　_____
   - (a) Angle Congruence Theorem
   - (b) definition of angle bisector
   - (c) Angle Measure Postulate
   - (d) Corresponding Angles Postulate

3. If H is the midpoint of DU, then $\overline{DH} \cong \overline{HU}$.　　　　　_____
   - (a) Segment Congruence Theorem
   - (b) definition of midpoint
   - (c) CPCF Theorem
   - (d) definition of congruence

4. If $r_m(\triangle RDO) = \triangle YTM$, then $\triangle RDO \cong \triangle YTM$.　　　　　_____
   - (a) definition of congruence
   - (b) Reflexive Property of Congruence
   - (c) CPCF Theorem
   - (d) definition of reflection

5. If $\angle 4$ and $\angle 7$ are vertical angles, then $\angle 4 \cong \angle 7$.　　　　　_____
   - (a) definition of vertical angles
   - (b) Vertical Angles Theorem
   - (c) Angle Congruence Theorem
   - (d) definition of congruence

▶ **LESSON MASTER 5-3B** *page 2*

In 6–11, $r_{\overleftrightarrow{OM}}(\triangle OMU) = \triangle OMD$. **Provide a justification for each conclusion.**

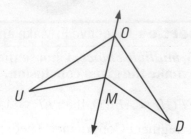

6. $\triangle OMU \cong \triangle OMD$

_____

7. $\overleftrightarrow{OM}$ is the perpendicular bisector of *UD*.

_____

8. $OD = OU$ _____

9. $r_{\overleftrightarrow{OM}}(O) = O$ _____

10. $\angle U \cong \angle D$ _____

11. $\overline{OM} \cong \overline{OM}$ _____

12. In the diagram at the right, *A*, *B*, and *C* are on ⊙*O*, and $\overline{OB}$ bisects $\angle AOC$. List three conclusions you can deduce and justify each conclusion.

a. _____ _____

b. _____ _____

c. _____ _____

13. Write a proof for the following.

Given: $\angle 3 \cong \angle 8$.
To prove: *m // n*.

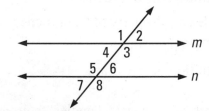

_____

_____

_____

_____

GEOMETRY © Scott, Foresman and Company

LESSON MASTER 5-4 B

Vocabulary

1. Refer to the diagram at the right.

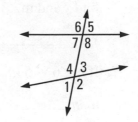

   a. Name an *interior angle.* _____

   b. Name an *exterior angle.* _____

   c. Name a pair of
      alternate interior angles. _____

   d. Name a pair of
      alternate exterior angles. _____

Skills Objective B: Construct equilateral triangles and the circle through three noncollinear points.

2. Construct an equilateral triangle with side $\overline{VR}$.

3. Construct the circle which passes through the points given.

Skills Objective C: Find angle measures using properties of alternate interior angles.

In 4 and 5, use the figure at the right in which $p \parallel q$.

4. If m∠6 = 57, find the measures of the other angles.

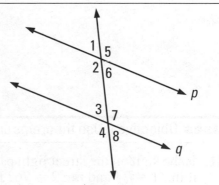

   _____

   _____

5. If m∠7 = 5x, find each of the following.

   a. m∠2 _____ b. m∠5 _____ c. m∠6 _____

In 6 and 7, use the figure at the right in which *s // t.*

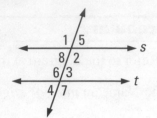

6. If m∠3 = 4x + 2 and m∠8 = 3x + 20, find x and m∠3.

x = _____   m∠3 _____

7. If m∠6 = 54n − 5 and m∠8 = 20n, find

   a. n. _____   **b.** m∠6. _____   **c.** m∠8. _____

Properties Objective F: Write proofs using the Transitive Properties of Equality or Congruence.

In 8–10, complete the proof by writing the argument.

8. Given: ∠1 ≅ ∠A.
   To prove: ∠2 ≅ ∠A.

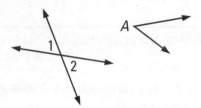

9. Given: B and C on ⊙Q; C is the midpoint of $\overline{QE}$.
   To prove: BQ = EC.

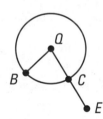

10. Given: △GHK is equilateral; r⟷(GH) = JH.
    To prove: $\overline{KG}$ ≅ $\overline{JH}$.

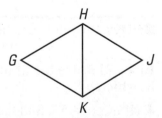

Uses Objective I: Use theorems on alternate interior angles in real situations.

11. Is the sign on the street light parallel to the ground if m∠1 = 74 and m∠2 = 76? Justify your answer.

   _____

   _____

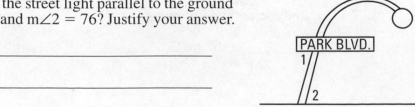

GEOMETRY © Scott, Foresman and Company

LESSON MASTER

Questions on SPUR Objectives

Skills Objective C: Find lengths using properties of perpendicular bisectors.

1. w is the $\perp$ bisector of $\overline{RS}$.

   a. Mark two pairs of congruent segments.

   b. Suppose $RJ = 8d$, $KS = 3d + 1$, and $JS = 24$.
   Find d, RJ and RK.

   _____ _____ _____

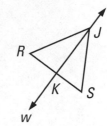

2. $\overleftrightarrow{DV}$ is the $\perp$ bisector of $\overline{UH}$. $UD = 6a + 1$,
   $DH = 4a + 15$, and $VH = 7a$. Find UV.

   _____

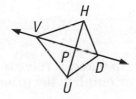

3. At the right, $Q = (-5, 0)$ and $G = (5, 0)$.

   a. Give an equation for
      the $\perp$ bisector of $\overline{QG}$.

      _____

   b. $QA = \sqrt{34}$. Find GA. _____

   c. Draw a segment whose length is
      equal to MQ.

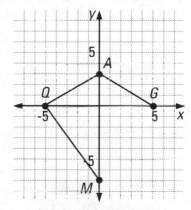

Properties Objective G: Write proof arguments using properties of reflection.

In 4 and 5, supply the justification for each step of the proof.

4. Given: $r_b(H) = T$.
   To prove: $YH = YT$.

   0. $r_b(H) = T$ _____

   1. $r_b(Y) = Y$ _____

   2. $YH = YT$ _____

Name _____

5. Given: $\overleftrightarrow{AB}$ is the ⊥ bisector of $\overline{MN}$.
To prove: $\angle MAB \cong \angle NAB$.

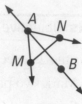

1. $r_{\overleftrightarrow{AB}}(M) = N$ _____

2. $r_{\overleftrightarrow{AB}}(A) = A; r_{\overleftrightarrow{AB}}(B) = B$ _____

3. $r_{\overleftrightarrow{AB}}(\angle MAB) = \angle NAB$ _____

4. $\angle MAB \cong \angle NAB$ _____

**In 6 and 7, refer to the diagram at the right.
Complete the proof by writing an argument.**

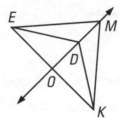

6. Given: $\overleftrightarrow{MO}$ is the ⊥ bisector of $\overline{EK}$.
To prove: $\triangle MED \cong \triangle MKD$.

7. Given: $r_{\overleftrightarrow{MO}}(E) = K$.
To prove: $\overline{DE} \cong \overline{DK}$.

─────────────────────────────────

Uses Objective I: Use the Perpendicular Bisector Theorem in real situations.

8. Do you think that the two diagonal braces
on the fence are equal in length? Explain
your reasoning.

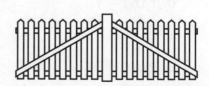

LESSON MASTER **Questions on SPUR Objectives**

Vocabulary

1. What is an *auxiliary figure*?

_____

_____

_____

Properties Objective H: Tell whether auxiliary figures are uniquely determined.

In 2–8, tell if the figure described is unique. If not, tell whether there is *more than one figure* or *no figure* satisfying the description.

2. midpoint of $\overline{UV}$

_____

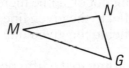

3. bisector of $\overline{MN}$

_____

4. diagonal $\overline{AC}$ bisecting $\angle A$

_____

5. point R between P and Q

_____

6. line parallel to $\overline{ZY}$ through W

_____

7. line through H and K perpendicular to m

_____

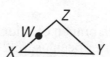

8. perpendicular bisector of $\overline{RT}$

_____

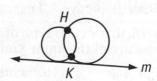

► **LESSON MASTER 5-6B** *page 2*

9. A student wished to draw as
   an auxiliary figure line *u*
   parallel to two given lines
   e and *r*. Explain if this is
   possible. Use a diagram if
   you wish.

   _____

   _____

Culture Objective J: Know the history and impact of postulates relating to
                parallel lines on the development of geometry.

In 10–12, complete the statements.

10. In Euclidean geometry, through a point
    not on a given line, there is (are) exactly
    __?__ line(s) parallel to the given line.   _____

11. In most non-Euclidean geometries, through
    a point not on a line there are either no lines
    parallel to the given line or __?__ line(s)
    parallel to the given line.   _____

12. According to the fifth postulate in Euclid's
    Elements, if m∠1 + m∠2 < 180, then lines
    ℓ and *m* __?__.

    _____

    _____

    _____

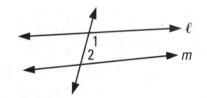

13. Have mathematicians been able to prove Euclid's
    fifth postulate from Euclid's other postulates?   _____

14. In which branch of science have non-Euclidean
    geometries been useful?   _____

Review Objective A, Lesson 3-3

**In 15–18, draw each type of angle, and give
the measure of the angle you drew.**

15. right angle   16. acute angle   17. obtuse angle   18. straight angle

_____   _____   _____   _____

Name

LESSON MASTER 5-7 B

Questions on SPUR Objectives

Skills Objective D: Use the Triangle-, Quadrilateral-, and Polygon-Sum Theorems to determine angle measures.

In 1–9, find the sum of the measures of the interior angles of each figure.

1. isosceles triangle ________

2. rectangle ________

3. pentagon ________

4. octagon ________

5. quadrilateral ________

6. scalene triangle ________

7. nonagon ________

8. 15-gon ________

9. hexagon ________

10. In $\triangle ABC$, $m\angle ABC = 40$ and $m\angle B = 111$. Find $m\angle C$. ________

11. In $\triangle QRS$, $m\angle Q = m\angle S$, and $m\angle R = 2x$. Find $m\angle Q$. ________

12. In quadrilateral $EFGH$, $m\angle E = 90$, $m\angle G = 104$, and $m\angle H = 123$. Find $m\angle F$. ________

13. In hexagon $UVWXYZ$, $m\angle U = m\angle V = m\angle W$, $m\angle X = 158$, $m\angle Y = 107$, and $m\angle Z = 83$. Find $m\angle U$. ________

14. The measures of the angles of a triangle are in the extended ratio 4:5:11. Find the measure of the smallest angle. ________

15. Refer to Figure 1 at the right. Find m∠SVE.

_____

16. Refer to Figure 2 at the right. Solve for *x*.

_____

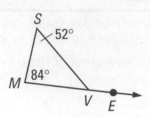
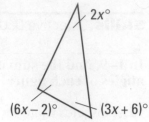

Figure 1   Figure 2

17. Find the measure of each angle of the hexagon pictured at the right.

∠A _____   ∠B _____   ∠C _____

∠E _____   ∠F _____

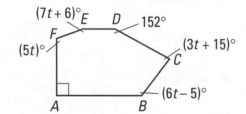

Culture Objective J: Know the history and impact of postulates relating to parallel lines on the development of geometry.

---

18. Does the Triangle-Sum Theorem hold for △NEQ on the earth's surface as pictured at the right? Explain.

_____

_____

_____

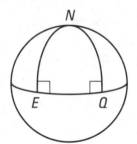

Review Objective B, Lesson 4-2

In 19–22, draw the reflection image of each polygon over the line. Circle each polygon that coincides with its image.

19.

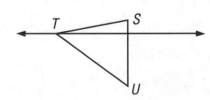

20.

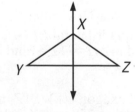

21.

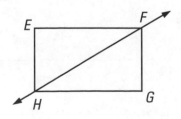

22.

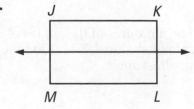

LESSON MASTER

6-1
B

Vocabulary

1. Suppose figure *Q* is *reflection-symmetric*. What does this mean?

Skills Objective A: Locate symmetry lines of geometric figures.

In 2–7, draw the symmetry line(s), if any, for the figure.

2.

3.

4.

5.

6.

7.

Properties Objective E: Apply properties of symmetry to assert and justify conclusions about symmetric figures.

In 8–13, *true or false*.

8. If $r_m (\angle X) = \angle X$, then *m* is the bisector of $\angle X$. _____

9. A circle has exactly two symmetry lines. _____

10. A symmetry line for $\overline{AB}$ is $\overleftrightarrow{AB}$. _____

11. If $r_e (\triangle RST) = \triangle XYZ$, then $r_e (\triangle XYZ) = \triangle RST$. _____

12. A line is not a reflection-symmetric figure. _____

13. Every triangle has at least one symmetry line. _____

► **LESSON MASTER 6-1B** *page 2*

14. *a* and *b* are symmetry lines for the polygon at the right.

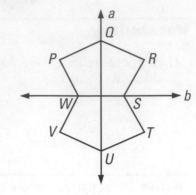

    a. Name three angles congruent to ∠*T*.

    _____

    b. How is *a* related to ∠*PQR*?

    _____

    c. $r_b(PQRSTUVW)$ = ____?____.   _____

    d. Name all the segments congruent to $\overline{VW}$.   _____

Uses Objective I: Locate and draw symmetry lines in real-world designs.

In 15–19, draw the symmetry line(s), if any, for the design.

15. Flag of Israel   **16.** Flag of Sweden   **17.** Flag of Japan

18.   **19.**

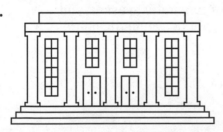

20. Is the drawing at the right reflection-symmetric? Explain why or why not.

_____

_____

_____

GEOMETRY © Scott, Foresman and Company

LESSON MASTER **Questions on SPUR Objectives**

Vocabulary

1. What is a *corollary?*

   _____

   _____

2. Refer to the isosceles triangle at the right.

   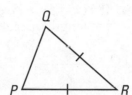

   a. Identify the *vertex angle.* _____

   b. Identify the *base angles.* _____

   c. Identify the *base.* _____

Skills Objective A: Locate symmetry lines of geometric figures.
Objective B: Draw polygons satisfying various conditions.

3. Draw an isosceles triangle with a vertex angle of 36°. Then draw the symmetry line for the triangle.

4. Draw an isosceles triangle with a base angle of 36°. Then draw the symmetry line for the triangle.

5. Draw a triangle with three symmetry lines. Show the symmetry lines.

Skills Objective C: Apply the theorems about isosceles triangles to find angle measures and segment lengths.

In 6–8, find the indicated measures in each triangle.

6.

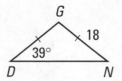

a. m∠N _____

b. m∠G _____

c. DG _____

7.

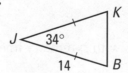

a. m∠K _____

b. JK _____

c. m∠B _____

8.

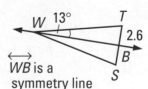

$\overleftrightarrow{WB}$ is a symmetry line

a. m∠S _____

b. m∠SBW _____

c. TS _____

9. At the right, △*YPQ* is isosceles with base $\overline{PQ}$.

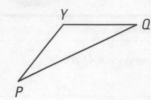

a. If m∠*P* = 10*x* and m∠*Y* = 52*x*, find the
   measure of each angle in △*YPQ*.

∠*P* _____   ∠*Q* _____   ∠*Y* _____

b. If *YQ* = 5*y* + 6, *QP* = 12*y* + 1.2, and *YP* = 10*y* − 11, find
   the length of each side of △*YPQ*.

$\overline{YQ}$ _____ $\overline{QP}$ _____ $\overline{YP}$ _____

Properties Objective F: Know the properties of various types of triangles.

10. At the right, △*URA* is isosceles with base
   $\overline{UR}$, and $\overline{AG}$ bisects ∠*UAR*. Name all
   pairs of congruent angles and segments.

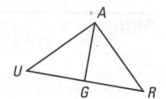

_____

_____

Properties Objective H: Write proofs using properties of isosceles triangles.

**In 11 and 12, complete the proof by giving
the argument.**

11. Given: Points *S* and *T* are on ⊙*O*.
   To prove: ∠*S* ≅ ∠*T*.

12. Given: △*FGH* is isosceles with symmetry line *m*.
   To prove: ∠1 ≅ ∠2.

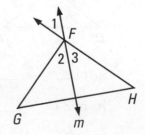

LESSON MASTER

6-3 B

Questions on SPUR Objectives

Skills Objective B: Draw polygons satisfying various conditions.

1. Draw a parallelogram that is not a rectangle.

2. Draw a rhombus that is not a square.

3. Draw an isosceles trapezoid that is not a parallelogram.

Skills Objective D: Apply theorems about quadrilaterals to find angle measures and segment lengths.

4. In quadrilateral *ABCD* at the right, find each length and angle measure.

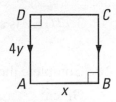

AD _____ CD _____ m∠D _____ m∠C _____

Properties Objective G: Know the properties of the seven special types of quadrilaterals.

In 5–7, classify the quadrilateral based only upon the markings given. Give the most specific name.

5.

6.

_____

7.

_____

8. Square *FOUR* is drawn at the right.

   a. Is *FOUR* also a kite? Why or why not?

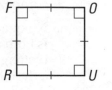

_____

_____

   b. Is *FOUR* also a trapezoid? Why or why not?

_____

Properties Objective H: Write proofs using properties of quadrilaterals.

9. Supply justifications for the conclusions
   in the argument written below.

   Given: $r_{\overleftrightarrow{TE}}(\triangle TEG) = \triangle TEV.$
   To prove: *TGEV* is a kite.

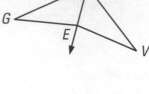

   Conclusions   Justifications

   0. $r_{\overleftrightarrow{TE}}(\triangle TEG) = \triangle TEV$ _____

   1. $\triangle TEG \cong \triangle TEV$ _____

   2. $\overline{TG} \cong \overline{TV}, \overline{EG} \cong \overline{EV}$ _____

   3. *TGEV* is a kite.   _____

10. Complete the proof by giving the argument.

    Given: $m\angle 1 = m\angle B = m\angle D.$
    To prove: *ABCD* is a parallelogram.

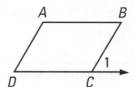

Representations Objective K: Draw and apply hierarchies of polygons.

11. Complete the hierarchy for the seven special
    types of quadrilaterals. Then answer *true* or
    false for the following statements.

    a. Every rhombus
       is a kite.   _____

    b. No quadrilateral
       is both a kite and
       a trapezoid.   _____

    c. No quadrilateral
       is both a
       rectangle and
       a rhombus.   _____

LESSON MASTER

6-4
B

Skills Objective A: Locate symmetry lines of kites and rhombuses.
Objective D: Apply theorems about kites and rhombuses to find angle
measures and segment lengths.

1. Draw the symmetry line(s) for kite
   QRST and mark all right angles and
   all congruent angles and segments.

2. Draw the symmetry line(s) for
   rhombus *ABCD* and mark all
   right angles and all congruent
   angles and segments.

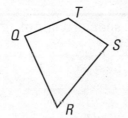

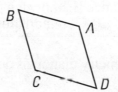

3. At the right, *M* and *Z* are the ends of kite *MGZX*,
   m∠2 = 46, and m∠*GZX* = 64. Find each measure.

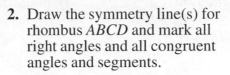

   a. m∠7 _____   **b.** m∠1 _____

   c. m∠3 _____   **d.** m∠5 _____

   e. m∠4 _____   **f.** m∠6 _____   **g.** m∠*ZGM* _____

4. In rhombus *UMNJ*, *UH* = 14 and m∠*UMH* = 31.

   a. Give as many segment lengths as possible.

   _____

   b. Give as many angle measures as possible.

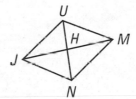

   _____

   _____

   c. Give as many pairs of parallel segments as possible.

   _____

   d. Give as many isosceles triangles as possible.

   _____

   e. Which triangles are congruent?

   _____

▶ **LESSON MASTER 6-4B** *page 2*

5. In rhombus *REJD*, m∠*DRE* = 82. Find each measure.

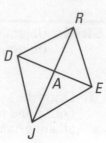

   a. m∠*DRA* _____   **b.** m∠*RDA* _____

   c. m∠*DJA* _____   **d.** m∠*DJE* _____

Properties Objective G: Know the properties of the seven special types of quadrilaterals.

---

6. How many symmetry diagonals does a kite have? _____

7. How many symmetry diagonals does a rhombus have? _____

Properties Objective H: Write proofs using properties of triangles and quadrilaterals.

---

8. Supply justifications for the conclusions in the argument written below.

   Given: ⊙*O* and ⊙*Q* with points *B*, *C*, and *Q* on ⊙*O*.
   To prove: *QCOB* is a kite.

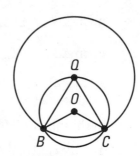

Conclusions	Justifications
1. $\overline{OB} \cong \overline{OC}$; $\overline{QB} \cong \overline{QC}$	_____
2. *QCOB* is a kite.	_____

9. Complete the proof by writing the argument.

   Given: $\overline{FW}$ and $\overline{SK}$ are ⊥ bisectors of
              each other.
   To prove: *SFKW* is a rhombus.

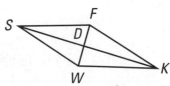

LESSON MASTER **Questions on SPUR Objectives**

6-5 B

Skills Objective A: Locate symmetry lines of geometric figures.

In 1–4, draw the symmetry line(s), if any, for the trapezoid.

1.   2.

3.   4.

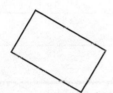

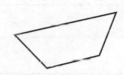

Skills Objective D: Apply theorems about quadrilaterals to find angle measures and segment lengths.

5. $\overline{RS}$ and $\overline{JK}$ are the bases of trapezoid $JKSR$, $m\angle K = 133$ and $m\angle R = 61$. Find $m\angle J$ and $m\angle S$.

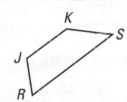

   $m\angle J$ _____ $m\angle S$ _____

6. $\overleftrightarrow{MN}$ is a symmetry line for trapezoid $ABCD$, $m\angle D = 74$, $AB = 28$, $AD = 12$, and $DC = 34.6$. Find each measure.

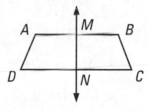

   a. $m\angle C$ _____   b. $m\angle A$ _____

   c. BC _____   d. MB _____

   e. DN _____   f. $m\angle AMN$ _____

7. In rectangle $EFGH$, $m\angle F = 2(6t + 3)$. Solve for t.

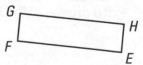

   _____

8. In $UVWX$, $m\angle U = 5x + 13$, $m\angle X = 129 - 3x$, $m\angle W = 64 - x$, and $m\angle V = 8x - 17$. Find the measure of each angle in $UVWX$.

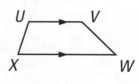

   $\angle U$ _____ $\angle V$ _____

   $\angle W$ _____ $\angle X$ _____

▶ **LESSON MASTER 6-5B** *page 2*

Properties Objective G: Know the properties of trapezoids.

9. Do any isosceles trapezoids have more than one symmetry line? Explain why or why not.

_____

_____

10. Can an isosceles trapezoid have a symmetry diagonal? Explain why or why not.

_____

_____

Properties Objective H: Write proofs using properties of trapezoids.

11. Supply justifications for the conclusions in the argument written below.

Given: $\overleftrightarrow{MN}$ is a symmetry line for isosceles trapezoid *TVHQ*.

To prove: $\triangle QMH$ is an isosceles triangle.

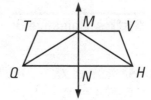

Conclusions	Justifications
1. $\overleftrightarrow{MN}$ is the $\perp$ bisector of $\overline{TV}$ and $\overline{QH}$.	_____
2. $r_{\overleftrightarrow{MN}}(Q) = H, r_{\overleftrightarrow{MN}}(M) = M$	_____
3. $MQ = MH$	_____
4. $\triangle QMH$ is an isosceles triangle.	_____

12. Complete the proof by writing the argument.

Given: $\overline{JP} \parallel \overline{KR}$, and $m\angle R = m\angle 1$.

To prove: $JK = PR$.

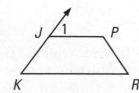

GEOMETRY © Scott, Foresman and Company

LESSON MASTER **6-6** B

Questions on SPUR Objectives

Vocabulary

1. Define *rotation-symmetric* figure.

_____

_____

_____

Skills Objective A: Locate symmetry lines and centers of symmetry of geometric figures.

In 2–7, if the figure has *n*-fold rotation symmetry, find *n*. Then draw and label the center of symmetry point *C*.

2.
_____

3.
_____

4.
_____

5.
_____

6.
_____

7.
_____

In 8–10, complete each statement.

8. If a figure has 5-fold rotation symmetry, then the least positive magnitude of a rotation that will map the figure onto itself is ___?___.

_____

9. If the least positive magnitude of a rotation that maps a figure onto itself is 60°, then the figure has ___?___-fold rotation symmetry.

_____

10. If a rotation of magnitude 90° maps a figure onto itself, then a rotation of magnitude ___?___ will also map the figure onto itself.

_____

11. Suppose a rotation of magnitude 30° maps a figure onto itself. Give the magnitudes of three other rotations that will map the figure onto itself.

_____

89 ▶

12. Draw a figure with 3-fold rotation symmetry that also has reflection symmetry.

13. Draw a figure with 3-fold rotation symmetry that does not have reflection symmetry.

Properties Objective E: Apply properties of symmetry to assert and justify conclusions about symmetric figures.

In 14 and 15, *true* **or** *false.*

14. If two symmetry lines for a figure intersect at O, then the figure has rotation symmetry with center O. _____

15. If a figure has 4-fold rotation symmetry, then it is reflection-symmetric. _____

16. If a figure has rotation symmetry, then can the least positive magnitude of a rotation that maps the figure onto itself be 27°? Explain why or why not.

_____

_____

Uses Objective I: Locate and draw symmetry lines in real-world designs.

In 17–19, refer to the design at the right.

17. Does the entire design have reflection symmetry? _____

18. Does the entire design have rotation symmetry? _____

19. Describe the symmetry in each portion of the design shown below.

a. _____

_____

b. _____

_____

90

LESSON MASTER

6-7
B

Vocabulary

1. What is a *regular polygon*?

_____

_____

_____

Skills Objective A: Locate symmetry lines and centers of symmetry of
geometric figures.
Objective B: Draw polygons satisfying various conditions.

**In 2–7, draw the figure described. Then draw the
symmetry line(s), if any. Finally, draw the center
of symmetry, if it exists, and label it *C*.**

2. a regular
quadrilateral

3. a regular pentagon

4. any polygon that is
equilateral, but not
regular

5. any polygon that is
equiangular but not
regular

6. a regular triangle

7. a regular octagon

Skills Objective C: Apply theorems about isosceles triangles to find angle
measures and segment lengths.
Objective D: Apply theorems about regular polygons to find angle
measures and segment lengths.

8. Find the measure of one interior angle of a regular

a. pentagon. _____   **b.** heptagon. _____   **c.** 16-gon. _____

9. *J* is the center of regular polygon *ABCDEFGHI*.
Find the measures of the angles of △*DEJ*.

_____

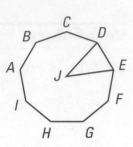

Properties Objective F: Know the properties of the various types of triangles
and regular polygons.

---

10. At the right, *QRSTUVWXYZ* is regular.

a. Name the center of
QRSTUVWXYZ.   _____

b. How many symmetry lines
does *QRSTUVWXYZ* have?   _____

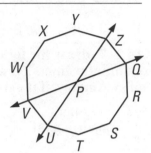

c. Are there any symmetry lines that do not contain
a vertex of *QRSTUVWXYZ*? If so, draw one.   _____

d. m∠*ZPQ* = _____   m∠*PZQ* = _____   m∠*VPZ* = _____

Properties Objective H: Write proofs using properties of triangles and
quadrilaterals.

---

11. Complete the proof by supplying the justifications.

Given: *UDTCE* is a regular pentagon.
To prove: ∠1 ≅ ∠2.

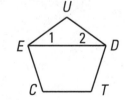

Conclusions	Justifications
1. $\overline{UE} \cong \overline{UD}$	_____
2. △*UED* is isosceles.	_____
3. ∠1 ≅ ∠2	_____

12. Complete the proof by giving the argument.

Given: *R* is the center of a regular
           octagon *STKAMHBN*.
To prove: △*RMN* is isosceles.

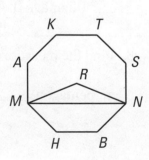

GEOMETRY © Scott, Foresman and Company

LESSON MASTER **6-8** **B**

Vocabulary

1. **a.** In ⊙*A* at the right, draw and label a
   chord. Give the name of the chord. _____

   b. Name the *minor arc* of the chord. _____

2. **a.** When is a tournament called a *round-robin* tournament?

   _____

   _____

   b. When does a team in a round-robin tournament get a *bye*?

   _____

   _____

Uses Objective J: Make a schedule for a round-robin tournament.

**In 3–10, consider a round-robin tournament for five
teams that play once a week.**

3. Place the five teams at equal intervals
   on the circle at the right.

4. Draw a chord and all chords parallel to it. Write
   the first week's pairings.

   _____

5. Rotate the chords $\frac{1}{5}$ of a revolution. Write the
   pairings for the second week.

   _____

6. Continue until all the teams have played each
   other. List the remainder of the weeks and the
   pairings for each week.

   _____

   _____

7. How many weeks are needed? _____

8. How many individual games are needed? _____

9. How many byes are needed? _____

10. How many weeks are needed for six teams? _____

In 11–14, consider a round-robin tournament for eight teams that play once a week.

11. In the space below, show the week-by-week pairings.

12. How many weeks are needed? _____

13. How many individual games are needed? _____

14. How many byes are needed? _____

Review Objective J, Lesson 2-7

In 15–20, can these numbers be the lengths of the sides of a triangle? Justify your answer.

15. 8, 6, 3 _____

16. 2, 8, 10 _____

17. 5, 4, 11 _____

18. 40, 40, 86 _____

19. 20, 36, 20 _____

20. 6, 12, 7 _____

LESSON MASTER 7-1 B

Skills Objective A: Draw triangles satisfying certain conditions and determine whether all such triangles are congruent.

In 1–8, use an automatic drawer or other drawing tools. Accurately draw a triangle satisfying the given conditions. Then complete the table on the next page by choosing the correct name for the condition and conjecturing whether all the triangles drawn with these conditions are congruent.

1. $\triangle RST$ with $RS = 4$ cm, $ST = 6$ cm, and $RT = 3.5$ cm

2. $\triangle ABC$ with m$\angle A = 44$, m$\angle B = 66$, and m$\angle C = 70$

3. $\triangle XYZ$ with $XY = 2.5$ in., $YZ = 1$ in., and m$\angle Y = 105$

4. $\triangle DEF$ with $DE = 3$ cm, $DF = 6$ cm, and m$\angle F = 25$

5. $\triangle OPQ$ with $PQ = 3$ in. and m$\angle Q = 90$

6. $\triangle UVW$ with m$\angle U = 80$ and m$\angle V = 52$

► **LESSON MASTER 7-1B** *page 2*

7. △*GHJ* with m∠*H* = 73,
   m∠*J* = 45, and *JH* = 5 cm

8. △*KMN* with m∠*M* = 120,
   m∠*N* = 22, and *KN* = 2.5 in.

Name for given condition	SSS	SSA	SAS	ASA	AAS	SA	AAA	AA
Question which involved this condition								
All triangles with this condition congruent?								

9. Explain how the AAA condition is similar to the AA condition.

   _____

   _____

   _____

Review Objective A, Lesson 5-1

10. Refer to the congruent triangles at the right. Correctly complete the following congruence statement.

    △ _____ ≅ △ _____

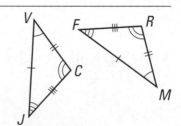

11. At the right, △*AND* is the image of △*BUT* under an isometry. Mark three pairs of congruent sides and three pairs of congruent angles.

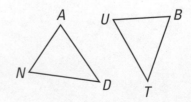

LESSON MASTER **7-2 B**

Skills Objective A: Draw triangles satisfying certain conditions and determine whether all such triangles are congruent.

In 1–6, conditions are given. Will all triangles satisfying the same conditions be congruent? Explain your answer.

1. In $\triangle JTP$, $m\angle T = 66$, $m\angle P = 51$, $JP = 3$ in.

_____

2. In $\triangle ABC$, $m\angle B = 27$, $m\angle C = 104$

_____

3. In $\triangle ESD$, $m\angle E = 38$, $ES = 7$ cm, $DE = 7$ cm

_____

4. In $\triangle ORM$, $OR = 4$ cm, $OM = 5.4$ cm, $MR = 8.8$ cm

_____

5. In $\triangle HKJ$, $m\angle H = 45$, $m\angle K = 78$, $HK = 38$ mm

_____

6. In $\triangle XYU$, $UY - 2$ in., $m\angle U = 42$, $YX = 1$ in.

_____

Properties Objective C: Determine whether triangles are congruent from given information.

In 7–10, use the marked diagram to tell whether the triangles are congruent. If they are congruent, write a congruence statement that indicates corresponding vertices.

7.

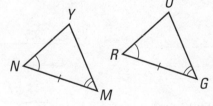

8.

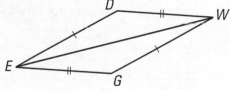

_____   _____

9.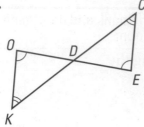

10.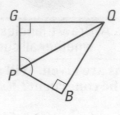

_____   _____

11. Give an additional piece of information that would guarantee that △ZHC ≅ △DMQ

    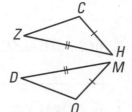

    a. by the SAS Congruence Theorem. _____

    b. by the SSS Congruence Theorem. _____

12. a. What additional piece of information would guarantee that △FTD ≅ △CRS? What theorem guarantees the congruence?

    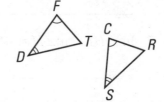

    _____

    b. Give a different piece of information that would guarantee that △FTD ≅ △CRS. What theorem guarantees the congruence?

    _____

Uses Objective I: Use theorems about triangles to explain real situations.

13. Junior Campers are making toy boats from hobby kits. The directions say to cut a canvas sail with the measurements shown. Will all the sails be congruent? Explain why or why not.

    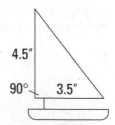

    _____

    _____

14. Luke ordered a triangular piece of glass with angles of 66°, 66°, and 48° to replace the broken piece in a light fixture. Will the new piece fit? Explain why or why not.

    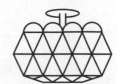

    _____

    _____

LESSON MASTER 7-3 B

Properties Objective D: Write proofs that triangles are congruent.
Objective E: Apply the triangle congruence and CPCF theorems to prove that segments or angles are congruent.

In 1 and 2, give a justification for each conclusion.

1. Given: *DTFS* is a rhombus.
   To prove: △*DES* ≅ △*FET*.

   Argument:

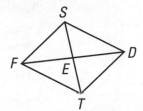

Conclusions	Justifications
0. *DTFS* is a rhombus.	_____
1. $\overline{DS} \cong \overline{FT}$	_____
2. $\overline{ST}$ is the ⊥ bisector of $\overline{FD}$; $\overline{FD}$ is the ⊥ bisector of $\overline{ST}$.	_____
3. $\overline{SE} \cong \overline{TE}$; $\overline{FE} \cong \overline{DE}$	_____
4. △*DES* ≅ △*FET*	_____

2. Given: ∠*J* ≅ ∠*K*; *N* is the midpoint of $\overline{JK}$.
   To prove: ∠*JMN* ≅ ∠*KMN*.

   Argument:

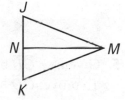

Conclusions	Justifications
0. ∠*J* ≅ ∠*K*	_____
1. $\overline{JM} \cong \overline{KM}$	_____
2. *N* is the midpoint of $\overline{JK}$.	_____
3. $\overline{JN} \cong \overline{KN}$	_____
4. △*JMN* ≅ △*KMN*	_____
5. ∠*JMN* ≅ ∠*KMN*	_____

► **LESSON MASTER 7-3B** *page 2*

In 3–6, complete the proof by giving the argument.

3. Given: $\overline{UQ} \parallel \overline{VR}$; $UP = RP$.
   To prove: $\triangle UQP \cong \triangle RVP$.

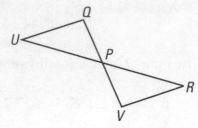

4. Given: $\odot C$.
   To prove: $\overline{XY} \cong \overline{ST}$.

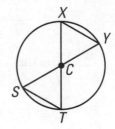

5. Given: $\overline{GH}$ bisects $\angle QGR$ and $\angle QHR$.
   To prove: $\overline{GQ} \cong \overline{GR}$.

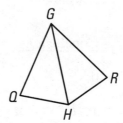

6. Given: Regular pentagon *ABCDE*.
   To prove: $\angle BAC \cong \angle EAD$.

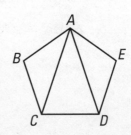

GEOMETRY © Scott, Foresman and Company

LESSON MASTER 7-4 B

Vocabulary

In 1 and 2, redraw the figure separating the pair of overlapping triangles. Label your drawing and mark the shared parts.

1.

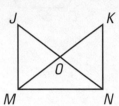

2.

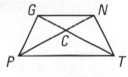

Properties Objective D: Write proofs that triangles are congruent.
Objective E: Apply the triangle congruence and CPCF theorems to prove that segments or angles are congruent.

---

3. Write a justification for each conclusion.
   Given: *GNTP* is an isosceles trapezoid with base angles ∠*GPT* ≅ ∠*NTP*.
   To prove: △*GTP* ≅ △*NPT*.

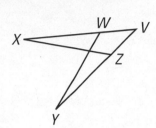

   Argument:

Conclusions	Justifications
1. $\overline{GP} \cong \overline{NT}$	_____
2. $\overline{PT} \cong \overline{PT}$	_____
3. △*GTP* ≅ △*NPT*	_____

In 4–7, complete the proof by giving the argument.

4. Given: *DN* = *YN*; *WN* = *FN*.
   To prove: ∠*W* ≅ ∠*F*.

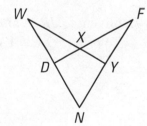

► **LESSON MASTER 7-4B** *page 2*

5. Given: *CDEFGH* is a regular hexagon.
   To prove: $\overline{FD} \cong \overline{EG}$.

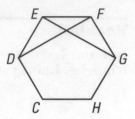

6. Given: $\odot S$; $\angle U \cong \angle K$.
   To prove: $\triangle SKT \cong \triangle SUM$.

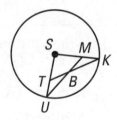

7. Given: $JR = MJ$; $\angle RYM \cong \angle MQR$.
   To prove: $\overline{QR} \cong \overline{YM}$.

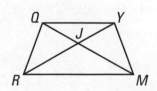

LESSON MASTER

7-5
B

Skills Objective A: Draw triangles satisfying certain conditions and determine whether all such triangles are congruent.

In 1–4, use an automatic drawer or other drawing tools.
Accurately draw a triangle satisfying the given conditions.
Tell whether all triangles meeting these conditions are
congruent. If all triangles meeting these conditions are
not congruent, show this with a second drawing.

1. $\triangle ABC$ with $AC = 3$ cm,
   $AB = 2.5$ cm, and m$\angle C = 45$

2. $\triangle RST$ with m$\angle R = 90$,
   $RS = 1.5$ in., and $ST = 2$ in.

_____

3. $\triangle MNO$ with m$\angle O = 90$ and
   $MO = 3.5$ cm

2. $\triangle XYZ$ with $XY = 20$ mm,
   $XZ = 25$ mm, and m$\angle Y = 105$

_____   _____

Properties Objective C: Determine whether triangles are congruent from given information.

In 5–7, use the marked diagram to tell whether the triangles
are congruent. If they are congruent, justify with a triangle
congruence theorem. Otherwise, write *not enough to tell*.

5.

6.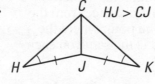
$HJ > CJ$

7.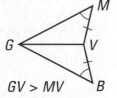
$GV > MV$

_____   _____   _____

▶ **LESSON MASTER 7-5B** *page 2*

Properties Objective D: Write proofs that triangles are congruent.
Objective E: Apply the triangle congruence and CPCF theorems to prove that segments or angles are congruent.

In 8 and 9, complete the proof by giving the argument.

8. Given: *GHTC* is an isosceles trapezoid with bases
   $\overline{GH}$ and $\overline{CT}$; $\overline{GM} \cong \overline{HN}$;
   $\overline{GM} \perp \overline{CT}$; $\overline{HN} \perp \overline{CT}$.
   To prove: $\triangle GMC \cong \triangle HNT$.

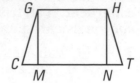

9. Given: $\overline{FN}$ is the $\perp$ bisector of $\overline{OE}$;
   $\overline{ON} \cong \overline{EF}$.
   To prove: $\overline{ON} /\!/ \overline{EF}$.

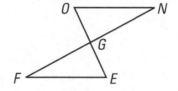

Uses Objective I: Use theorems about triangles to explain real situations.

---

10. Cables $\overline{AB}$ and $\overline{XY}$ on the suspension bridge pictured at the right are the same length. End supports $\overline{AC}$ and $\overline{XZ}$ are equal in length and are perpendicular to the ground. Explain why the distance from the base of the support to the point where the cable meets the ground is the same on each side of the bridge.

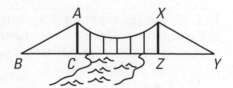

_____

_____

LESSON MASTER 7-6 B

Vocabulary

1. a. What is a *tessellation*?

_____

_____

b. What is the *fundamental region* of a tessellation?

_____

_____

_____

Uses Objective J: Draw tessellations of real objects.

2. A brick patio is tiled with rectangular bricks, as shown at the right. The length of each rectangle is twice its width. Draw part of a tessellation that will yield a different rectangular-brick pattern for the patio.

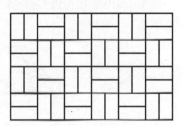

In 3–5, draw part of a tessellation using the given figure.

3. equilateral triangles   **4.** scalene triangles   **5.** quadrilaterals with no right angles

6. Can a regular octagon be used as a fundamental region for a tessellation? Explain your answer.

_____

_____

▶ **LESSON MASTER 7-6B** *page 2*

In 7 and 8, the tessellation is a tile pattern found in the Alhambra in Granada, Spain.

7. Shade a possible fundamental region in the tesselation below.

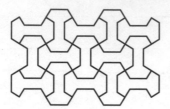

8. Use the fundamental region below to draw part of a tessellation.

9. Doreen is needle-pointing the pattern shown below. Outline a possible fundamental region.

10. Draw part of a tessellation using the figure below as the fundamental region.

LESSON MASTER 7-7 B

Properties Objective F: Apply properties of parallelograms.

1. Consider the symmetry of a parallelogram.

   a. Does every parallelogram have reflection symmetry?
   If so, describe the line(s) of reflection.

   _____

   _____

   b. Does every parallelogram have rotation symmetry?
   If so, describe the center and the magnitude(s) of
   the rotation(s).

   _____

   _____

2. Refer to parallelogram *QRST* at the right.

   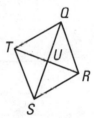

   a. If m∠*QTS* = 102, find as many other angle
   measures as you can.

   _____

   b. If m∠*STR* = 48 and m∠*QSR* = 40, find as many other
   angle measures as you can.

   _____

   c. If *QT* = 12 and *QS* = 22, find as many other lengths
   as you can.

   _____

   d. If *UR* = 4 and *RQ* = 7, find as many other lengths
   as you can.

   _____

3. At the right, if *AB* = 32, *BD* = 52, and
   CD = 5*x* + 2, solve for *x*.

   _____

   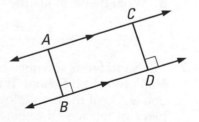

4. *KMNJ* is a parallelogram. Solve for

   a. *a.* _____

   b. *b.* _____

   c. *x.* _____

   d. *y.* _____

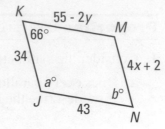

5. a. At the right, draw a parallelogram *EFGH* with congruent diagonals.

   b. What type of special parallelogram is *EFGH*?

   _____

   c. Justify your answer to Part **b**.

_____

_____

_____

_____

_____

_____

Uses Objective K: Use theorems about parallelograms to explain real situations.

6. Mrs. Parisi is making draperies for the windows shown at the right. She measured the distance along the left side of the windows from the drapery rod to the floor.

   a. What does she know about the distance along the right side of the windows from the drapery rod to the floor?

   _____

   b. What theorem justifies Part **a**?

   _____

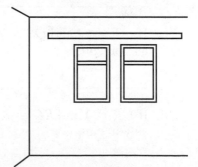

7. Mr. Santiago is sewing a banner for Napleton High School. If the measure of one angle of the parallelogram-shaped piece of fabric in the center is 45, what are the measures of the other three angles?

_____

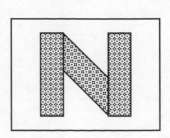

LESSON MASTER 7-8 B

Properties Objective G: Determine whether conditions are sufficient for parallelograms.

In 1–10, use the diagram at the right. Tell whether sufficient conditions are given for *ABCD* to be a parallelogram. If your answer is *yes,* write the sufficient condition.

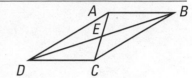

1. $AB = DC$ _____

2. $\angle DAB \cong \angle BCD$ _____

3. E is the midpoint of $\overline{BD}$ and $\overline{AC}$. _____

4. $\angle DAB \cong \angle BCD$, $\angle ABC \cong \angle CDA$ _____

5. $AB = BC, CD = AD$ _____

6. $AB = BD$ _____

7. $AB = DC, BC = AD$ _____

8. $\overline{BC} \parallel \overline{AD}, \overline{AB} \parallel \overline{DC}$ _____

9. $\overline{BC} \parallel \overline{AD}, \overline{AB} \cong \overline{DC}$ _____

10. $\overline{BC} \parallel \overline{AD}, \overline{BC} \cong \overline{AD}$ _____

In 11 and 12, a conditional is given. **a. Draw an instance of the conditional. b. Tell whether you think the conditional is always true. If it is, explain why you think so. If not, draw a counterexample.**

11. If three sides of a quadrilateral are congruent, then the quadrilateral is a parallelogram.

   a.   b.

12. If a quadrilateral has two pairs of consecutive angles that are supplementary, then the quadrilateral is a parallelogram.

   a.   b.

13. Provide the argument for the proof.
Given: △*RQP* ≅ △*SPQ*.
To prove: *QSPR* is a parallelogram.

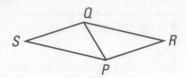

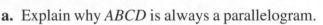

Uses Objective K: Use theorems about parallelograms to explain real situations.

14. The log tool of a fireplace set pivots at *A*, *B*, *C*, and *D*;
and *AB* = *BC* = *CD* = *DA*.

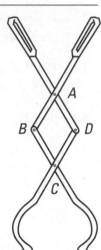

a. Explain why *ABCD* is always a parallelogram.

_____

_____

b. As ∠*B* gets smaller, what happens to ∠*D*
and ∠*BAD*? Explain your answer.

_____

_____

c. If the handles are pushed closer together, does the opening
for the logs increase or decrease in size? Explain your answer.

_____

_____

_____

15. A Girl Scout tied a knot in a piece of rope and then
tied four more knots 8 ft, 14 ft, 22 ft, and
28 ft from the first knot. She drove a spike into the
ground through each of the first four knots, keeping
the rope tight between the spikes and bringing the
last knot to meet the first. Did the rope form a
parallelogram? Explain why or why not.

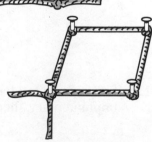

_____

_____

LESSON MASTER 7-9 B

Questions on SPUR Objectives

Skills Objective B: Determine measures of angles in polygons using exterior angles.

1. Draw an exterior angle at each vertex of △EFG below. Then give the sum of the measures of the angles you drew.

2. Draw an exterior angle at each vertex of WXYZ below. Then give the sum of the measures of the angles you drew.

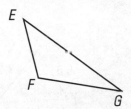

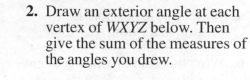

_____

_____

In 3–11, find the value of the variable(s).

3.

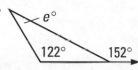

4.

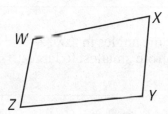

5.

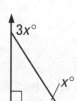

_____

_____

_____

6.

7.

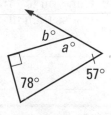

8.

_____

_____

_____

9.

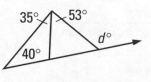

10.

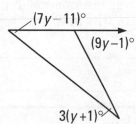

11.

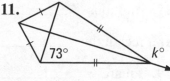

_____

_____

_____

Properties Objective H: From given information, deduce which sides or angles of triangles are smallest or largest.

12. **a.** Which angle measure is greater, m∠1 or m∠2? _____

    b. What theorem justifies your answer to Part **a**?

    _____

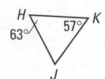

13. Name the angles in △XYZ in order from smallest to largest.

    _____ _____ _____

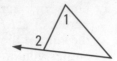

14. Name the sides of △HJK in order from smallest to largest.

    _____ _____ _____

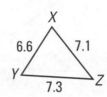

15. In △PQR,

    a. find x. _____

    b. find m∠PRQ. _____

    c. tell which side of △PQR is longest. _____

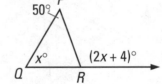

16. **a.** In △ABC, which angle has the greater measure, ∠A or ∠B? _____

    b. Can you tell from the given information if m∠C is less than m∠B? Why or why not?

    _____

    _____

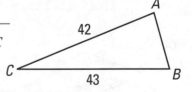

Review Objective G, Lesson 6-3

In 17–21, for each term, complete the following definition:
A quadrilateral is a (given term) if and only if ___?___.

17. rhombus _____

18. rectangle _____

19. square _____

20. trapezoid _____

21. kite _____

Name _____

Skills Objective A: Calculate perimeters of parallelograms, kites, and equilateral polygons given appropriate lengths and vice versa.

In 1–9, give the perimeter of each figure.

1. a rectangle with length 8 cm and width 2.5 cm _____

2. an equilateral triangle with one side of length 15 in. _____

3. a square-shaped region $\frac{1}{4}$ yard on a side _____

4. a regular hexagon with one side of length 16 mm _____

5. a parallelogram with one side of length 12 and the adjacent side half as long _____

6. a regular octagon with side $(y + 7)$ _____

7. an equilateral pentagon with side length $(4a + 13)$ _____

8. a rectangle with one dimension $n + 2$ and the other dimension $2n - 1$ _____

9. a kite with the length of a shorter side $4m$ and the length of a longer side 5 more than twice the length of a shorter side _____

10. The perimeter of an equilateral triangle is 13.5 m. Find the length of a side. _____

11. The perimeter of a parallelogram is 48, with the length of a shorter side 10. Find the length of a longer side. _____

12. The perimeter of a rhombus is 34 mm. What is the length of a side? _____

13. The longer sides of a rectangle are 3 times as long as the shorter sides. If the perimeter is 100 feet, what are the dimensions of the rectangle? _____

14. The perimeter of a regular hexagon is $84h + 12$. What is the length of a side? _____

15. Pictured at the right is kite *KITE*. If its perimeter is 72 cm, what are the lengths of its sides?

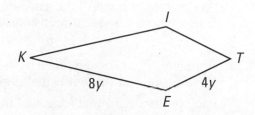

_____

▶ **LESSON MASTER 8-1B** *page 2*

16. The perimeter of a kite is 120 inches, and the length
of one side is 18 inches. Is this enough information to
find the lengths of the other three sides of the kite?
If so, find the lengths. If not, tell why not.

_____

_____

Uses Objective H: Apply perimeter formulas for parallelograms, kites, and
equilateral polygons to real-world situations.

---

17. The Parthenon in Athens, Greece, was completed
in 432 B.C. It is about 69.5 m long and 30.9 m wide.
Find its perimeter.   _____

18. The Pentagon, outside Washington, D.C., is shaped
like a regular pentagon with each side 921 feet long.
Find the perimeter.   _____

19. The base of the Great Pyramid of Khufu, near Cairo,
Egypt, is shaped like a square. If the perimeter is
about 922.4 m, find the length of a side.   _____

20. The Taj Mahal in Agra, India, is octagonal, with a
perimeter of 212 m. Four sides each measure about
44.5 m, and the remaining sides are each the same
length. Find the length of a remaining side.   _____

21. A stockade fence is to be supported at 6-foot intervals
by vertical posts. If the area to be fenced is a rectangle
54 feet by 72 feet, how many posts will be needed?   _____

22. Sue Ling wishes to sew braid trim 3 inches from the
edges of a 72-in. × 108-in. table cloth. How many
yards of trim will she need?   _____

23. The molding for an ornate gold picture frame with
outside dimensions of 5 inches and 7 inches costs $12.
At this rate, what will the same molding cost for a
frame whose outside dimensions are 3 times as long?   _____

24. For an outdoor display, Jose wishes to outline a
large 6-pointed star with small lights. The sides of
each point are $3\frac{1}{2}$ feet long, and he plans to place the
lights 4 inches apart. How many lights will he need?   _____

LESSON MASTER 8-2 B

Skills Objective C: Calculate areas of squares and rectangles given relevant lengths of sides and vice versa.

1. Rectangle *ABCD* is 25 mm wide and 40 mm long.

   a. Find Area (*ABCD*) in square millimeters. _____

   b. Find Area (*ABCD*) in square centimeters. _____

2. Find the area of a square with side length 14 cm. _____

3. A rectangle has a perimeter of 36 and a shorter side measures 8. Find the area of the rectangle. _____

4. The perimeter of a square is $16s + 24$. Find its area. _____

5. The area of a rectangle is 99 cm². One dimension is 22 cm. What is the other? _____

6. The area of a square is 324 square centimeters. Find the length of a side. _____

7. The length of a rectangle is 3 times its width. If its area is 108 square feet, find its dimensions. _____

Properties Objective G: Relate various formulas for area.

8. Explain how the formula for the area of a square can be derived from the formula for the area of a rectangle.

_____

_____

9. Find the area of the shaded region in the figure at the right.

   _____

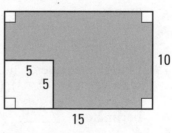

10. Given a square with side length s, how many times as great is the area of a square whose side is 3 times s? _____

11. How does the area of a rectangle change if its width is doubled and its length is halved? _____

12. How does the area of a rectangle change if its width is doubled and its length is tripled? _____

▶ **LESSON MASTER 8-2B** *page 2*

Uses Objective I: Apply formulas for areas of squares and rectangles to real-world situations.

13. The width of a soccer field can vary from about 46 m to about 91 m, while the length can vary from about 91 m to about 119 m. What is the range for possible areas for a soccer field? _____

14. A room measures 15 feet by 21 feet.

   a. How many square tiles 9 inches on a side will be needed to cover the floor? _____

   b. What will be the total cost, excluding tax, for the tiles if they are priced at 79¢ each? _____

15. Rolls of sod measure 18 in. by 6 ft. How many rolls will be needed for a football field $53\frac{1}{3}$ yd by 120 yd? _____

16. What will be the total cost, without tax, to carpet a 12-ft × 18-ft living room if the cost per yd² is $18.95 plus $6.50 per yd² for padding and installation? _____

17. Cathy has 60 feet of chain link to make a rectangular pen for her dog Daisy.

   a. Find the dimensions of the largest pen she can make. _____

   b. What is the area of that pen? _____

Representations Objective K: Determine the areas of polygons on a coordinate plane.

18. Find the perimeter and the area of *MONKEY*.

   perimeter _____

   area _____

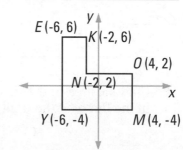

19. Find the perimeter and the area of the quadrilateral with vertices (-2, -3), (-2, 5), (4, 5), and (4, -3).

   perimeter _____   area _____

20. A floor plan for a doll-house living room is shown on the grid at the right. If the unit of measure is centimeters, find the area of its floor.

   _____

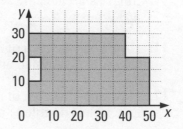

LESSON MASTER

8-3
B

Vocabulary

1. The area of a region is the ___?___ of the
   estimates made using finer and finer grids.   _____

2. Define *lattice point*.

   _____

3. In the area formula $A = (I + \frac{1}{2}B) \times U$, what does
   each variable represent?

   a. A _____

   b. I _____

   c. B _____

   d. U _____

Skills Objective B: Describe or apply a method for determining the area of an
irregularly shaped region.

In 4–6, estimate the area of the irregular region.
The side length of one small square is given.

4. 10 in. _____ **5.** .5 km _____ **6.** 40 m _____

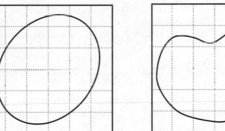 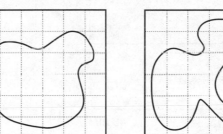

7. Estimate the area of the figure
   at the right.

   a. Use the left-hand grid.

   _____

   b. Use the right-hand grid.

   _____

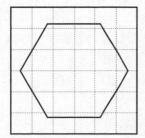 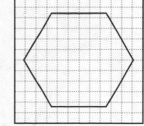

   side of squares = 1 in.   side of squares = $\frac{1}{2}$ in.

   c. Which answer is more accurate? Justify your answer.

► **LESSON MASTER 8-3B** *page 2*

**In 8–13, estimate the area of the state or country.
The side length of a small square is given in miles.**

8.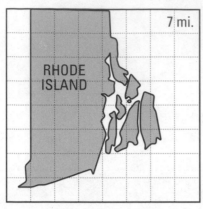
7 mi.
RHODE ISLAND

_____

9.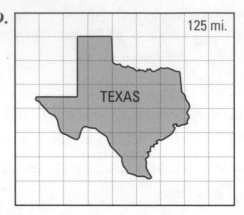
125 mi.
TEXAS

_____

10.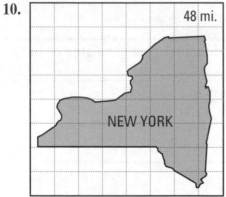
48 mi.
NEW YORK

_____

11.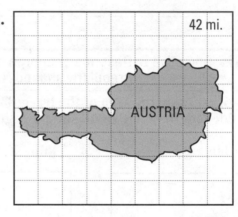
42 mi.
AUSTRIA

_____

12.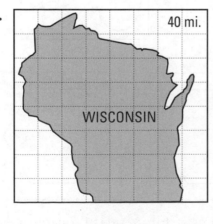
40 mi.
WISCONSIN

_____

13.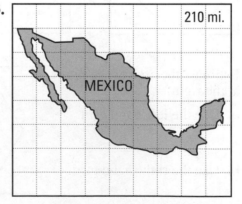
210 mi.
MEXICO

_____

14. What are the approximate dimensions in feet
of a square lot with an area of a half acre?
(640 acres = 1 square mile, 1 mile = 5280 feet)   _____

LESSON MASTER

8-4
B

Vocabulary

1. Define *altitude of a triangle*. _____

_____

_____

2. The length of an altitude is also called the _____ .

Skills Objective C: Calculate areas of triangles given relevant lengths of sides and vice versa.

In 3–5, find the area of △BUG.

3.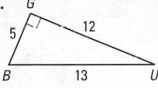

4.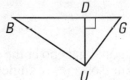

DU = 8 cm
DG = 6 cm
BD = 12 cm

5.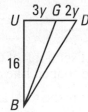

Area (△DUB) = 80 ft²

_____ _____ _____

6. If Area (△LON) = 150 units², find *IN*.

_____

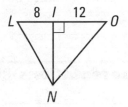

7. The two legs of a right triangle measure 8 cm and 25 cm. Find the area of the triangle. _____

8. The area of a right triangle is 36 in². If the length of one leg is 6 in., what is the length of the other leg? _____

Properties Objective G: Relate various formulas for area.

9. a. Give a formula for the area of kite *KITE* at the right.

_____

b. If *KT* = 36 and *IE* = 24, find Area (*KITE*). _____

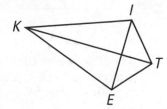

10. Given △ABC and △DEF with AB = DE, m∠C = 80 and m∠F = 120, can Area △ABC = Area △DEF? Why or why not?

_____

_____

Uses Objective I: Apply formulas for areas of triangles to real-world situations.

11. The flag of Antigua shown at the right is a rectangle 3 feet high and $4\frac{1}{2}$ feet wide. The two solid-colored red triangles are congruent. How much material is needed for each red triangle?

_____

12. The rectangular Congo flag pictured at the right is 225 cm wide and 150 cm high. What percent of the flag is the yellow stripe which is enclosed by the red and the green isosceles triangles?

_____

13. The roof sections of the hexagonal gazebo at the right are shaped like congruent isosceles triangles.

   a. What is the total area of the roof?

   _____

   b. What will be the approximate cost for roof shingles if the price is $12.99 per bundle and 3 bundles cover 100 square feet?

   _____

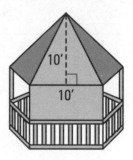

Representations Objective K: Determine the areas of triangles on a coordinate plane.

14. A triangle has vertices (-5, 7), (4, 7), and (1, 2).

   a. Draw the triangle on the grid at the right.

   b. Find the area of the triangle.

   _____

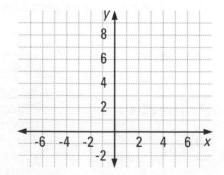

15. The three sides of a triangle are on the x-axis, the y-axis, and the line with equation $8x + 5y = 40$.

   a. Draw the triangle on the grid at the right.

   b. Find the area of the triangle.

   _____

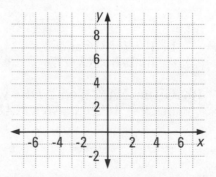

LESSON MASTER 8-5 B

Vocabulary

1. Define *altitude of a trapezoid*.

_____

_____

Skills Objective C: Calculate areas of trapezoids and parallelograms given relevant lengths of sides and vice versa.

In 2–6, use the information in the drawing to find the area of the trapezoid.

2. $\sqrt{6y}$

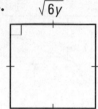

3.   12

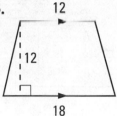

12

18

4.   16

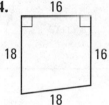

18   16

18

_____   _____   _____

5. $8\sqrt{5}$

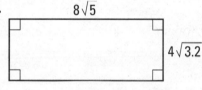

$4\sqrt{3.2}$

6.   8.5

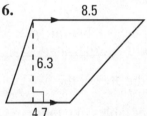

6.3

4.7

_____   _____

7. A rhombus has a perimeter of 84 cm and an area of 252 cm². Find the length of the altitude.   _____

8. An isosceles trapezoid has an area of 144 in². Its altitude measures 9 in. Give a possible combination of lengths for the bases of the trapezoid.   _____

Properties Objective G: Relate various formulas for area.

9. How is the formula for the area of a trapezoid derived from the triangle area formula? Draw a diagram to illustrate your explanation.

_____

_____

10. How is the formula for the area of a parallelogram related to the formula for the area of a trapezoid?

_____

_____

_____

Skills Objective I: Apply formulas for areas of trapezoids and parallelograms to real-world situations.

In 11 and 12, use the diagrams to estimate the area of the state. Dimensions are given in miles.

11.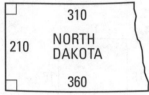

12.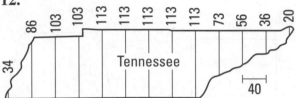

_____   _____

13. The tables in a pre-school classroom are shaped like isosceles trapezoids as shown at the right.

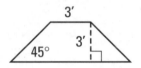

    a. If two of these tables are placed with their longer bases aligned, what shape is formed?   _____

    b. What is the area of the two tables in Part **a**?   _____

14. Suppose four tables like those in Question 13 are put together with their sides matched and their longer bases on the perimeter.

    a. What shape is formed by the perimeter?   _____

    b. What is the area of the figure in Part **a**?   _____

Representations Objective K: Determine the areas of trapezoids and parallelograms on a coordinate plane.

In 15 and 16, find the area of the region.

15.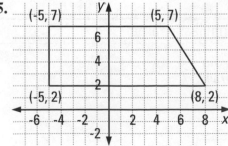

16.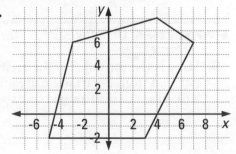

_____   _____

LESSON MASTER **8-6 B**   **Questions on SPUR Objectives**

Vocabulary

1. State the *Pythagorean Theorem*.

_____

_____

_____

2. State the *Pythagorean Converse Theorem*.

_____

_____

_____

Skills Objective D: Apply the Pythagorean Theorem to calculate lengths and areas in right triangles and other figures.

In 3–5, a triangle is given. a. Find the length of the missing side. b. Find the area.

3.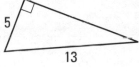
5
13

4.
24
7

5.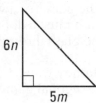
6*n*
5*m*

a. _____   a. _____   a. _____

b. _____   b. _____   b. _____

6. Find the perimeter and the area of a rhombus with diagonals measuring 20 in. and 32 in.

perimeter _____   area _____

Skills Objective E: Apply the Pythagorean Converse Theorem.

In 7–9, could the numbers be the lengths of sides of a right triangle?

7. 4, 5, 7 _____   **8.** 9, 40, 41 _____   **9.** 20, 21, 29 _____

10. Find the perimeter and the area of a right triangle with a hypotenuse of 25 mm and one side 7 mm long.

perimeter _____   area _____

11. Given $A = (5, 2)$ and $B = (8, 2)$, give possible integer coordinates for C such that $BC = \sqrt{34}$.   _____

Uses Objective H: Apply the Pythagorean Theorem to real-world situations.

12. The minute hand of Big Ben is 14 feet long and the hour hand is 9 feet long. What is the distance between the tips of the hands at 3:00 P.M.? _____

13. The north-south distance from South Bend, Indiana, to Indianapolis is about 140 miles. Richmond is about 73 miles due east of Indianapolis. What is the distance between South Bend and Richmond "as the crow flies"? _____

14. Four guy wires are to be placed from the top of a 40-meter-tall radio tower to points 12 meters from the center of the base of the tower. What is the toal length of wire needed? _____

15. The top of a tree broken by a storm just touches the ground 12 feet from the base of the tree. If the tree had been 36 feet tall, how much is still standing? _____

16. The glass for a window is 7.5 feet wide. About how high must a doorway be in order for a contractor to get the glass through the door if the doorway is 3 feet wide? _____

17. Barney wants to use felt to cover the top of a regular-hexagonal game table. Each side is 3 feet long.

   a. What is the area to be covered? _____

   b. Felt comes 72 inches wide. Can Barney cover the table top without having a seam in the felt? _____

18. How much ribbon is needed to wrap the package as shown below?

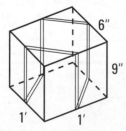

19. Find the length of wire needed to brace the two poles shown below.

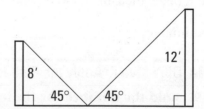

_____   _____

Culture Objective L: Identify cultures in which the Pythagorean Theorem is known to have been studied.

In 20 and 21, *true or false*.

20. In Japan, the Pythagorean Theorem is called "The Theorem of Three Triangles." _____

21. Leonardo Da Vinci gave a proof of the Pythagorean Theorem. _____

LESSON MASTER

8-7
B

Vocabulary

1. **a.** Define *circumference*. _____

   b. Define *pi*. _____

Skills Objective F: Calculate lengths and measures of arcs and the circumference of a circle given measures of relevant lengths and angles and vice versa.

---

2. *Multiple choice.* Which expression shows the exact circumference of a circle with a radius of 30 cm? _____

   (a) 30π cm   (b) 188.5 cm   (c) 60π cm   (d) 15π cm

3. Give the circumference of a circle with a diameter of 23 m

   a. exactly. _____   **b.** to the nearest meter. _____

In 4–7, the circumference of a circle is given. Find the desired length.

4. 242π, radius _____   5. 8.75 ft, diameter _____

6. 22π mm, diameter _____   7. $17y$, radius _____

In 8–10, find the diameter of the circle with the given arc measure and length.

8. $60°$, 16π cm _____   9. $45°$, 12 in. _____   10. $135°$, 6π _____

11. In the circle below, $CB = 8$ and $\overset{\frown}{AB} = 6$. Find m $\overset{\frown}{AB}$.

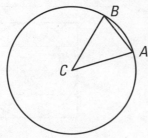

12. In the circle below, how much longer is $\overset{\frown}{CD}$ than $\overline{CD}$?

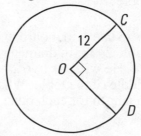

_____   _____

13. By how much is the circumference of a circle with the given diameter increased if the radius is increased by 1 meter?

   a. 20 meters _____   **b.** 2000 meters _____

Uses Objective J: Apply formulas for the circumference of a circle to real situations.

14. The sizes of many flower bulbs are given by circumference. Find the diameter for each bulb with the given measure.

   a. tulip, 12 cm _____   **b.** crocus, 8 cm _____

   c. amaryllis, 34 cm _____

15. In center-point irrigation, a long pipe describes a circle as it rotates to water a field. What is the circumference of the circle described by an irrigation pipe $\frac{1}{4}$ mile long? _____

16. A track for automobile racing is shown at the right. Each end portion is a half-circle with diameter .477 mi, and the two side sections are straight-line segments with length .5 mi.

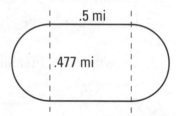

   a. What is the total length of the track? _____

   b. How many laps must a car make to travel 500 miles? _____

17. Kitty is making cone-shaped cardboard party hats by cutting sections out of circles with 6-in. radii as shown at the right. How much trim will she need to go around the curved edge of each hat?

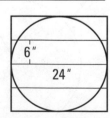

   _____

18. The *bore* of a tree is the diameter of its trunk. How much greater is the circumference of a tree with a 3-inch bore than the circumference of a tree with a 2-inch bore? _____

19. Erik plans to use 6-in. board to make a round table 24 in. in diameter as shown at the right. He will use two 24-in. boards for the middle of the table. What is the minimum length for each outer board?

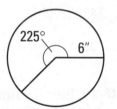

   _____

20. How many times must Pedro ride around a 70-meter-diameter circular track in order to cover 1 kilometer? _____

21. In a half mile, how many more wheel revolutions are made by a 20" child's bike than by a 26" adult's bike? _____

LESSON MASTER   **8-8** B

Skills Objective F: Calculate the area of a circle given measures of relevant lengths and angles and vice versa.

In 1–3, estimate to the nearest tenth the area of the circle described.

1. a radius of 8 inches

   _____

2. a circumference of 24π units

   _____

3. a diameter of 4√3 cm

   _____

4. The area of a circle is 12.96π square units. Find its diameter. _____

5. The area of a circle is 50 square inches. Find its radius. _____

6. Find the area of a semi-circle with diameter 26 m. _____

7. In ⊙ O at the right, find the area of the region bounded by $\overline{OA}$, $\overline{OB}$, and $\widehat{AB}$.

   _____

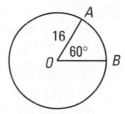

Properties Objective G: Relate various formulas for area.

---

8. Which has greater area, a circle with diameter of 6 feet or an equilateral triangle with a side of 6 feet? Justify your answer.

   _____

   _____

In 9 and 10, find the area of the shaded region.

9.

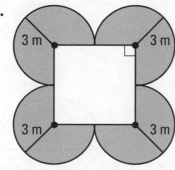

   _____

10.

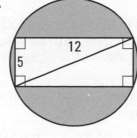

   _____

▶ **LESSON MASTER 8-8B** *page 2*

Properties Objective J: Apply formulas for the area of a circle to real situations.

11. The free-throw circle and rectangular lane of a basketball court are shown at the right. In high-school and college, the lane is 12 feet wide, while in professional basketball the lane is 16 feet wide. Find the total area of the region on

    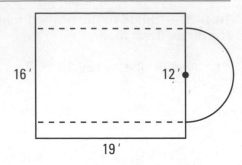

    a. a high school/college court. _____

    b. a professional court. _____

12. Suppose a radio station can transmit within a 100-km radius from its broadcast tower. What is the area of the transmission region? _____

13. Another radio station claims that it can reach people in an area of 25,000 square kilometers. What is the radius of its transmission area? _____

14. Find the area of the region that can be watered by a center-point irrigation system with a $\frac{1}{4}$-mile pipe

    a. in square miles. _____

    b. in square feet. _____

    c. in acres. _____

15. The usable portion of a CD has an outer radius of 5.7 cm and an inner radius of 2.3 cm. Find the area of the usable portion of the CD. _____

16. A window in the shape of a half circle is to be installed over a door frame which is 40 inches wide. What is the area of the glass needed for the window? _____

17. A circular drop-leaf table is shown at the right. Find the area of

    a. the table with leaves up (as pictured).

    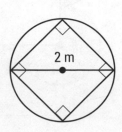

    _____

    b. the table with leaves down (a square). **c.** one leaf.

    _____ _____

LESSON MASTER 9-1 B

Vocabulary

1. What is *solid geometry?*

_____

_____

_____

Properties Objective F: Apply the properties of planes.

In 2–5, *true* or *false*. Justify your answer by stating the appropriate assumption from the Point-Line-Plane Postulate.

2. There are at least two different planes containing ∠*DEF*.

_____

_____

_____

3. If point *A* is on planes *M* and *N*, then *M* ∩ *N* is a line.

_____

_____

_____

4. Given plane *E*, there is at least one point in space *not* in *E*.

_____

_____

_____

5. If points *S* and *T* lie in plane *Z*, then
$\overline{ST}$ may not lie in plane *Z*.

_____

_____

_____

► **LESSON MASTER 9-1B** *page 2*

**In 6–10, match the situation with the assumption it most
closely illustrates.**

(a) **Unique Line Assumption**   (b) **Number Line Assumption**

(c) **Dimension Assumption**   (d) **Flat Plane Assumption**

(e) **Unique Plane Assumption**   (f) **Intersecting Planes Assumption**

6. The glass panels in a revolving door meet
   along the center post.   _____

7. A tricycle offers a stable ride.   _____

8. A ruler might show inches or centimeters.   _____

9. There is only one straight route from Train
   Station A to Train Station B.   _____

10. The line joining two points on a sheet of
    cardboard is on the cardboard.   _____

In 11–14, tell if the figure must be contained in exactly one plane.

11.

_____

12.

W

_____

13.

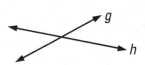

_____

14.

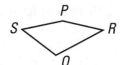

_____

Review Objective C: Lessons 3-6 and 3-7

**In 15 and 16, refer to the diagram at
the right.**

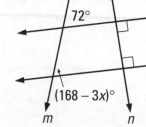

15. Is *u // v* ? Justify your answer.

_____

_____

16. Solve for *x*. Justify your answer. _____

_____

LESSON MASTER 9-2 B

Vocabulary

1. When is a line perpendicular to a plane?

   _____

   _____

2. Define *parallel planes*.

   _____

   _____

3. Define *skew lines*.

   _____

   _____

Skills Objective A: Draw common 3-dimensional shapes.

In 4–9, draw the figure.

4. two parallel planes

5. a line perpendicular to a plane

6. a line intersecting a plane at a 45° angle

7. a dihedral angle

8. two intersecting planes that are not perpendicular

9. a line parallel to a plane

▶ **LESSON MASTER 9-2B** *page 2*

Properties Objective F: Apply the properties of planes.

10. **a.** At the right, *m* and *n* are in plane *D*. *a* ⊥ *m* and *a* ⊥ *n*. Is *a* ⊥ *D*? Explain your answer.

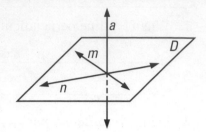

_____

_____

_____

_____

b. Is *a* perpendicular to any other lines in *D*? Explain your answer.

_____

_____

c. Is *m* ⊥ *n*? Explain your answer.

_____

_____

d. Why can't you apply the Two Perpendiculars Theorem from Chapter 3 to conclude that *m* // *n*?

_____

_____

11. Provide the argument for the proof.

Given: $\overline{GE}$ ⊥ plane *S* at *E*; *E* is the midpoint of $\overline{XY}$; *X*, *E*, and *Y* are in plane *S*.

To prove: △*GXE* ≅ △*GYE*.

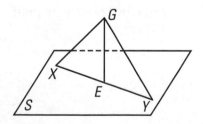

GEOMETRY © Scott, Foresman and Company

LESSON MASTER

9-3 B

Questions on SPUR Objectives

Vocabulary

1. a. Define *cylinder*. _____

_____

 b. Define *prism*. _____

_____

In 2–5, refer to the prism at the right.

2. a. How many edges
 are there? _____

 b. Name any two edges. _____

3. a. How many vertices
 are there? _____

 b. Name any two vertices. _____

4. a. How many faces are there? _____

 b. Name two lateral faces. _____

 c. Name faces in two parallel planes. _____

5. What type of prism is this? _____

6. What is the difference between a 3-dimensional
 surface and a solid?

_____

_____

_____

Skills Objective A: Draw prisms and cylinders.

In 7–12, sketch the indicated surface.

7. a cube   **8.** a right cylinder   **9.** an oblique cylinder

Name _____

10. a right rectangular prism

11. a right triangular prism

12. a regular hexagonal prism

Skills Objective D: Given appropriate lengths, calculate areas and lengths in prisms and cylinders.

---

13. Refer to the box at the right.

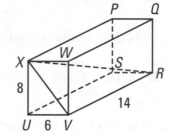

 a. Name all segments with length 14. _____

 b. Find *XV*. _____

 c. Find *XR* to the nearest tenth. _____

14. Refer to the oblique cylinder at the right.

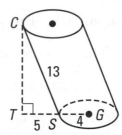

 a. Find its height. _____

 b. Find the area of its base. _____

Uses Objective H: Recognize prisms and cylinders in the real world.

In 15–18, tell which 3-dimensional figure most resembles the real-world object. Be as specific as you can.

15. the top story of the house pictured at the right

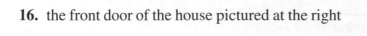

_____

16. the front door of the house pictured at the right

_____

17. the cabinet pictured at the right

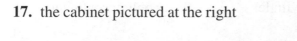

_____

18. the lamp shade pictured at the right

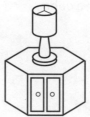

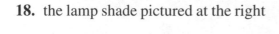

_____

LESSON MASTER

9-4
B

Questions on SPUR Objectives

Vocabulary

1. **a.** Define *cone*. _____

   _____

   b. Define *pyramid*. _____

   _____

In 2–5, refer to the pyramid at the right.

2. **a.** Name its base. _____

   b. Name its vertex. _____

3. **a.** Name its base edges.

   _____

   b. Name its lateral edges.

   _____

4. **a.** How many faces are there? _____

   b. How many lateral faces are there? _____

   c. Name any two lateral faces. _____

5. What type of pyramid is this? _____

In 6–8, refer to the cone at the right.

6. **a.** Name its base. _____

   b. Name its vertex. _____

7. **a.** Name a lateral edge. _____

   b. Name its axis. _____

8. What type of cone is this? _____

Skills Objective A: Draw pyramids and cones.

In 9–11, sketch the indicated surface.

9. a right cone

10. a right square pyramid

11. a truncated cone

Skills Objective D: Given appropriate lengths, calculate areas and lengths in pyramids and cones.

12. Refer to the regular triangular pyramid with base *S* at the right.

   a. Find the perimeter of its base. _____

   b. Find its slant height. _____

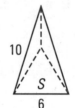

13. Refer to the truncated regular square pyramid at the right.

   a. What is the ratio of the lengths of the base edges? _____

   b. What is the ratio of the areas of its bases? _____

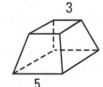

14. Refer to the cone at the right.

   a. Find its altitude. _____

   b. Find the area of its base. _____

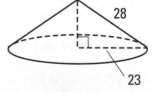

Uses Objective H: Recognize pyramids and cones in the real world.

In 15–18, tell which 3-dimensional figure most resembles the real-world object. Be as specific as you can.

15. a teepee _____

16. a soft-drink cup _____

17. Egyptian pyramid _____

18. a cow bell _____

LESSON MASTER

9-5
B

Vocabulary

1. Define *sphere*.

_____

_____

2. Define *plane section*.

_____

_____

_____

Skills Objective A: Draw spheres.
Objective B: Draw plane sections of common 3-dimensional shapes.

3. Use the sphere pictured at the right.

   a. Draw and label Q, the center of the sphere.

   b. Draw and label $\overline{QR}$, a radius not in $\odot Q$.

   c. Draw and label $\odot G$, a great circle different from $\odot Q$.

   d. Draw and label $\odot S$, a small circle.

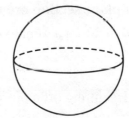

In 4–6, sketch the plane section and describe its shape.

4. parallel to the base of a regular pentagonal prism

   _____

5. neither parallel to nor intersecting the bases of an oblique cylinder

   _____

6. perpendicular to the base of a right cone but not through the vertex

   _____

Skills Objective D: Given appropriate lengths, calculate areas and lengths in spheres.

7. The diameter of a sphere is 16 in. What is the area of a great circle of the sphere? _____

8. Refer to the right prism pictured at the right. A plane section is formed when a plane cuts through the prism and is parallel to the bases. What is the area of the plane section? _____

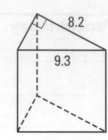

9. Refer to the cone pictured at the right. A plane section is formed when a plane cuts through the center of the base and is perpendicular to the base. What is the area of the plane section? _____

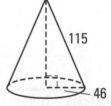

Uses Objective H: Recognize 3-dimensional figures in the real world.

In 10–12, tell which 3-dimensional figure and what kind of plane section are most representative of the situation.

10. cutting a tomato in half

_____

11. cutting off a piece of pipe

_____

12. making an oblique cut through a pencil

_____

Review Objective A, Lesson 6-1

In 13–18, draw the symmetry line(s), if any, for the figure.

13.

14.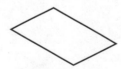

15.

16.

17.

18.

LESSON MASTER

9-6 B

Vocabulary

1. Define *reflection image in space*.

_____

_____

_____

_____

2. When are two 3-dimensional figures congruent?

_____

_____

3. When is a 3-dimensional figure reflection-symmetric?

_____

_____

Properties Objective G: Determine symmetry planes in 3-dimensional figures.

In 4–12, a 3-dimensional figure is given. a. Tell if the figure has bilateral symmetry. b. If so, give the number of symmetry planes.

4.

oblique cone

a. _____

b. _____

5.

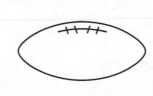

football

a. _____

b. _____

6.

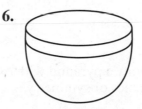

mixing bowl

a. _____

b. _____

7.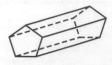

regular pentagonal
prism

a. _____

b. _____

8.

triangular
pyramid

a. _____

b. _____

9.

pliers

a. _____

b. _____

10.

bird

a. _____

b. _____

11.

truncated right cone

a. _____

b. _____

12.

cube

a. _____

b. _____

13. Draw a prism with exactly one
plane of symmetry.

14. Draw a pyramid with exactly four
planes of symmetry.

15. Draw a real-world object with an
infinite number of symmetry planes.

LESSON MASTER

9-7
B

Skills Objective C: Give views of a figure from the top, sides, or front.

In 1–4, a figure is given. Sketch views of the figure from the given direction. a. top b. front c. right side d. bottom

1. 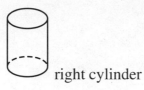 right cylinder

a.   b.

c.   d.

2. 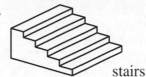 stairs

a.   b.

c.   d.

3. 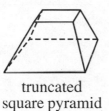 truncated square pyramid

a.   b.

c.   d.

4. 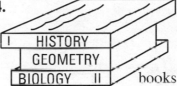 books

a.   b.

c.   d.

Skills Objective E: From 2-dimensional views of a figure determine the
3-dimensional figure.

In 5–8, name a surface with the views shown.

5.

   top   front   side   _____

6.

   top   front   side   _____

7.

   top   front   side   _____

8.

   top   front   side   _____

9. A building is made of congruent prefabricated boxes.
   Three views of the building are given.

   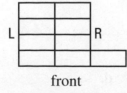   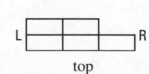

   front   left side   top

   a. How tall in stories
      is the building?   _____

   b. How long in sections is the
      building from front to back?   _____

   c. At the right, sketch a possible
      shape of the building.

LESSON MASTER 9-8 B

Vocabulary

1. Define *polyhedron*.

_____

_____

_____

2. Define *regular polyhedron*.

_____

_____

_____

3. List the regular polyhedra. For each one describe
the faces and tell how many faces it has.

_____

_____

_____

_____

_____

Representations Objective J: Make a surface from a net and vice versa.

In 4–7, sketch the surface that can be made from each net.

4.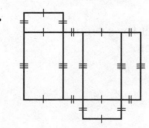

5.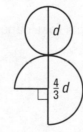

▶ **LESSON MASTER 9-8B** *page 2*

6.

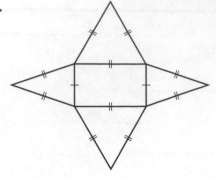

7.

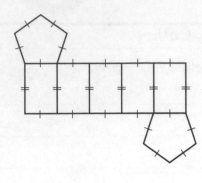

8. Draw a net for a right cylinder whose height is equal to the diameter of a base.

9. Draw a net for a regular triangular prism.

10. Draw two different nets for a cube.

11. Draw a net for a regular tetrahedron.

LESSON MASTER 9-9 B

Uses Objective I: Apply the Four-Color Theorem to maps.

1. a. State the *Four-Color Theorem*.

_____

_____

_____

_____

b. In what year was the Four-Color Theorem proved? _____

In 2 and 3, color each map using as few colors as possible.

2.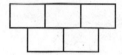

3.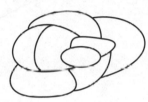

4. Draw a map with seven regions that can be colored with only <u>two</u> colors.

5. Draw a map with seven regions that requires <u>four</u> colors to be colored.

6. At the right is a map of some of the central states in the United States. Color it using the least number of colors.

► **LESSON MASTER 9-9B** *page 2*

7. At the left is a map of Mexico and Central America. Color it using exactly three colors. Then label as many countries as you can.

Representations Objective K: Interpret maps of the world.

8. How is a Mercator-projection map made?

_____

_____

9. a. Name a property that is not preserved
on a Mercator-projection map.   _____

   b. Name a property that is preserved
on a Mercator-projection map.   _____

10. Describe two problems with using a map of the
world that is made up of gores.

_____

_____

_____

LESSON MASTER 10-1 B

Vocabulary

1. What is the difference between the *surface area* and the *lateral area* of a 3-dimensional figure?

_____

_____

_____

Skills Objective A: Calculate lateral areas and surface areas of cylinders and prisms from appropriate lengths, and vice versa.

**In 2–9, a figure is described.   a. Give its lateral area.
b. Give its surface area.**

2. a box with length 12 in., width 7 in., and height 8 in.

   a. _____

   b. _____

3. a right cylinder with base radius 5 cm and height 8.5 cm

   a. _____

   b. _____

4. a right pentagonal prism with base area 72 mm², base perimeter 32 mm, and height 35 mm

   a. _____

   b. _____

5. a right cylinder with base circumference 18π ft and height 10 ft

   a. _____

   b. _____

6. a cube with edge 3 yd

   a. _____

   b. _____

7. a cube with edge *e*

   a. _____

   b. _____

8.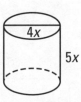

   right cylinder

   a. _____

   b. _____

9.

   right triangle prism

   a. _____

   b. _____

In 10 and 11, a net for a 3-dimensional figure is
shown.   a. Give the lateral area of the figure.
b. Give the surface area of the figure.

10.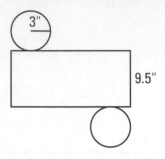

11.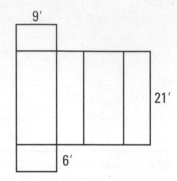

a. _____

b. _____

a. _____

b. _____

Uses Objective H: Apply formulas for lateral and surface area of prisms and
cylinders to real situations.

---

12. A section of concrete sewer pipe is 4 ft in diameter
and 8 ft long. Find the lateral area of the pipe.   _____

13. A wooden toy box measures .75 m
by .6 m by .5 m. Find the surface area
of the toy box.

_____

14. Refrigerated biscuit dough comes in a cylindrical can
with diameter 2.5 in. and height 8 in. The bases are
aluminum and the lateral face is cardboard.

a. How many square inches of aluminum
are used?   _____

b. How many square inches of cardboard
are used?   _____

15. Pipe organs often have large wooden pipes shaped like
long, narrow boxes without bases. One of the largest
organ pipes, in Liverpool Cathedral, England, is
about 36 ft long, 2 ft 9 in. wide, and 3 ft 2 in. deep.
Find its lateral area.   _____

LESSON MASTER 10-2 B

Skills Objective B: Calculate lateral areas and surface areas of pyramids and cones from appropriate, lengths, and vice versa.

In 1–8, a figure is described.   a. Give its lateral area.
b. Give its surface area.

1. a regular square pyramid with slant height of 2 yd and base edge of 1 yd

a. _____

b. _____

2. a right cone with radius 6 cm and slant height of 9 cm

a. _____

b. _____

3. a regular square pyramid with slant height of 5 in. and base area of 49 in²

a. _____

b. _____

4. a right cone with circumference of base 14π ft and slant height of 8 ft

a. _____

b. _____

5. a regular square pyramid with slant height of *t* and base edge of *u*

a. _____

b. _____

6. a right cone with radius *j* and slant height of 2*j*

a. _____

b. _____

7.

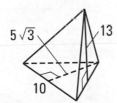

regular triangular pyramid
slant height 13, base edge 10,
altitude of base 5√3

a. _____

b. _____

8.

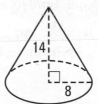

right cone

a. _____

b. _____

9. Find the lateral area of a regular hexagonal pyramid with a slant height of 9 and a base edge of 8. _____

10. The slant height of a regular square pyramid is 20 mm and its lateral area is 560 mm². What is the length of a base edge? _____

11. Pictured at the right are a right cone and regular square pyramid.

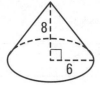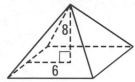

a. Find the slant height of each.

_____

b. Find the lateral area of each.

_____

c. What is the ratio of the lateral area of the cone to the lateral area of the pyramid? _____

d. Find the surface area of each.

_____

e. What is the ratio of the surface area of the cone to the surface area of the pyramid? _____

Uses Objective H: Apply formulas for lateral and surface area of pyramids and cones to real situations.

12. A paper weight is shaped like a regular square pyramid with a base edge of 8 cm and a height of 6.5 cm. Find its surface area. _____

13. A clown's hat is in the shape of a right cone with a radius 3.5 in. and a height 10 in. Find its lateral area. _____

14. A watch crystal, shown at the right, is shaped like the lateral sides of a regular pyramid having a 12-sided base. If the slant height is 17 mm and the perimeter of the base is 96 mm, what is its lateral area? _____

15. Paper covers for ice-cream cones are made of heavy paper. Cone A has a radius of 1 in. and a slant height of 4 in. Cone B has a radius of 1.25 in. and a slant height of 3.5 in. Which cone contains more paper? _____

LESSON MASTER 10-3 B

Vocabulary

1. A glass bottle is filled with sand.

   a. Is the volume of the bottle better represented by
      the amount of glass or the amount of sand? _____

   b. Is the surface area of the bottle better represented
      by the amount of glass or the amount of sand? _____

Skills Objective A: Calculate volumes of rectangular prisms from appropriate
lengths, and vice versa.

**In 2–7, give the volume of the boxes with the
given dimensions.**

2. 6 cm, 11 cm, 8 cm

3. 2.4 in., 6 in., 6 in.

4. $\frac{2}{3}$ yd, $\frac{1}{2}$ yd, $2\frac{3}{4}$ yd

_____   _____   _____

5. 11 mm, 11 mm, 11 mm

6. x, $2x$, $3x$

7. 5 in., 5 ft, 5 yd

_____   _____   _____

8. Refer to the boxes at the right.

   a. Find the surface area of
      each box.

   _____

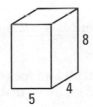 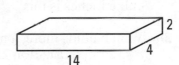

   b. Find the volume of each box. _____

   c. Study your answers in Parts a and b.
      What do you notice?

   _____

9. Refer to the boxes at the right.

   a. Find the surface area of
      each box.

   _____

 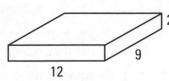

   b. Find the volume of each box. _____

   c. Study your answers in Parts **a** and **b**.
      What do you notice?

   _____

▶ **LESSON MASTER 10-3B** *page 2*

10. The volume of a box is 624 units³. Two of the
    dimensions are 6 units and 13 units. Find the
    third dimension.   _____

Skills Objective C: Calculate cube roots.

**In 11–16, give the cube root of the number. Round inexact
answers to the nearest tenth.**

11. 512   _____   12. 117.649   _____

13. 7000   _____   14. 0.14887   _____

15. 45   _____   16. 100   _____

17. Find the length of the edge of a cube whose
    volume is 4,096 m³.   _____

18. The volume of a cube is about 614 ft³. What is
    the area of a face, to the nearest tenth?   _____

Uses Objective I: Apply formulas for volumes of rectangular prisms to real
situations.

19. A carton contains 16 ounces of cream. How many
    cubic inches is this?   _____

20. Which holds more, a metal foot locker 26 in. by 14 in.
    by 12 in., or a carton 22 in. by 16 in. by 13 in.?   _____

21. The inside dimensions of a freezer are 32 in. by
    28 in. by 60 in. Find its volume in cubic feet.   _____

22. The dimensions of each brick
    at the right are 2 in., 3.5 in.,
    and 8 in.

    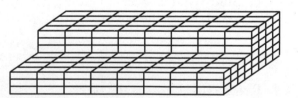

    a. Find the volume of a
       single brick.

    _____

    b. Find the total volume of the 2 steps shown.   _____

    c. How many gallons of water would be displaced
       if the steps shown were built totally submerged
       into a pond?   _____

GEOMETRY © Scott, Foresman and Company

LESSON MASTER  10-4 B

Properties Objective E: Determine what happens to the surface area and volume of a figure when its dimensions are multiplied by some number(s).

1. A box has a volume of 450 m³.

   a. If one dimension of the box is doubled, what is the volume of the larger box? _____

   b. If two dimensions of the box are doubled, what is the volume of the larger box? _____

   c. If all three dimensions of the box are doubled, what is the volume of the larger box? _____

2. A box has a volume of 200 ft³.

   a. If one dimension of the box is multiplied by 5, what is the volume of the larger box? _____

   b. If one dimension of the box is multiplied by 5 and another dimension is doubled, what is the volume of the larger box? _____

   c. If one dimension of the box is multiplied by 5, another dimension is doubled, and the third dimension is tripled, what is the volume of the larger box? _____

3. What happens to the volume of a box if all three dimensions are

   a. tripled? _____

   b. multiplied by 5? _____

   c. multiplied by $\frac{1}{2}$? _____

   d. multiplied by k? _____

4. A box has dimensions ℓ, w, and h. If the dimensions are changed as indicated, give the volume of the new box.

   a. Just the length is multiplied by 4. _____

   b. Its length is multiplied by 3, its width by 6, and its height by 10. _____

   c. Five is added to each dimension. _____

▶ **LESSON MASTER 10-4B** *page 2*

Representations Objective J: Represent products of two (or three) numbers or expressions as areas of rectangles (or volumes of boxes), and vice versa.

In 5–10, a diagram is shown.   **a.** Write the multiplication of polynomials represented by the diagram.   **b.** Find the product of the polynomials.

5.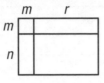

a. _____

b. _____

6.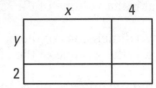

a. _____

b. _____

7.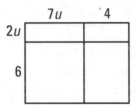

a. _____

b. _____

8.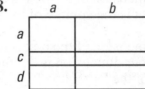

a. _____

b. _____

9.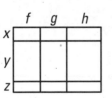

a. _____

b. _____

_____

10.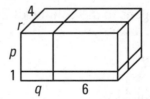

a. _____

b. _____

_____

11. The sum of the areas of the four small rectangles at the right is $x^2 + 7x + 6$. If the length of the largest rectangle is $x + 6$, what is the width?   _____

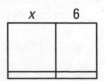

12. a. Draw a diagram that models $(x + 2)(x + 7)$.

 b. Give the product. _____

LESSON MASTER 10-5 B

Skills Objective A: Calculate volumes of cylinders and prisms from appropriate length, and vice versa.

In 1–5, calculate the volume of the figure with the specified dimensions.

1.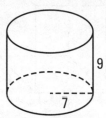

2.
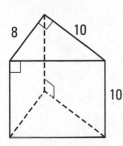

3.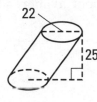

_____   _____   _____

4.

circumference 25π mm

5.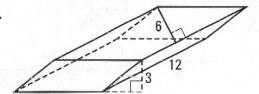

_____   _____

6. What is the area of the base of a prism that has a volume of 140 m^3 and a height of 7 m? _____

7. What is the radius of a cylinder that has a volume of 108π ft^3 and a height of 3 ft? _____

8. What is the volume of a regular hexagonal prism with a base area of 24√3 cm^2 and a height of 12 cm? _____

9. What is the length of a base edge of an oblique square prism with a height of 42 in. and a volume of 168 in^3? _____

10. A square prism and a cylinder have the same height of 13 mm and the same volume of 832 mm^3. Which is greater, the base edge of the prism or the diameter of the base of the cylinder? _____

▶ **LESSON MASTER 10-5B** *page 2*

Properties Objective G: Know the conditions under which Cavalieri's Principle can be applied.

11. *Multiple choice.* List all of the rectangular prisms below that may be paired with the one at the right under Cavalieri's Principle.

_____

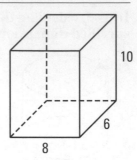
10
6
8

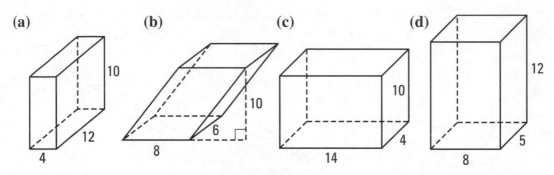

(a) 10, 12, 4 **(b)** 10, 8, 6 **(c)** 10, 14, 4 **(d)** 12, 8, 5

Uses Objective I: Apply formulas for volumes of prisms and cylinders to real situations.

12. In terms of volume, list the cans at the right in order from the smallest to largest.

____ ____ ____

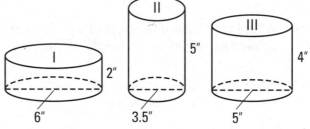

13. Find the volume of the flower tray at the right. Its end pieces are shaped like isosceles trapezoids.

_____

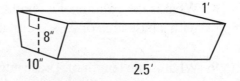

14. How many gallons of oil can be stored in a cylindric tank 8 feet long with a 5-foot diameter? (1 cubic foot = 7.5 gallons)

_____

15. Find the total weight of 30 steel rods shaped like regular hexagonal prisms with 3-inch sides and 20 feet long. The density of steel is 490 pounds per cubic foot.

_____

LESSON MASTER 10-6 B

Properties Objective F: Develop formulas for specific figures from more general formulas.

1. a. What is the special formula for the volume of a cylinder?

_____

b. Explain how the formula in Part **a** was derived from the basic formula for the volume of a cylindric surface.

_____

_____

_____

2. a. What is the special formula for the surface area of a right cone?

_____

b. Explain how the formula in Part **a** was derived from the basic formula for the lateral area of a right conical surface.

_____

_____

_____

In 3–8, write a specific lateral-area formula for each figure.

3.

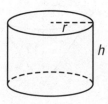

right cylinder

_____

4.

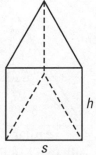

regular triangular prism

_____

5.

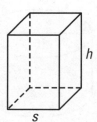

right square prism

_____

6.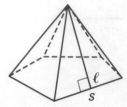

regular
pentagonal pyramid

_____

7.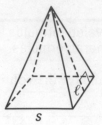

regular square
pyramid

_____

8.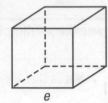

cube

_____

In 9–11, give a formula for each measure.

9.

surface area of
the right cone

_____

10.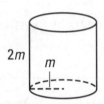

lateral area of
right cylinder

_____

11.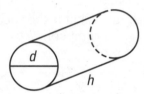

volume of right
cylinder

_____

Review Objective A, Lesson 10-1; Objective B, Lesson 10-2

**In 12–14, a figure is shown. a. Give its lateral area.
b. Give its surface area.**

12.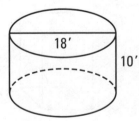

right cylinder

a. _____

b. _____

13.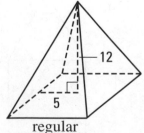

regular
square pyramid

a. _____

b. _____

14.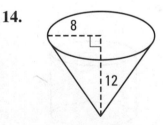

right cone

a. _____

b. _____

LESSON MASTER

10-7 B

Skills Objective B: Calculate volumes of pyramids and cones from appropriate lengths, and vice versa.

In 1–9, find the volume of the figure.

1.

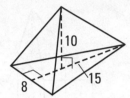

10

8   15

triangular pyramid

_____

2.

9

12

right cone

_____

3.

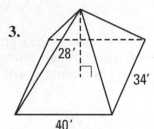

28'

34'

40'

rectangular pyramid

_____

4.

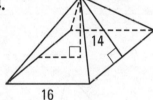

14

16

right square pyramid

_____

5.

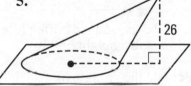

26

cone with circumference
of base 36π

_____

6.

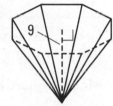

9

octagonal pyramid
with base area of 180

_____

7.

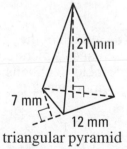

21 mm

7 mm

12 mm

triangular pyramid

_____

8.

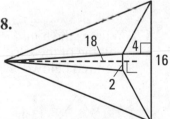

18   4

16

2

trapezoidal pyramid

_____

9.

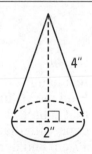

4"

2"

right cone

_____

10. A cone has a volume of 504π cm³ and a height
of 14 cm. What is the diameter of its base?

_____

11. A square pyramid has a base edge of 8.2 m and a volume of 3362 m³. What is its height?   _____

12. A hexagonal pyramid has a height of 15 in. and a volume of $720\sqrt{3}$ in³. What is the area of the base?   _____

13. Pictured at the right is a square pyramid sitting on a box. What is the ratio of the volume of the pyramid to the volume of the box?

_____

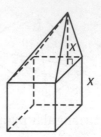

Uses Objective I: Apply formulas for volumes of pyramids and cones to real situations.

---

14. Determine the volume of a cone-shaped coffee filter that has a diameter of 4 in. and a height of 4 in.   _____

15. Mr. Hong needs to calculate the volume of his garage to determine which exhaust fan he should buy. If the overall height of the garage is 17 ft, find the volume, ignoring wall and roof thicknesses.

_____

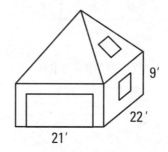

16. A *wall pocket* is a vase that hangs on the wall. Find the volume of one that is half of a right cone with diameter 17 cm and height 22 cm.

17. What is the total volume of the silo pictured below?

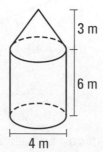

18. Which of the candles pictured below contains more wax?

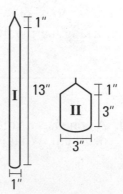

_____   _____   _____

LESSON MASTER 10-8 B

Skills Objective D: Calculate the volume of a sphere from appropriate lengths, and vice versa.

1. Refer to the sphere and the cylinder containing two cones shown at the right.

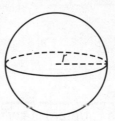 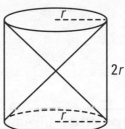

   a. Inside the cylinder, shade the space that has the same volume as the sphere.

   b. Complete the following. Given a cylinder with radius r and height $2r$ containing two cones each with radius r and height r, the volume of a sphere with radius r is equal to the volume of ___?___ minus the volume of ___?___.

   _____   _____

In 2–4, draw the sphere with the given dimension. Then find its volume.

2. radius = 18 mm   3. radius = 1.5 cm   4. diameter = 1 in.

   _____   _____   _____

5. The radius of a sphere is 26 in.

   a. Find the volume of the sphere to the nearest cubic inch.   _____

   b. Find the volume of the sphere to the nearest tenth of a cubic foot.   _____

6. The circumference of a great circle of a sphere is 28π cm. What is its volume?   _____

▶ **LESSON MASTER 10-8B** *page 2*

In 7–10, give the radius of the sphere with the given volume. Round inexact answers to the nearest tenth.

7. $\frac{32}{3}\pi$ cubic units   8. 288π in^3

_____   _____

9. 52 ft^3 10. 1262 m^3

_____   _____

Properties Objective E: Determine what happens to the volume of a sphere when its dimensions are multiplied by some number(s).

---

11. Refer to the sphere at the right. What would happen to its volume

   a. if the radius were doubled? _____

   b. if the radius were tripled? _____

   c. if the radius were multiplied by ten? _____

   d. if the radius were halved? _____

   e. if the radius were multiplied by *k*? _____

Uses Objective I: Apply the formula for volume of a sphere to real situations.

---

12. Find the volume of each ball.

   a. tennis ball, 6.4 cm in diameter   _____

   b. table-tennis ball, 3.8 cm in diameter   _____

   c. baseball, 23.5 cm in circumference   _____

13. How many ounces of water are displaced if 120 glass marbles are dropped into a 20-gallon aquarium, and the diameter of each marble is $\frac{1}{2}$ in.?   _____

14. The diameter of an inflatable beach ball is 16 in. If a person blowing it up exhales 120 cubic inches of carbon dioxide with each breath, how many breaths will it take to fill the ball?   _____

LESSON MASTER 10-9 B

Skills Objective D: Calculate the surface area of a sphere from appropriate lengths, and vice versa.

1. Refer to the sphere with great circle G shown at the right. What is the ratio of the surface area of the sphere to the area of $\odot G$?

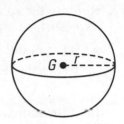

_____

In 2–9, find the surface area of a sphere with the given dimension.

2. radius = 7

_____

3. radius = 18 mm

_____

4. diameter = 38 cm

_____

5. diameter = 5

_____

6. circumference of great circle = 16π ft

_____

7. area of great circle $\approx 225\pi$ in^3

_____

8. volume = 972π cm^3

_____

9. volume $\approx$ 11,500 cubic units

_____

10. The radius of a sphere is 58 in.

   a. Find the surface area of the sphere to the nearest square inch. _____

   b. Find the surface area of the sphere to the nearest tenth of a square foot. _____

11. The surface area of a sphere is 688 cm^2. What is its radius to the nearest tenth of a centimeter? _____

▶ **LESSON MASTER 10-9B** *page 2*

Properties Objective E: Determine what happens to the surface area of a sphere when its dimensions are multiplied by some number(s).

12. Refer to the sphere at the right. What would happen to its surface area

    a. if the radius were doubled? _____

    b. if the radius were tripled? _____

    c. if the radius were multiplied by 10? _____

    d. if the radius were halved? _____

    e. if the radius were multiplied by k? _____

Uses Objective I: Apply the formula for the surface area of a sphere to real situations.

13. Estimate the surface area of each planet to the nearest million square miles.

    a. Venus, radius ≈ 3750 miles   _____

    b. Mars, radius ≈ 2100 miles   _____

    c. Jupiter, radius ≈ 44,500 miles   _____

14. The diameter of a plastic beach ball is 18 in. It is made up of 12 gores, each a different color. How many square inches of plastic are used for each gore? _____

15. The United States launched its first communications satellite, *Echo I*, in 1960. Find the area of the thin metal that coated this 100-foot diameter balloon. _____

Review Objective C, E, and H, Lessons 2-2 and 2-3

In 16–19 a conditional statement is given.   **a.** Tell if the conditional is true.   **b.** tell if its converse is true.

a = I am 16 years old today. c = I am a teenager.

b = I cannot vote in the next year's d = I will be 17 in a year.
    national election.

16. $a \Rightarrow b$ **a.** _____   **b.** _____   17. $a \Rightarrow d$ **a.** _____   **b.** _____

18. $c \Rightarrow a$ **a.** _____   **b.** _____   19. $b \Rightarrow c$ **a.** _____   **b.** _____

LESSON MASTER 11-1 B

Properties Objective D: Follow the Law of Detachment and the Law of Transitivity to make conclusions.

In 1–5, use both mathematical statements. a. What (if anything) can you conclude? b. What law(s) of reasoning did you use?

1. (1) If the measure of an angle is between 0 and 90, then the angle is acute.

   (2) m∠X = 62

   a. _____

   b. _____

2. (1) If *EFGH* is a rhombus, it is also a parallelogram.

   (2) *EFGH* is a parallelogram.

   a. _____

   b. _____

3. (1) If $b = 12$, then $c = 20$.

   (2) If $a = 2b$, then $b = 12$.

   a. _____

   b. _____

4. (1) If Figure *A* is the image of Figure *B* under a reflection, Figure *A* is congruent to Figure *B*.

   (2) △*WXY* is the reflection image of △*RST*.

   a. _____

   b. _____

5. (1) If $p > 0$ and $q > 0$, then $pq > 0$.

   (2) $pq > 0$

   a. _____

   b. _____

▶ **LESSON MASTER 11-1B** *page 2*

6. Consider the statements below.

    (1) If a quadrilateral is a rectangle, then it has two
        lines of symmetry.
    (2) If a figure has two lines of symmetry, then it
        has rotation symmetry.
    (3) *SYMT* is a rectangle.

    a. Apply the Law of Transitivity to the first two
       statements and write a conclusion.

    _____

    _____

    b. Apply the Law of Detachment to statement 3 and the
       statement you wrote in Part **a** to write a conclusion.

    _____

Properties Objective H: Apply the Law of Detachment and the Law of
                Transitivity in real situations.

**In 7–10, using all the given statements, what (if anything)
can you conclude?**

7. (1) Marty drives to school whenever he has an early
       chemistry lab.
   (2) Marty has early chemistry labs every Wednesday.

   _____

8. (1) After basketball practice, Jennie goes to the Snack Shack.
   (2) Jennie went to the Snack Shack yesterday.

   _____

9. (1) If Beatriz does well in her next recital, she'll get to be in
       the orchestra next year.
   (2) If Beatriz plays "Ode to Joy," she is sure to do well.
   (3) Beatriz will play "Ode to Joy."

   _____

10. (1) City Hall is closed on national holidays.
    (2) Building permits are issued only at City Hall.
    (3) Today is July 4.

    _____

LESSON MASTER 11-2 B

Properties Objective D: Follow the Law of the Contrapositive to make
conclusions.

**In 1–5, use both given statements. a. What (if anything) can
you conclude? b. What law(s) of reasoning did you use?**

1. (1) If a triangle is equilateral, then it is isosceles.
   (2) $\triangle ABC$ is not isosceles.

   a. _____

   b. _____

2. (1) If Figure 1 is the reflection image of Figure 2, then
       Figure 1 does not have the same orientation as Figure 2.
   (2) $J'K'L'M'$ has the same orientation as $JKLM$.

   a. _____

   b. _____

3. (1) If the measure of an angle is greater than 90, then
       the angle is obtuse.
   (2) $m\angle C$ is not greater than 90.

   a. _____

   b. _____

4. (1) If $m = 15$, then $m^2 = 225$.
   (2) $m^2 = 225$

   a. _____

   b. _____

5. (1) The diagonals of a kite are perpendicular.
   (2) In $QRST$, $\overline{QS} \perp \overline{RT}$.

   a. _____

   b. _____

6. Assume the statements below are all true. What final
   conclusion can you reach using all three statements?

   (1) $r \Rightarrow i$ (2) $i \Rightarrow d$ (3) not-d

   _____

7. What final conclusion can you reach using all
   three statements?

   (1) A reflection or composite of reflections is an isometry.
   (2) If a transformation is an isometry, then distance is preserved.
   (3) W is a transformation that does not preserve distance.

   _____

Properties Objective E: Write the converse, inverse, or contrapositive of a
conditional.

**In 8 and 9, a statement is given. a. Write its converse.
b. Write its inverse. c. Write its contrapositive.
d. Assuming the original statement is true, which of
a, b, and c are also true?**

8. If $\angle X$ and $\angle Y$ are vertical angles, then m$\angle X$ = m$\angle Y$.

   a. _____

   b. _____

   c. _____

   d. _____

9. If you are a teen, you were born after 1975.

   a. _____

   b. _____

   c. _____

   d. _____

Properties Objective H: Apply the Law of the Contrapositive in real situations.

**In 10 and 11, using both given statements, what (if anything)
can you conclude using the laws of logic?**

10. (1) If Joe does not get a scholarship, he will not attend Yale.
    (2) Joe will attend Yale.

    _____

11. (1) Today I bought a leather purse.
    (2) If I don't get a raise, I won't buy a leather purse.

    _____

LESSON MASTER 11-3 B

Properties Objective D: Follow the Law of Ruling Out Possibilities to make conclusions.

1. Explain the *Law of Ruling Out Possibilities.*

_____

_____

In 2 and 3, what can you conclude from the given statements?

2. (1) $x > 19$ or $x \leq 19$.
(2) x is not greater than 19.

_____

3. (1) $\angle U$ is either right or obtuse.
(2) m$\angle U \neq 90$

_____

In 4–6 use all the given statements. a. What (if anything) can you conclude? b. What law(s) of reasoning did you use?

4. (1) F is either a circle or a sphere.
(2) A sphere is a 3-dimensional figure.
(3) F is not a 3-dimensional figure

a. _____

b. _____

5. (1) b is either even or odd.
(2) An odd number has an odd square.
(3) b^2 is not odd.

a. _____

b. _____

6. (1) N is either a rotation or a translation.
(2) A rotation is the composite of two reflections over two intersecting lines.
(3) The two lines of reflection defining transformation N do not intersect.

a. _____

b. _____

Name _____

► **LESSON MASTER 11-3B** *page 2*

Properties Objective H: Apply the Law of Ruling Out Possibilities in real situations.

In 7–9, using all the given statements, what (if anything) can you conclude using the laws of logic?

7. (1) Mr. Harner gets either a 20% or a 30% discount.
   (2) 30% discounts are not given to store employees.
   (3) Mr. Harner is a store employee.

   _____

8. (1) Margaret is a freshman, a sophomore, a junior, or a senior.
   (2) Margaret's grade level does not begin with "s."
   (3) Freshmen may not take U.S. History.
   (4) Margaret is taking U.S. History.

   _____

9. (1) Elena, Kiyoko, and Douglas are each taking a different science course: Chemistry, Physics, or Biology.
   (2) Kiyoko is not taking Chemistry.
   (3) Douglas is taking either Physics or Biology.

   _____

10. Make a grid using the clues below to determine who participates in what sport. Ajay, Maxine, Kenny, Lindsey, and Susan each play a different sport. The sports are basketball, soccer, tennis, baseball, and swimming.

    (1) Maxine does not play soccer.
    (2) Susan plays either tennis or she swims.
    (3) Ajay plays either basketball or tennis, or he swims.
    (4) Kenny does not play a sport with a ball.

    basketball _____

    soccer _____

    tennis _____

    baseball _____

    swimming _____

GEOMETRY © Scott, Foresman and Company

LESSON MASTER **11-4** **B**

Vocabulary

1. What is *direct reasoning?* _____

_____

_____

_____

2. What is *indirect reasoning*? _____

_____

3. What are *contradictory* statements? _____

_____

Properties Objective D: Follow the Law of Indirect Reasoning to make conclusions.

In 4–6, you are given two statements *p* and *q*. Are *p* and *q* contradictory? Explain your answer.

4. *p*:   ∠*E* and ∠*F* are supplementary angles.
   q: ∠*E* and ∠*F* are vertical angles.

_____

_____

5. *p*:   △*RST* is equiangular.
   q: △*RST* is scalene.

_____

_____

_____

6. *p*:   perimeter of square *ABCD* = *x* units.
   q: area of square *ABCD* = *x* square units.

_____

_____

Properties Objective F: Write indirect proofs.

7. Use an indirect argument to prove that a right triangle *cannot* have an obtuse angle.

8. Use an indirect argument to prove that $\sqrt{7} \neq \frac{111}{42}$.

9. Finish the proof with an indirect argument.

   Given: In acute triangle *UOE*, $\overleftrightarrow{DN}$ is the perpendicular bisector of $\overline{EO}$.

   To prove: $\overleftrightarrow{DN}$ is *not* parallel to $\overline{UO}$.

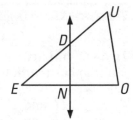

Properties Objective H: Apply the Law of Indirect Reasoning in real situations.

10. Pam has three coins. They are either all the same, or all different. They may be pennies, nickels, dimes, and quarters. The sum of their values is an odd number. Use an indirect proof to show that Pam has *no* dimes.

GEOMETRY © Scott, Foresman and Company

LESSON MASTER 11-5 B

Properties Objective F: Write indirect proofs involving coordinates.

1. If $V = (-3, 0)$, $M = (0, -4)$, $T = (0, 3)$, and $J = (4, 0)$, use an indirect proof to show that $\overleftrightarrow{VM}$ is *not* parallel to $\overleftrightarrow{TJ}$.

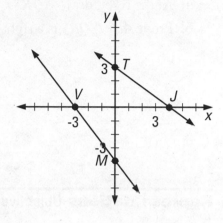

2. Let $A = (0, 4)$, $B = (6, 0)$, $C = (0, -4)$, and $D = (-6, 0)$. Use an indirect proof to show that $ABCD$ is *not* a square.

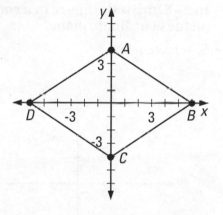

Properties Objective G: Use coordinate geometry to deduce properties of figures and prove theorems.

3. Given $E = (1, 4)$, $F = (4, 3)$, $G = (-1, -3)$, and $H = (-4, -2)$.

   a. At the right, draw $EFGH$.

   b. Prove that $EFGH$ is a parallelogram.

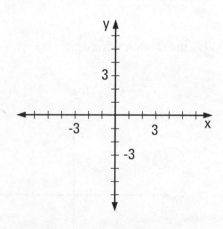

4. Given $Q = (-4, -4)$, $R = (-1, -5)$, and
$S = (1, 1)$.

   a. At the right, draw $\triangle QRS$.

   b. Prove that $\triangle QRS$ is a right triangle.

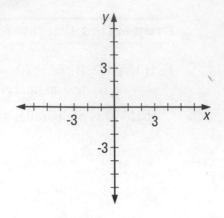

Representations Objective K: Give convenient locations for triangles and quadrilaterals in the coordinate plane.

In 5–8, draw the figure in a convenient location on the coordinate plane.

5. a rectangle

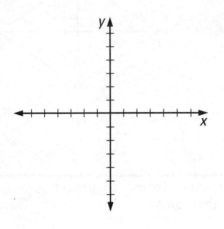

6. a kite

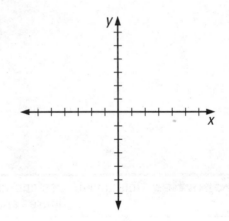

7. an isosceles triangle

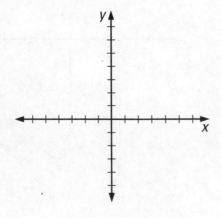

8. a square

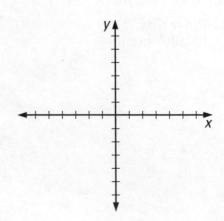

LESSON MASTER 11-6 B

Skills Objective A: Determine the length of a segment in the coordinate plane.

In 1–6, find the distance between the given points.

1. (-6, 1) and (4, 5) _____

2. (7, 0) and (2, 12) _____

3. (12, 0) and (26, 0) _____

4. (-3, -8) and (9, -1) _____

5. (2.3, 6.1) and (-1.4, 0.3) _____

6. (32, -40), and (51, -16) _____

7. What is the length of a diagonal of rectangle *FNET* at the right?

_____

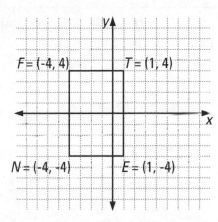

Properties Objective F: Write indirect proofs involving the use of the Distance Formula.

8. Let $A = (-2, 5)$, $B = (3, 6)$, $C = (3, 0)$, and $D = (-2, -1)$.

   a. Draw *ABCD* at the right.

   b. Use an indirect proof to show that *ABCD* is *not* a rhombus.

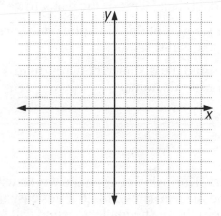

9. Given $E = (7, 1)$, $F = (-3, 5)$, and $G = (4, 7)$. Use an indirect proof to show that E and F do *not* both lie on the circle with center G.

Properties Objective G: Use coordinate geometry to deduce properties of figures and prove theorems.

10. Given *GHJK* as shown at the right. Prove that *GHJK* is a kite.

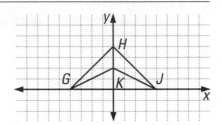

Uses Objective I: Apply the Distance Formula in real situations.

11. Judd lives 4 blocks north and 6 blocks east of the water tower. Marta lives 2 blocks south and 7 blocks west of the water tower.

   a. Represent this situation on the grid at the right.

   b. Find the distance between Judd's and Marta's homes.

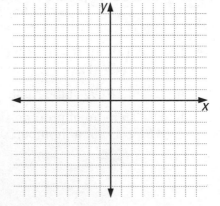

   _____

12. Mrs. Kurinsky's car phone works within a 75-mile radius of her office. She made a sales call 26 miles east and 58 miles south of her office. From there, she made a second call by driving 8 miles north and 17 miles west. Then she drove 14 miles west and 3 miles south for lunch at a restaurant. Could Mrs. Kurinsky use her car phone from the parking lot of the restaurant? Explain your answer.

   _____

LESSON MASTER

11-7 B

Representations Objective J: Graph and write an equation for a circle given its center and radius, and vice versa.

In 1–10, write an equation for the circle satisfying the given conditions.

1.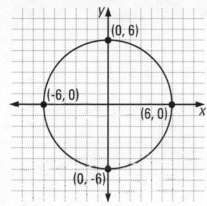

_____

2.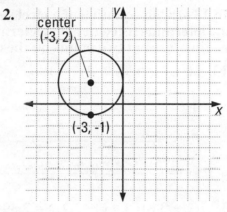

_____

3. radius 15, center (5, -3)

_____

4. radius 3.5, center (2, 0)

_____

5. diameter 22, center (0, 0)

_____

6. radius 4, center (-1, -2.8)

_____

7. center (2, 5), containing (13, 5)

_____

8. center (-1, 6), containing (2, 1)

_____

9. radius r, center (18, -7)

_____

10. radius 25, center (h, k)

_____

11. a. Draw the circle with radius 4 and center at (-2, -3)

b. Give two points on the circle.

_____

c. What is an equation for this circle?

_____

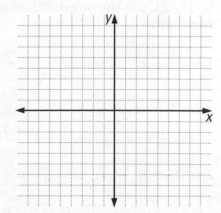

12. Which of these points are on the circle with
center (-5, 4) and radius 13? _____

$A = (8, 4)$ $B = (0, 16)$ $C = (-18, 4)$

$D = (-17, -1)$ $E = (-13, 13)$ $F = (16, 0)$

In 13–18, an equation of a circle is given.
a. Determine its center. b. Determine its
radius. c. Find two points on the circle.

13. $(x - 4)^2 + (y - 2)^2 = 196$

    a. _____

    b. _____

    c. _____

14. $(x - 8)^2 + (y + 2)^2 = 4$

    a. _____

    b. _____

    c. _____

15. $(x + 3.8)^2 + (y + 2.2)^2 = 2.89$

    a. _____

    b. _____

    c. _____

16. $x^2 + y^2 = 94$

    a. _____

    b. _____

    c. _____

17. $x^2 + (y - 8)^2 = 18$

    a. _____

    b. _____

    c. _____

18. $(x + 19)^2 + y^2 = 1$

    a. _____

    b. _____

    c. _____

Review Objective D, Lesson 2-4.

In 19–21, use the number line at
the right.

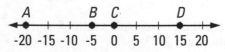

19. Give the coordinate of the midpoint of each segment.

    a. $\overline{AC}$ _____   **b.** $\overline{BD}$ _____   **c.** $\overline{AB}$ _____

    d. $\overline{BC}$ _____   **e.** $\overline{CD}$ _____   **f.** $\overline{AD}$ _____

20. Give the coordinate of E if A is the midpoint of $\overline{BE}$. _____

21. Give the coordinate of F if B is the midpoint of $\overline{DF}$. _____

LESSON MASTER 11-8 B

Skills Objective A: Determine the coordinates of the midpoint of a segment in the coordinate plane.

In 1–8, determine the coordinates of the midpoint of the segment described.

1. endpoints (-8, 4) and (5, 5) _____

2. endpoints (0, 0) and (-10, -3) _____

3. endpoints (4, 9) and (19, 9) _____

4. endpoints (2.8, -13) and (-6.6, -4.2) _____

5. $\overline{AB}$ at the right _____

6. $\overline{CD}$ at the right _____

7. $\overline{EF}$ at the right _____

8. $\overline{FG}$ at the right _____

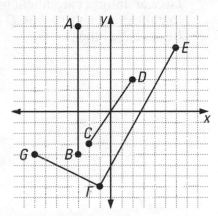

9. Find the midpoint of $\overline{PQ}$ given that $P = (-4, -4)$ and that Q is the midpoint of the segment with endpoints (-12, 9) and (6, 0). _____

Skills Objective B: Apply the Midpoint Connector Theorem.

10. **a.** In $\triangle XYZ$ at the right, D and E are midpoints of $\overline{XY}$ and $\overline{XZ}$, respectively. If $YZ = \frac{1}{2}$, find $\overline{DE}$.

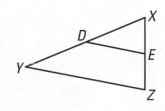

_____

b. What other relationship exists between $\overline{DE}$ and $\overline{YZ}$? _____

c. Name an angle congruent to $\angle XDE$. Justify your answer.

_____

_____

▶ **LESSON MASTER 11-8B** *page 2*

11. In △*JKM* at the right, *P*, *Q*, and *R* are midpoints of the sides, as shown. If *JK* = 22, and *PR* = 17, give all other segment lengths that can be found.

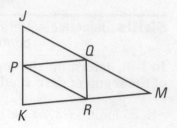

_____

_____

Properties Objective G: Use coordinate geometry to deduce properties of figures and prove theorems.

---

12. Use *ABCD* pictured at the right. Give an indirect argument to prove that the diagonals of *ABCD* do *not* bisect each other.

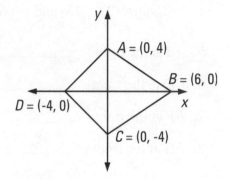

13. Given △*UVW* at the right with *M* and *N*, the midpoints of $\overline{UW}$ and $\overline{UV}$, respectively. Without using the Midpoint Connector Theorem, prove each statement.

   a. $\overline{MN} \parallel \overline{WV}$

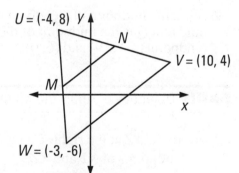

   b. $MN = \frac{1}{2} WV$

LESSON MASTER 11-9 B

Vocabulary

1. Complete each statement.

   a. Points in space can be located using a __?__ system.

   _____

   b. The three axes of the system in Part **a** are the _____ ,

   the _____ , and the _____ .

   c. (x, y, z), which specifies a point's position, is called __?__.

   _____

Skills Objective C: Plot points, find distances between them, and find coordinates of midpoints in 3-dimensional space.

In 2 and 3, a pair of points is given. a. Plot the points.
b. Find the coordinates of the midpoint of the segment
joining the points. c. Find the distance between the points.

2. $A = (5, 4, 2)$ and $B = (-3, -1, 7)$

   a.

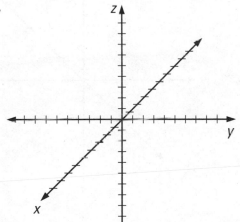

   b. _____

   c. _____

3. $P = (-6, 3, 0)$ and $Q = (4, -3, -2)$

   a.

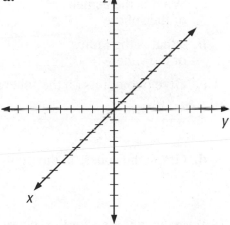

   b. _____

   c. _____

▶ **LESSON MASTER 11-9B** *page 2*

Uses Objective I: Apply the Box Diagonal Formulas in real situations.

4. A gift box measures 15 cm by 20 cm by 70 cm. Will an umbrella 75 cm long fit in the box? Explain your answer.

_____

_____

5. A foot locker measures 2.5 ft by 1.75 ft by 1.5 ft. Will a baseball bat 39 in. long fit in the locker? Explain your answer.

_____

_____

Representations Objective J: Graph and write an equation for a sphere given its center and radius, and vice versa.

6. A sphere has the equation $(x + 2)^2 + (y + 4)^2 + (z - 3)^2 = 25$.

   a. What is the center of the sphere? _____

   b. What is the radius of the sphere? _____

   c. Give two points on the sphere.

   _____

   d. Graph the sphere at the right.

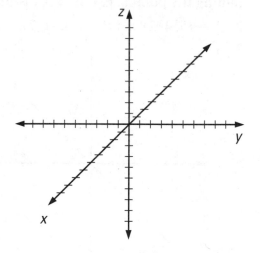

7. Write an equation for the sphere graphed at the right with center (0, 0, -2).

_____

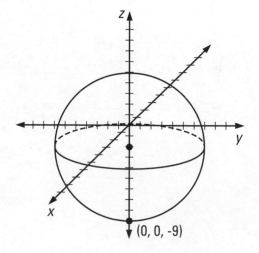

(0, 0, -9)

LESSON MASTER

12-1 B

Representations Objective G: Perform and analyze size transformations on figures in the coordinate plane.

1. Let $Q = (-3, 4)$, $R = (1, 3)$, $S = (2, -2)$, and $T = (-2, -3)$.

   a. Graph $QRST$ at the right.

   b. Give the coordinates of Q', R', S', and T', where $Q'R'S'T'$ is the image of $QRST$ under S_2.

   _____

   _____

   c. Graph $Q'R'S'T'$.

   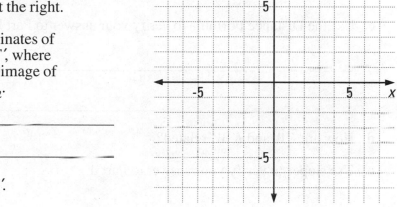

   d. What is a relationship between QR and $Q'R'$? _____

   e. How are $\overline{QR}$ and $\overline{Q'R'}$ related? _____

2. Let $A = (8, -2)$, $B = (0, 0)$, and $C = (-2, 8)$.

   a. Graph $\triangle ABC$ at the right.

   b. Give the coordinates of A', B', and C', where $\triangle A'B'C' = S_{.75}(\triangle ABC)$.

   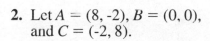

   _____

   _____

   c. Graph $\triangle A'B'C'$.

   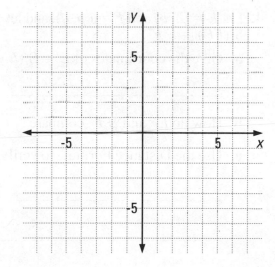

   d. What is a relationship between AC and $A'C'$? _____

   e. How are $\overline{BC}$ and $\overline{B'C'}$ related? _____

▶ **LESSON MASTER 12-1B** *page 2*

3. Let $H = (-2, -4)$, $K = (1, 3)$, and $W = (4, -4)$, and let
$S_{2.5}(\triangle HKW) = H'K'W'$.

  a. Give the coordinates of H', K', and W'.

  _____

  b. What is a relationship between HW and $H'W'$? _____

  c. Use the Distance Formula to verify your answer to Part **b**.

  _____

  _____

  d. How are $\overline{KW}$ and $\overline{K'W'}$ related? _____

  e. Use slopes to verify your answer to Part **d**.

  _____

  _____

  f. What is the image of (m, n) under $S_{2.5}$? _____

4. Let $E = (a, b)$ and $F = (p, q)$, and let
$S_k(EF) = E'F'$.

  a. Give the coordinates of $E' = S_k(E)$ and $F' = S_k(F)$.

  _____

  b. How do EF and $E'F'$ compare? _____

  c. Use the Distance Formula to verify your answer to Part **b**.

  _____

  _____

  d. How are $\overline{EF}$ and $\overline{E'F'}$ related? _____

  e. Use slopes to verify your answer in Part **d**.

  _____

  _____

GEOMETRY © Scott, Foresman and Company

LESSON MASTER 12-2 B

Vocabulary

1. Define *size transformation*. _____

_____

_____

_____

2. When is a size transformation

   a. an expansion? _____

   b. a contraction? _____

   c. the identity transformation? _____

Skills Objective A: Draw size-transformation images of figures.

In 3–6, draw the image of the figure under a size transformation with the designated magnitude and center.

3. magnitude .25, center *C*

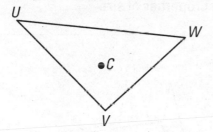

4. magnitude 3, center *R*

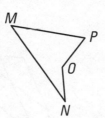

▶ **LESSON MASTER 12-2B** *page 2*

5. magnitude 1.5, center *H*

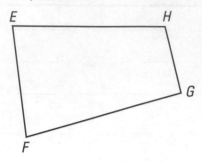

6. magnitude $\frac{3}{5}$, center *E*

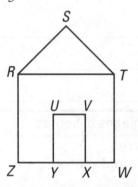

● *E*

Properties Objective C: Recognize and apply properties of size
transformations.

---

7. At the right, the dashed figure is
the image of the solid one under a
size transformation S. Use a ruler
to locate the center *C* and determine
the magnitude of S.

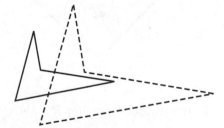

_____

8. △ *A′B′C′* is a size change image of △ *ABC*.

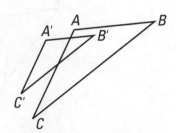

   a. Is the size change a contraction or
      an expansion?

   _____

   b. If *AC* = 40 and *A′C′* = 24, what is the
      magnitude of the size change?

   _____

   c. Use the value in Part **b** to find *AB* if *A′B′* = 21. _____

LESSON MASTER

12-3
B

Skills Objective A: Draw size-transformation images of figures.

In 1–3, draw the image of the figure under a size transformation with the designated magnitude and center.

1. $k = 2.5$, center Z

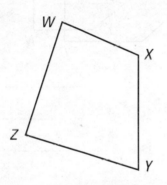

2. $k = .75$, center G

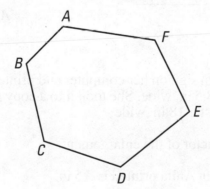

Properties Objective C: Recognize and apply properties of size
transformations.

---

3. Give three properties preserved by size transformations.

_____

4. Give a property that is *not* preserved by all size transformations.

_____

5. At the right, *HUGE* is the
   image of *TINY* under a size
   transformation with center *C*.
   UH = 18, *IT* = 12, *IC* = 9,
   and m∠*HEG* = 144. Find
   each of the following.

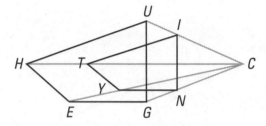

   a. the magnitude of the size change _____

   b. *UI* _____

   c. m∠*TYN* _____

6. At the right, S(△*OAB*) = △*ODC*, *OD* = 8, *DA* = 14,
   OB = 16.5, and *AB* = 11. Find the lengths of as
   many other segments as you can.

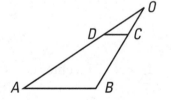

   _____

   _____

7. Anita designed a campaign sign on her computer and printed
   it out on a sheet of paper 8.5 in. wide. She took it to a copy
   store to be made into a poster 18 in. wide.

   a. Find the size change factor of the enlargement. _____

   b. The lettering on the sign Anita printed is .75 in.
      tall. About how tall is it on the poster? _____

   c. If Anita's sign is 11 in. long, what is the
      minimum length the poster can be so that
      nothing from the original sign is cut off? _____

LESSON MASTER 12-4 B

Vocabulary

1. **a.** What is a *ratio*? _____

   _____

   b. Give three examples of ratios.

   _____

2. **a.** What is a *proportion*? _____

   _____

   b. Give three examples of proportions.

   _____

   c. Write a proportion and label
   its means and its extremes.

Skills Objective B: Use proportions to find missing parts in similar figures.

3. $\triangle AWD$ is the image of $\triangle UPO$ under a
   size change. Write three equal ratios
   involving the sides of these triangles.

   _____

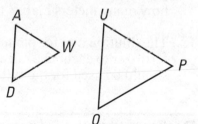

**In 4 and 5, $\triangle MGT$ is the image of $\triangle VRS$
under a size change.**

4. If $MG = 14$, $VR = 10$,
   and $MT = 21$, find VS. _____

5. *Multiple choice.* Which
   equation is a proportion? _____

   (a) $\dfrac{GT}{RS} = \dfrac{VS}{MT}$ (b) $\dfrac{MT}{GT} = \dfrac{VS}{VR}$

   (c) $\dfrac{GT}{RS} = \dfrac{MT}{VS}$ (d) $\dfrac{MT}{GT} = \dfrac{RS}{VR}$

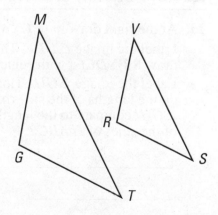

► **LESSON MASTER 12-4B** *page 2*

In 6 and 7, *UVWXYZ* is the image of *ABCDEF* under a size change.

6. If $XY = 20.4$, $FA = 42$, and
   $DE = 30.6$, find ZU.

   _____

7. If $WX = 30$, $VU = 44$, and $BA = 67.5$,
   what other segment length can you
   determine? Find that length.

   _____

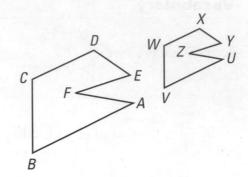

Uses Objective E: Identify and determine proportional lengths and distances in real situations.

8. If 2.5 pounds of roast beef cost $9.98, what
   should 6 pounds of roast beef cost?   _____

9. A computer printer prints 100 pages in
   12 minutes. At that rate, how long would it
   take to print 750 pages?   _____

10. If you read p pages in 10 hours, at that rate,
    how many pages can you read in s hours?   _____

11. A souvenir model of the Eiffel Tower in Paris is
    $\frac{1}{2000}$ the actual size. If the model is 15 cm tall,
    how many meters high is the Eiffel Tower?   _____

12. The dilution rate for plant fertilizer is 1.5 oz of
    fertilizer to each 32 oz of water. How much water
    should be used for the full 24-oz bottle of fertilizer? _____

Review Objective D, Lesson 4-5, and Objective A, Lesson 12-2

13. At the right draw $r_k \circ r_u(\triangle ABC)$.
    Label the image $\triangle DEF$. Then
    draw $S_2(\triangle DEF)$ with center O.
    Label the image $\triangle GHI$. How
    do the lengths of the sides of
    $\triangle GHI$ compare to the lengths
    of the sides of $\triangle ABC$?

    _____

    _____

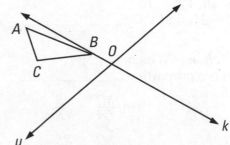

LESSON MASTER

Questions on SPUR Objectives

Vocabulary

1. Define *similar figures*.

   _____

   _____

   _____

2. What is a *similarity transformation*?

   _____

   _____

3. What is a *ratio of similitude*?

   _____

   _____

Skills Objective B: Use proportions to find missing parts in similar figures.

4. △*XYZ* is the image of △*DEF* under a similarity transformation. Find each of the following.

   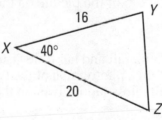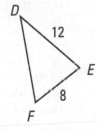

   a. *YZ* _____

   b. *DF* _____

   c. another angle measure _____

   d. a ratio of similitude _____

5. *QTSR ~ POMN*. Find as many missing lengths as possible.

   _____

   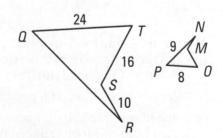

6. △GYT ~ △UFZ, with the ratio of similitude 4.5,
   FZ = 31.5, and GT = 5.

   a. Find as many other segment lengths
   as possible.   _____

   b. If m∠Y = 62 and m∠Z = 40, find as many
   other angle measures as possible.

   _____

7. Parallelograms *ABCD* and *DEFG* are similar.

   a. Complete the following. The ratio of
   similitude is ___?___ or ___?___ .

   _____   _____

   b. Find *BC*.   _____

   c. Find m∠A.   _____

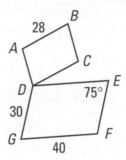

Uses Objective E: Identify and determine proportional lengths and distances in
real situations.

8. A slide measures 35 mm by 23 mm. The full picture
   is projected on a screen and measures 120 cm long.
   What is the width of the picture on the screen?   _____

9. Lucy is 5 ft 5 in. tall and her little sister Gwen is
   4 ft 2 in. tall. In a photograph of the two sisters, Lucy
   is 6.25 in. tall. How tall is Gwen in the photograph?   _____

10. A scale model of the solar system shows Mercury
    24 inches from the sun. The actual distance is
    about 36 million miles. Earth is about 93 million
    miles from the sun. In the model, how far should
    Earth be from the sun?   _____

11. On the 2-in.-by-2-in. photograph of a United States
    passport, the size of a person's face from the chin to
    the top of the head must not be less than 1 in. nor
    greater than $1\frac{3}{8}$ in. If a person's face measures 3.5 in.
    in a photograph, by what range of scale factors must
    the photograph be reduced for use on a passport?   _____

GEOMETRY © Scott, Foresman and Company

LESSON MASTER 12-6 B

Properties Objective D: Use the Fundamental Theorem of Similarity to find lengths, perimeters, areas, and volumes in similar figures.

1. At the right, *ABCD ~ UVWX*.

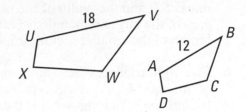

a. What is the ratio of similitude? _____

b. What is the ratio of their perimeters? _____

c. What is the ratio of their areas? _____

2. *EFGHIJ ~ ONMLKJ* with a ratio of similitude of $\frac{3}{5}$. The area of *EFGHIJ* is 32 square units and the perimeter of *OMNLKJ* is 14 units.

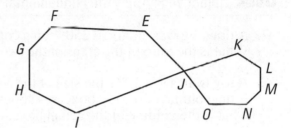

a. What is the area of *OMNLKJ*? _____

b. What is the perimeter of *EFGHIJ*? _____

3. Two figures are similar with a ratio of similitude of 4.2.

a. What is the ratio of corresponding lengths? _____

b. What is the ratio of their perimeters? _____

c. What is the ratio of their areas? _____

d. What is the ratio of their volumes? _____

e. What is the ratio of corresponding angle measures? _____

▶ **LESSON MASTER 12-6B** *page 2*

4. Two quadrilaterals are similar and have perimeters
   of 33 cm and 13.2 cm. If the area of the larger
   quadrilateral is 61.5 cm², find the area of the smaller.   _____

5. Two rectangles are similar. The width of the smaller
   one is 8 ft and the width of the larger is 10 ft. If the
   area of the larger rectangle is 660 ft², what is the
   length of the smaller rectangle?   _____

6. Two right triangles are similar and have areas of
   36 m² and 144 m². If the hypotenuse of the larger
   triangle is 30 m long, what is the length of the
   hypotenuse of the smaller triangle?   _____

Uses Objective F: Apply the Fundamental Theorem of Similarity in real situations.

7. A drawing was enlarged 250% on a copy machine.
   What is the ratio of the areas of the two drawings?   _____

8. A toy train set is 1.5% the size of the actual train.
   If the volume of the toy boxcar is about 12.3 in³,
   what is the volume of the actual boxcar?   _____

9. Two solid busts of Beethoven are similar and made
   out of the same material. Their heights are 22 cm
   and 38 cm. If the smaller bust weighs 14 kg,
   what is the weight of the larger?   _____

10. A parade featured a 7-meter-tall balloon of Perky
    Penguin. Plastic souvenirs, similar to the balloon,
    were 12 cm tall. If the surface area of the souvenir is
    600 cm², what is the surface area of the large balloon?

    _____

11. The kites at the right are similar. Their
    areas are 1900 in² and 1372.75 in². If the
    longer brace of the larger kite is 4 ft 2 in.
    long, what is the length of the longer brace
    of the smaller kite?

    _____

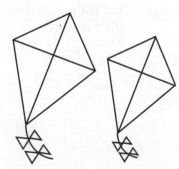

LESSON MASTER **Questions on SPUR Objectives**

12-7 B

Uses Objective F: Apply the Fundamental Theorem of Similarity in real situations.

In 1 and 2, consider Alice's assortment of size-changing pills from *Alice in Wonderland*. Suppose Alice is 5 ft tall, weighs 100 pounds, and drinks an 8-ounce glass of orange juice every day.

1. If Alice takes a pill that makes her 6 times as large,

   a. how tall would Alice be? _____

   b. how much would Alice weigh? _____

   c. how much orange juice would she drink every day? Give your answer to the nearest *gallon*. _____

2. If Alice takes a pill that makes her $\frac{1}{6}$ as large,

   a. how tall would Alice be? _____

   b. how much would Alice weigh? _____

   c. how much orange juice would she drink every day? _____

3. Two similar American flags are 2 ft long and 6 ft long. If the area of the red fabric on the smaller flag is 124 in², what is the area of the red fabric on the larger one? _____

4. If a 16-inch pizza costs $13.50, about how much should a 10-inch pizza cost? _____

5. If an 8-inch pizza serves 2 people, how many people can be served from a 16-inch pizza? _____

6. Two similar storage sheds are 3.8 m and 5.6 m tall.

   a. If the materials for a new roof on the smaller one cost $850, what would the materials for a new roof on the larger one cost? _____

   b. The exhaust fan for the larger one moves twice as much air per minute as the fan for the smaller one. Will it do as good a job ventilating the shed? Explain your answer.

   _____

   _____

   _____

7. Gilberto made a solid model of a volcano out of papier-maché. He used 8 sheets of newspaper for the papier-maché. Now he wants to make a similar volcano twice as tall.

   a. How many sheets of newspaper will he need? _____

   b. How will the area of the bases of the two volcanoes compare?

   _____

8. Mr. Crane picked two pumpkins from his garden. They appeared to be similar in shape. The larger one weighed 16 pounds and the smaller weighed 2 pounds. What was the ratio of their diameters? _____

9. Two aluminum cans are similar. The larger uses 1.8 times the aluminum as the smaller. If the larger holds 48 ounces, what is the capacity of the smaller? _____

10. The areas of two similar ice skating rinks are 1200 ft² and 1728 ft². The fence surrounding each is the same height. If it takes 9 gallons of paint to paint the fence around the smaller rink, how much paint is needed for the fence around the larger rink? _____

11. If it takes 1200 gallons to fill a cylindrical swimming pool, how much would it take to fill a similar swimming pool with double the radius? _____

12. A wooden crate has a volume of 2 m³. By what factor should each dimension be multiplied to make a similar crate with a volume of 54 m³? _____

Review Objective B, Lesson 12-5

13. △SDM ~ △TGK

   a. Write three equal ratios involving the sides of these triangles.

   _____

   b. Write three equations involving angle measures.

   _____ _____

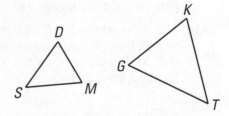

LESSON MASTER 13-1 B

Vocabulary

1. State the *SSS Similarity Theorem.*

_____

_____

_____

Properties Objective F: Determine whether or not triangles are similar using the SSS Similarity Theorem.

In 2–5, *true or false.*

2. Triangles with sides measuring 3, 5, and 7 and
   6, 10, and 14 are similar.   _____

3. Triangles with sides measuring 1.5, 1.5, and
   3.5 and 6, 10, and 12 are similar.   _____

4. Triangles with sides measuring 5 ft, 6 ft, and 7 ft
   and 6 ft, 5 ft, and 7 ft are similar.   _____

5. Triangles with sides measuring 3 cm, 4 cm, and 5 cm
   and 6 m, 8 m, and 10 m are similar.   _____

In 6–13, determine whether or not the triangles in each
pair are similar. If so, write a similarity statement using
the correct order of vertices. Justify your answer.

6. 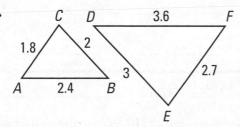   7.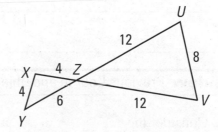

_____   _____

_____   _____

8.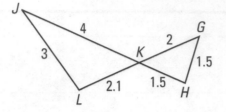

_____

_____

9.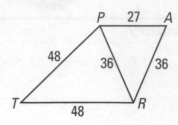

_____

_____

10.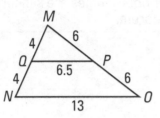

_____

_____

11.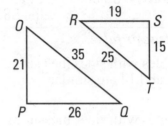

_____

_____

12.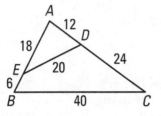

_____

_____

13.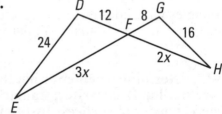

_____

_____

Review Previous Course and Objective B, Lesson 12-4

14. Consider the proportion $\frac{12}{18} = \frac{72}{108}$.

 a. Name the means.   **b.** Name the extremes.

_____   _____

 c. Write three other proportions using these numbers.

_____

15. If $\frac{a}{b} = \frac{c}{d}$, give an instance of each case.

 a. $\frac{a-b}{b} = \frac{c-d}{d}$ **b.** $\frac{a+b}{b} = \frac{c+d}{d}$

_____   _____

LESSON MASTER 13-2 B

Vocabulary

1. State the *AA Similarity Theorem*. _____

_____

2. State the *SAS Similarity Theorem*. _____

_____

_____

3. Explain why there is no ASA Similarity Theorem. _____

_____

Properties Objective F: Determine whether or not triangles are similar using the AA and SAS Similarity Theorems.

In 4–9, determine whether or not the triangles in each pair are similar. If so, write a similarity statement using the correct order of vertices. Justify your answer.

4.

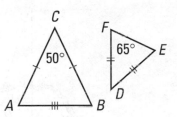

_____

_____

5.

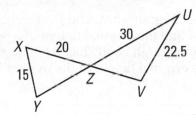

_____

_____

6.

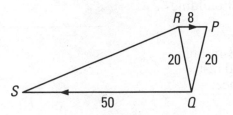

_____

_____

7.

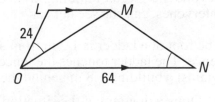

_____

_____

8.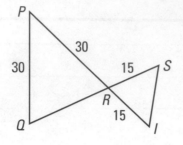

9.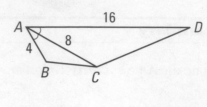

_____   _____

_____   _____

10. At a ground distance of 1.5 miles from takeoff, a plane's altitude is 1000 yards. Assuming a constant angle of ascent, find the plane's altitude 5 miles from takeoff.   _____

11. Use the information in the diagram to find the width of the river.

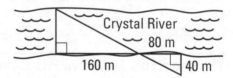

_____

12. A man standing 5 meters from a 6-meter pole casts a 2.5-meter shadow, the tip of which aligns with the tip of the pole's shadow. How tall is the man?   _____

13. The diagram shows how an archaeologist can find the original height of a pyramid, even though its top has worn away. Find the original height of the pyramid.

_____

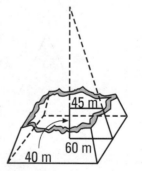

14. A tourist on the observation deck of an 800-foot building looks toward a 600-foot building which is one block away. Her car is parked two blocks beyond the shorter building. If no other building intervenes, can she see her car?   _____

15. The foot of a ladder is 1.2 m from a 1.8-m-high fence. The ladder touches the fence and rests against a building 1.8 m behind the fence.

 a. Draw a diagram of the situation.

 b. Determine how far up the building the top of the ladder can reach.   _____

 c. How long is the ladder?   _____

Name _____

Vocabulary

In 1 and 2, complete the *Side-Splitting Theorem* and its converse.

1. If a line is ___?___ to a side of a triangle and intersects the other two sides in distinct points, it splits these sides into ___?___ segments.

_____   _____

2. If a line intersects $\overline{OP}$ and $\overline{OQ}$ in distinct points X and Y so that $\dfrac{OX}{XP} = \dfrac{OY}{YQ}$,

   then $\overline{XY}$ is _____ to $\overline{PQ}$.

3. At the right, draw a picture of the situation in Question 2.

Skills Objective A: Find lengths in figures by applying the Side-Splitting Theorem and the Side-Splitting Converse Theorem.

---

4. Given $\triangle XYZ$ at the right, in which $RS \parallel YZ$, find each missing length.

   a. $XR = 8; XS = 6; XZ = 15; XY =$ _____

   b. $XS = 6; XR = 9; XY = 15; XZ =$ _____

   c. $XS = 6; SZ = 4; XR = 8; RY =$ _____

   d. $XR = 6n; RY = 2n; XS = 9; SZ =$ _____

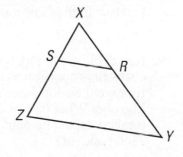

5. In the diagram at the right, $h \parallel j \parallel k$. Find each missing length.

   a. $AC = 9; BC = 6; DF = 15; EF =$ _____

   b. $AB = 4; BC = 13; EF = 39; DE =$ _____

   c. $AB = 5y; DE = 2y; EF = 12; BC =$ _____

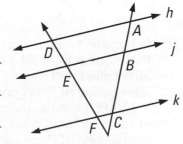

6. Given $\triangle ADM$ at the right, in which $OP \parallel AD$, tell whether each statement is true.

   a. $\dfrac{x}{y} = \dfrac{z}{w}$ _____

   b. $\dfrac{x + y}{y} = \dfrac{z + w}{z}$ _____

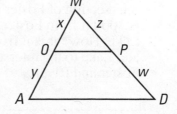

7. Name all pairs of parallel lines in the
figure at the right.

_____

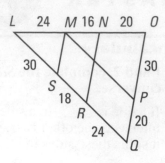

Uses Objective H: Use the Side-Splitting Theorem to find lengths and distances in
real situations.

---

8. A half-mile ramp begins 2596 ft
from a bridge. There is a support
under a toll plaza which is located
1500 ft up the ramp.

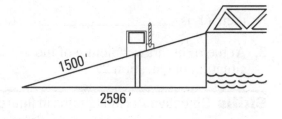

   a. How far is the base of the support
   from the lower end of the ramp? _____

   b. How high is the support? _____

9. Residents are to pay for new
curbs in proportion to the
footage their lots have on
Latrobe. What part of the
total cost must be paid by
each resident?

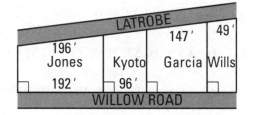

Jones _____ Kyoto _____ Garcia _____ Wills _____

10. In the street map at the right,
River Street is parallel to Lake
Street and Pond Street. The
intersection of River and State
is 1200 ft from the intersection
of Lake and State, and the
intersection of Pond and State
is another 800 ft. The
intersection of Foster and Pond
is 1000 ft from Foster and
Lake. How far is it from Foster
and Lake to the intersection of
Foster and River?

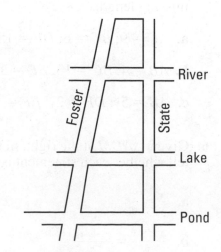

_____

LESSON MASTER 13-4 B

Vocabulary

In 1 and 2, given the positive numbers a and b,

1. define the *geometric mean*. _____

2. define the *arithmetic mean*. _____

3. For the set $\{4, 9\}$, find the

    a. arithmetic mean. _____   **b.** the geometric mean. _____

4. State the *Right-Triangle Altitude Theorem*. _____

_____

_____

_____

_____

Skills Objective B: Calculate lengths using the Right-Triangle Altitude Theorem.

5. Given △MOP at the right, find each length.

    a. $MP = 3$; $MN = 12$; $MO =$ _____

    b. $PN = 4$; $MN = 9$; $ON =$ _____

    c. $PN = 28$; $PM = 7$; $OP =$ _____

    d. $OP = 8$; $MP = NP$; $MN =$ _____

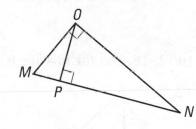

6. Given the diagram at the right, find each length.

    a. $a = 30$; $c = 50$; $h =$ _____

    b. $h = 12$; $m = 9$; $b =$ _____

    c. $a = 24$; $m = 4$; $b =$ _____

    d. $b = 8$; $m = 12$; $c =$ _____

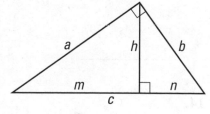

7. Find d in the diagram at the right.

_____

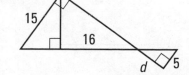

8. Use the diagram at the right to find each length.

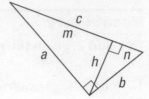

   a. $a = 7\sqrt{5}$; $h = 14$; $c = $ _____; $n = $ _____

   b. $a = 6\sqrt{5}$; $b = 3\sqrt{5}$; $m = $ _____; $n = $ _____

Review Objective D, Lesson 5-7, and Objective D, Lesson 8-6

---

9. Find the sum of the measures of the angles
   in a 15-sided polygon.   _____

10. Polygon *PQRSTU* at the right is a regular
    hexagon. Give the measure of each angle.

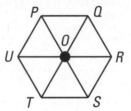

    a. m∠*OPQ* _____

    b. m∠*ROT* _____

11. Polygon *ABCDEFGH* at the right is a regular
    octagon. Give the measure of each angle.

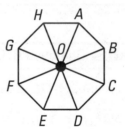

    a. m∠*ODE* _____

    b. m∠*DOC* _____

In 12–15, find the missing length.

12.

_____

13.

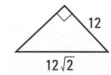

_____

14.

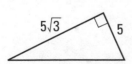

_____

15.

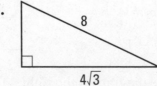

_____

LESSON MASTER 13-5 B

Vocabulary

1. In the diagram at the right, _____

   is *inscribed* in _____.

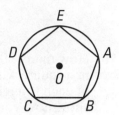

In 2 and 3, complete the theorems.

2. According to the *Isosceles Right Triangle Theorem*, in an isosceles right triangle,

   _____

3. The *30-60-90 Triangle Theorem* states that in a 30-60-90 triangle,

   _____

   _____

Skills Objective C: Calculate lengths of sides in isosceles right triangles and in 30-60-90 triangles.

In 4–9, find the missing lengths.

4.

   $x =$ _____ ; $y =$ _____

5.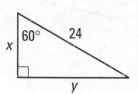

   $x =$ _____ ; $y =$ _____

6.

   $x =$ _____ ; $y =$ _____

7.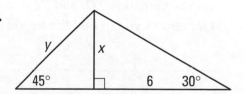

   $x =$ _____ ; $y =$ _____

8.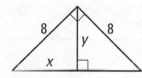

   perimeter of square = _____

9.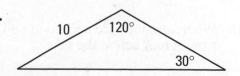

   perimeter = _____

9. A regular octagon's sides are extended to form
   a square as shown. Each side of the octagon is
   3 units long. Find the length of a side of the square.

   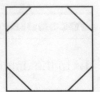

   _____

10. How many 30-60-90 triangles can be drawn
    in a square with 6-cm sides, if the hypotenuse
    of each triangle is 6 cm? Draw a diagram to
    show how you would arrange the triangles.

    _____

Review Objective F and H, Lessons 13-1 and 13-2

**In 11–14, tell whether or not the triangles are similar.
If so, justify with a similarity theorem.**

11.

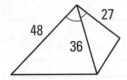

_____

12.

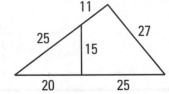

_____

13.

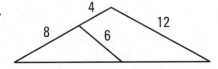

_____

14.

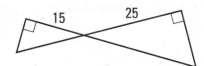

_____

15. Explain how measuring the shadows $\overline{DS}$,
    cast by yardstick $\overline{YD}$, and $\overline{RE}$, cast by tree
    $\overline{TR}$, allows you to find the height of the tree.

    _____

    _____

    _____

16. What measures are needed to find the distance
    from *A* to *B* across the lake?

    _____

    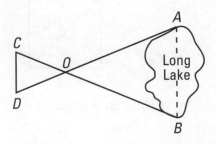

LESSON MASTER

13-6
B

Questions on SPUR Objectives

Skills

In 1–3, use the figure at the right.

1. Which side is adjacent to ∠C? _____

2. Which side is opposite ∠B? _____

3. Which angle is opposite $\overline{AB}$? _____

4. *Trigonometry* literally means _____.

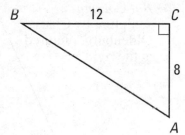

Skills Objective D: Determine tangents of angles.

5. Consider △ABC at the right.

   a. Give tan B. _____

   b. Give tan A. _____

   c. From tan B, estimate m∠B. _____

   d. From tan A, estimate m∠A. _____

Skills Objective E: Estimate or determine exact values of the tangent ratio.

In 6–8, give exact values.

6. tan 30° _____   7. tan 45° _____   8. tan 60° _____

In 9–14, estimate to the nearest thousandth.

9. tan 40° _____   10. tan 72° _____

11. tan 25° _____   12. tan 58° _____

13. tan 33.24° _____   14. tan 16.7° _____

In 15 and 16, use △KLM at the right. a. Estimate the tangent of the given angle to the nearest hundredth. b. Determine the measure of the angle.

15. a. tan K _____

    b. m∠K _____

16. a. tan M _____

    b. m∠M _____

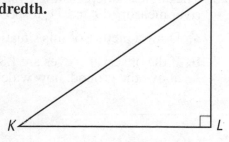

Properties Objective G: Know the definition of tangent.

17. Use △*RST* at the right. Do *not* measure.

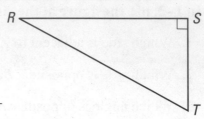

   a. Give the tangent of ∠*R*. _____

   b. $\frac{RS}{TS}$ is the tangent of which angle? _____

   c. How is tan *R* affected if m∠*R* increases? _____

Skills Objective I: Use tangents to determine unknown lengths in real situations.

18. How tall is Chicago's *Bat Column*, a sculpture by Claes Oldenburg, pictured at the right?

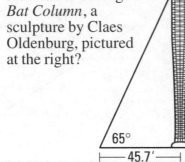

65°

├──── 45.7' ────┤

_____

19. How tall is the San Jacinto Monument, shown at the right?

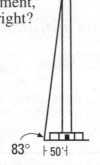

83° ├ 50'┤

_____

20. How tall is the Leaning Tower of Pisa, shown at the right?

86° ↖ 4.3 m

_____

21. How wide is the river below?

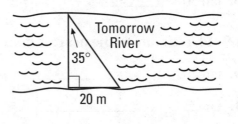

Tomorrow River

35°

20 m

_____

22. The angles of depression to the near and far banks of a river measure 49 and 11, respectively.

   a. Draw a picture of this situation.

   b. If the observer's eyes are 1.8m above the ground, how wide is the river?

_____

GEOMETRY © Scott, Foresman and Company

LESSON MASTER **13-7 B**

Questions on SPUR Objectives

Skills Objective D: Determine sines and cosines of angles.

1. Use △ABC at the right.

   a. Find BC. _____

   b. Find sin B. _____

   c. Find sin A. _____

   d. Find cos B. _____   e. Find cos A. _____

   f. Estimate m∠B. _____   g. Estimate m∠A. _____

Skills Objective E: Estimate or determine exact values of sine and cosine ratios.

In 2–7, give exact values.

2. sin 30° _____   3. sin 45° _____   4. sin 60° _____

5. cos 30° _____   6. cos 45° _____   7. cos 60° _____

In 8–15, estimate to the nearest thousandth.

8. sin 40° _____   9. cos 40° _____

10. cos 65° _____   11. sin 83° _____

12. sin 47.8° _____   13. cos 56.1° _____

14. sin 70.5° _____   15. cos 29.6° _____

In 16–18, use △DEF at the right. Do _not_ use a protractor.

16. Determine the approximate measure of each angle.

   a. m∠D _____   b. m∠F _____

17. Calculate each sine to the nearest hundredth.

   a. sin D _____   b. sin F _____

18. Calculate each cosine to the nearest hundredth.

   a. cos D _____   b. cos F _____

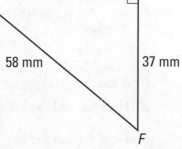

209 ▶

► **LESSON MASTER** 13-7B *page 2*

Properties Objective G: Know the definitions of sine and cosine.

19. Define *sin A*.

_____

_____

In 20–23, use △ *RST* at the right.

20. Write a ratio for each function.

   a. sin *R* _____   **b.** cos *R* _____

21. $\frac{RS}{RT}$ is the sine of which angle? _____

22. $\frac{TS}{RT}$ is the cosine of which angle? _____

23. How is sin *R* affected if m∠*R* increases? _____

Uses Objective I: Use sines and cosines to determine unknown lengths in
real situations.

24. From a point at the foot of a hill, the angle of elevation
of the top is 15°. The distance from the foot of the hill
to the top is 150 meters. Find the height of the hill.   _____

25. A 30-foot ladder leans against a building making an angle
of 72° with the ground.

   a. How high on the building does the ladder reach?   _____

   b. How far from the building is the end of the ladder?   _____

26. The tailgate of a tractor-trailer rig is 1 m off the ground.
The greatest incline for efficiently loading the truck is 10°.
How long should the ramp be for a 10° incline?   _____

27. A plane takes off at an angle of 24° with the ground.

   a. How far has it traveled in a horizontal distance
   after it has traveled 3 miles?   _____

   b. How high, in feet, is the plane after it has traveled
   3 miles?   _____

28. A biker pedaled up a slope of 6° for 150 meters and
then another 100 meters at a slope of 9°.

   a. How far did the biker travel in a horizontal distance?   _____

   b. How far did the biker climb vertically?   _____

LESSON MASTER 13-8 B

Skills Objective D: Use the SAS area formula.

In 1–4, find the area of the triangle.

1.

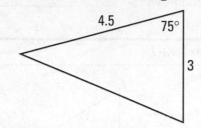

2.

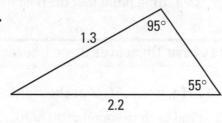

_____   _____

3.

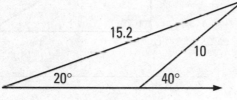

4.

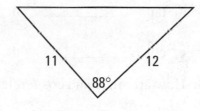

_____   _____

5. Find the area of a regular pentagon with sides
   8 centimeters long.   _____

6. Find the area of a regular decagon with sides
   8 centimeters long.   _____

Uses Objective J: Determine components of vectors in real situations.

7. A hurricane is moving 30 mph in
   a direction 23° west of north. Find
   the components of its velocity.   _____   _____

8. An oil tanker traveled 32 knots
   (nautical miles) per hour on a course
   38° north of west. Find the
   components of its velocity.   _____   _____

9. The Fox River flows at a rate of
   5 kilometers per hour in a direction
   80° south of east. Find components
   of the river's velocity.   _____   _____

10. A helicopter pilot wants to reach a point 3 km south
    and 6 km east of the takeoff location.

    a. In which direction should the helicopter take off? _____

    b. How far will the helicopter travel? _____

11. A sailboat traveled 45 miles on a course 35° north of east
    and then traveled 60 miles on a course 75° north of east
    before the wind died down. Find the actual distance from
    its starting point that the boat lost its wind power.   _____

Review Objectives D and I, Lesson 13-6 and 13-7

In 12–14, use △*FGH* at the right.

12. Find each trigonometric ratio.

    a. tan *F* _____   **b.** sin *H* _____

    c. cos *H* _____   **d.** sin *F* _____

13. How are sin *H* and cos *F* related?   _____

14. How is cos *F* affected if m∠*F* increases?   _____

15. The string of a kite forms an angle of 68° with the ground.
    If 250 m of string have been let out, how high is the kite?   _____

16. A mine shaft forms a 15° angle with the ground and reaches
    a point 150 feet below the surface. How long is the shaft?   _____

17. If the sun's rays make an angle of 70° with the ground, how
    long is the shadow of a person who is 180 cm tall?   _____

18. From the top of a 100-foot lookout tower, a forest ranger
    spotted a fire at a 25° angle of depression. How far was
    the fire from the base of the lookout tower?   _____

19. The angle of elevation from an observer on the roof of the
    Grande Hotel to the roof of the Rio Stock Exchange is a
    10° angle. The buildings are 300 meters apart. How much
    taller is the Rio Stock Exchange than the Grande Hotel?   _____

20. A 90-foot escalator makes an angle of 18° with the lower
    level of a parking garage. How high does the escalator
    rise vertically?   _____

21. A ladder mounted on a fire truck is 6 ft above the ground.
    If the maximum length of the ladder is 120 ft and the
    measure of the largest safe angle the ladder can make
    with the truck is 75, how high will the ladder reach?   _____

LESSON MASTER

14-1
B

Vocabulary

1. Give the measure or range of measures for each arc.

　　a. minor arc　　　_____

　　b. major arc　　　_____

　　c. semicircle　　　_____

2. In the circle at the right, draw each of the following.

　　a. an angle that intercepts $\overset{\frown}{JK}$

　　b. the chord of $\overset{\frown}{JK}$

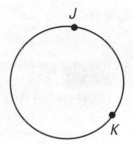

3. a. What is an *inscribed polygon*?

_____

_____

　　b. Draw an inscribed pentagon in the circle at the right.

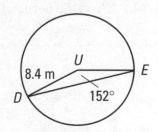

Skills Objective A: Calculate lengths of chords and arcs.

In 4–6, refer to ⊙U at the right. Find the indicated measure.

4. $m\overset{\frown}{DE}$ _____

5. *UE* _____

6. *DE* _____

In 7–11, use ⊙*O* at the right. **a. Find the length of
the chord of the indicated arc. b. Find the length
of the indicated arc.**

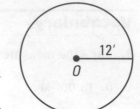

7. a 60° arc   **a.** _____   **b.** _____

8. a 90° arc   **a.** _____   **b.** _____

9. a 120° arc   **a.** _____   **b.** _____

10. a 42° arc   **a.** _____   **b.** _____

11. a 165° arc   **a.** _____   **b.** _____

12. Regular octagon *ABCDEFGH* is inscribed in
    circle *Q*, whose radius is 10 in. What is the
    perimeter of *ABCDEFGH*?

    _____

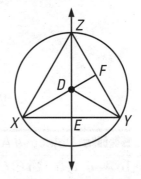

Properties Objective F: Make deductions from properties of radii and chords,
and know sufficient conditions for radii to be
perpendicular to them.

In 13–16, equilateral triangle *XYZ* is inscribed in ⊙*D*,
m∠*XDE* = m∠*YDE*, and $\overline{DF}$ is perpendicular
to $\overline{YZ}$. **Justify the given statement.**

13. m$\widehat{XY}$ = m$\widehat{YZ}$ = m$\widehat{XZ}$

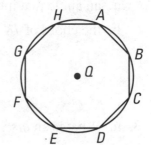

_____.

_____

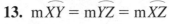

14. $\overleftrightarrow{ZE}$ is the perpendicular bisector of $\overline{XY}$.

_____

15. *YF* = *ZF*

_____

16. $\widehat{XY}$ ≅ $\widehat{YZ}$

_____

LESSON MASTER

14-2 B

Vocabulary

1. What is an *inscribed angle*?

_____

_____

_____

Skills Objective B: Calculate measures of inscribed angles from measures of
intercepted arcs and vice versa.

Objective C: Calculate measures of angles between chords from measures
of intercepted arcs, and vice versa.

In 2–10, find the indicated measure.

2.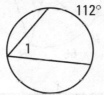

m∠1 _____

3.

m$\widehat{UV}$ _____

4.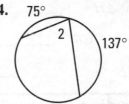

m∠2 _____

5.

m∠3 _____

6.

m∠4 _____

7.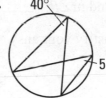

m∠5 _____

8.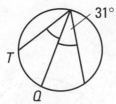

m$\widehat{TQ}$ _____

9.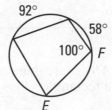

m$\widehat{EF}$ _____

10.

m∠6 _____

11. Find the measures of as many arcs and angles of the figure as you can.

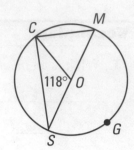

_____

_____

_____

_____

12. Find the measures of the following arcs and angles of ⊙C.

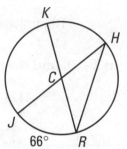

   a. $\overarc{HR}$ _____

   b. m∠H   _____

   c. m∠HCR   _____

   d. $\overarc{JH}$ _____

Properties Objective G: Make deductions from properties of angles formed by chords.

13. Refer to the circle at the right.

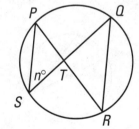

   a. Find m∠R. _____

   b. Justify your answer to Part **a.**

_____

_____

_____

_____

14. The diagonals of quadrilateral *ABCD* are diameters of ⊙O. Explain why *ABCD* is a rectangle.

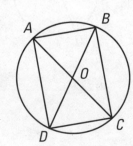

_____

_____

_____

_____

LESSON MASTER

14-3
B

Skills Objective D: Locate the center of a circle given sufficient information.

In 1 and 2, use the right-angle method to find the center *O* of the circle.

1.

2.

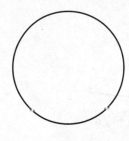

3. Use the perpendicular bisector method to find the center of the circle.

4. Use the perpendicular bisector method to find the center of the circle that contains this arc.

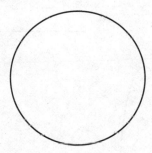

In 5 and 6, draw a circle through the three given points.

5.

6.

In 7 and 8, draw a circle through the three vertices of the triangle.

7.

8.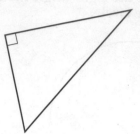

Uses Objective I: Given the angle width of a lens and the width of an object, determine the set of points from which the object just fits in the picture.

---

9. A stage is 65 feet wide. A photographer, using a camera with a picture angle of 53°, wants to just fit the stage in a picture. How far back from the center of the front of the stage would the photographer need to stand?

_____

In 10–12, the top view of a ship, 1050 feet long, is shown. A photographer at sea wants to take a picture of this using a camera with an 84° field of vision.

10. Locate all points where the photographer's boat could be located to fit the ship exactly in the picture.

11. **a.** If the photographer wants to be directly in front of the middle of the ship, point *M*, how far from this point will the photographer need to be?

_____

b. Locate this point *P* on the diagram.

12. Because of various obstacles, suppose the photographer can maneuver the boat no farther than 500 feet from the middle of the ship. The photographer has a variety of camera lenses. To fit the ship, what is the minimum size for the angle of vision on the lens?

_____

LESSON MASTER

14-4
B

Vocabulary

1. What is a *secant*? _____

_____

Skills Objective C: Calculate measures of angles between chords or secants from measures of intercepted arcs, and vice versa.

In 2–10, find the indicated measure.

2.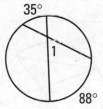

35°

1

88°

m∠1 _____

3.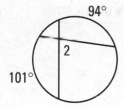

94°

2

101°

m∠2 _____

4.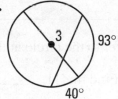

3

93°

40°

m∠3 _____

5.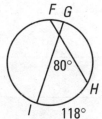

F G

80°

H

I 118°

m$\widehat{FG}$ _____

6.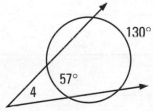

130°

57°

4

m∠4 _____

7.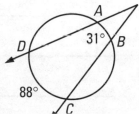

A

D 31° B

88°

C

m$\widehat{AB}$ _____

8.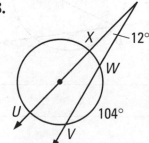

X 12°

W

U

104°

V

m$\widehat{UV}$ _____

9.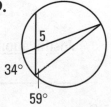

5

34°

59°

m∠5 _____

10.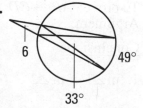

6

49°

33°

m∠6 _____

11. Find the measure of the
indicated angle in the diagram
at the right.

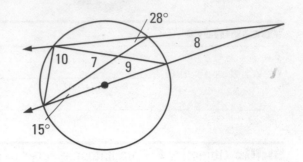

  a. ∠7 _____

  b. ∠8 _____

  c. ∠9 _____

  d. ∠10 _____

Properties Objective G: Make deductions from properties of angles formed by
chords or secants.

12. Refer to the circle at the right.

  a. Find m∠11. _____

  b. Explain how you found your answer to Part **a.**

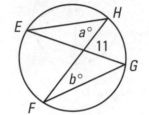

  _____

  _____

  _____

  _____

13. Complete the following argument that proves
that parallel secants intercept congruent arcs.

Given: Secants $\overleftrightarrow{AC}$ and $\overleftrightarrow{BD}$ are parallel.
To prove: $\widehat{AB} \cong \widehat{CD}$
Argument:

Conclusions	Justifications
1. $m\angle 1 = m\angle 2$	_____
2. $m\angle 1 = \frac{1}{2}m\widehat{AB}$; $m\angle 2 = \frac{1}{2}m\widehat{CD}$	_____
3. $\frac{1}{2}m\widehat{AB} = \frac{1}{2}m\widehat{CD}$	_____
4. $m\widehat{AB} = m\widehat{CD}$	_____
5. $\widehat{AB} \cong \widehat{CD}$	_____

GEOMETRY © Scott, Foresman and Company

LESSON MASTER 14-5 B

Vocabulary

1. a. Define *tangent to a circle*. _____

_____

b. Define *tangent to a sphere*. _____

_____

Properties
Objective F: Make deductions from properties of radii and tangents, and know sufficient conditions for radii to be perpendicular to them.

In 2 and 3, complete the statement using the diagram at the right.

2. If $\overline{MG} \perp \overleftrightarrow{GP}$, then ____?____.

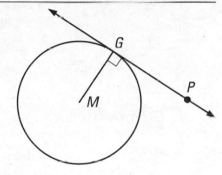

_____

_____

3. If $\overleftrightarrow{GP}$ is tangent to $\odot M$ at G, then ____?____.

_____

4. Refer to $\odot W$ with tangents $\overline{ZY}$ and $\overline{ZX}$.

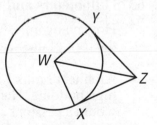

a. What kind of triangles are $\triangle XZW$ and $\triangle YZW$? _____

b. Justify your answer to Part **a**.

_____

_____

c. Prove $\triangle XZW \cong \triangle YZW$.

_____

_____

d. What does Part **c** imply about $\overline{ZY}$ and $\overline{ZX}$? Why?

_____

5. In ⊙*B*, $\overline{AC}$ is tangent at *C*.

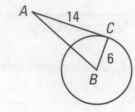

   a. Find *AB*. _____

   b. Find the area of △ *ABC*. _____

6. Complete the following argument that proves that tangents at the endpoints of a diameter are parallel.

   Given: ⊙*O* has diameter $\overline{GH}$, *m* is tangent at *G*, and *n* is tangent at *H*.

   To prove: *m* // *n*

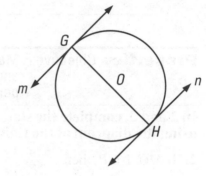

   Conclusions   Justifications

   1. $\overline{GH} \perp m$, $\overline{GH} \perp n$ _____

   2. *m* // *n*   _____

Uses Objective J: Determine the maximum distance that can be seen from a particular elevation.

In 7–10, assume the radius of the earth is 3960 miles or 6375 kilometers and that there are no hills or obstructions.

7. How many miles would a person be able to see from the roof of the Sears Tower in Chicago, at 1454 feet? _____

8. Architect Frank Lloyd Wright once designed a mile-high building. Had it been built, how many miles would a person have been able to see from the top? _____

9. How far above the earth is a plane if a pilot can see 300 kilometers? _____

10. To the nearest hundred feet, Mt. Foraker in Alaska, at 17,400 feet, is twice as high as Guadalupe Peak in Texas, at 8700 ft. Can a person see twice as far from the top of Mt. Foraker as from the top of Guadalupe Peak? Why or why not?

_____

_____

LESSON MASTER 14-6 B

Skills Objective C: Calculate measures of angles between chords, secants, or tangents from measures of intercepted arcs, and vice versa.

In 1–9, find the indicated measure. You may assume tangents from the diagrams.

1.

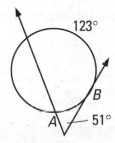

m∠1 _____

2.

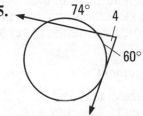

m∠2 _____

3.

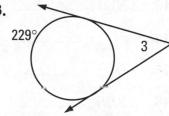

m∠3 _____

4.

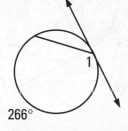

m$\widehat{AB}$ _____

5.

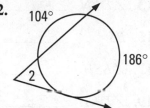

m∠4 _____

6.

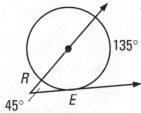

m$\widehat{ER}$ _____

7.

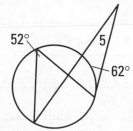

m∠5 _____

8.

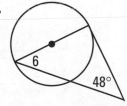

m∠6 _____

9.

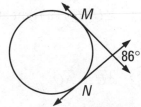

m$\widehat{MN}$ _____

▶ **LESSON MASTER 14-6B** *page 2*

In 10–19, refer to ⊙*O* at the right.
$\overline{HS}$ and $\overline{HK}$ are tangents. Find
the indicated measure.

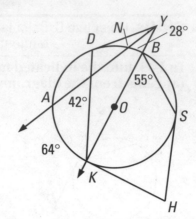

10. $\overset{\frown}{DN}$ _____ 11. $\overset{\frown}{AD}$ _____

12. ∠*NYB* _____ 13. ∠*DYN* _____

14. $\overset{\frown}{KS}$ _____ 15. $\overset{\frown}{BS}$ _____

16. ∠*H* _____ 17. ∠*BSH* _____

18. ∠*BKH* _____ 19. ∠*DKH* _____

Properties Objective F: Make deductions from properties of radii and
tangents, and know sufficient conditions for radii to be
perpendicular to them.
Objective G: Make deductions from properties of angles formed by
chords, tangents, or secants.

---

20. Complete the following argument.

Given: ⊙*P* and ⊙*Q* intersect at *A* and *B*,
⊙*P* contains *Q*, and ⊙*Q* contains *P*.
To prove: $\overline{AU}$ is tangent to ⊙*Q*.

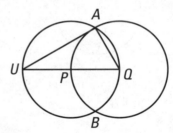

Conclusions   Justifications

1. ∠*UAQ* is a right angle.   _____

_____

2. $\overline{AU} \perp \overline{AQ}$ _____

_____

3. $\overline{AU}$ is tangent to ⊙*Q*.   _____

_____

LESSON MASTER 14-7 B

Questions on SPUR Objectives

Skills Objective E: Apply the Secant Length Theorem and the Tangent Square Theorem.

In 1–3, refer to ⊙O at the right.

1. If $UV = 6$, $VR = 4$, and $VS = 12$, find VT. _____

2. If $TS = 27$, $UV = 9$, and $VR = 8$, find VS. _____

3. For the measures given in Question 2, what is the power of point V? _____

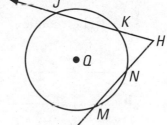

In 4–6, refer to ⊙Q at the right.

4. If $HK = 10$, $HM = 32$, and $HN = 12$, find HJ. _____

5. If $KJ = 14$, $MN = 9$, and $HN = 8$, find HK. _____

6. For the measures given in Question 5, what is the power of point H? _____

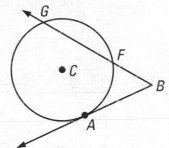

In 7–9, refer to ⊙C at the right.

7. If $AB = 14$ and $BG = 20$, find BF. _____

8. If $BF = 6$ and $FG = 9$, find AB. _____

9. For the measures in Question 8, what is the power of point B? _____

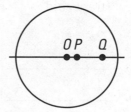

10. Consider ⊙O with radius 10.

   a. What is the power of point O? _____

   b. What is the power of point P, if P is 2 units from O? _____

   c. What is the power of point Q, if Q is 7 units from O? _____

   d. As a point inside a circle gets farther and farther from the center, what appears to happen to the power of the point?

   _____

   e. What is the power of a point *on* ⊙O? _____

11. Extend Question 10 by drawing the line $\overleftrightarrow{OP}$. As a point
    outside a circle gets farther and farther from the center,
    what happens to the power of the point?

_____

_____

Review Objectives A, C, and F, Chapter 8

**In 12–17, a figure is given. a. Find its perimeter (or
circumference). b. Find its area.**

12.

    right triangle

    a. _____

    b. _____

13.

    square

    a. _____

    b. _____

14. 6.77

    circle

    a. _____

    b. _____

15. Study Questions 12–14. Complete the following statements.
    The three figures shown have the same, or nearly the same
    ___?___. The figure with the least perimeter is the ___?___.

_____   _____

16.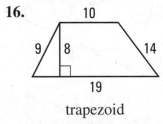

    trapezoid

    a. _____

    b. _____

17.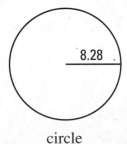

    circle

    a. _____

    b. _____

18.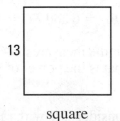

    square

    a. _____

    b. _____

19. Study Questions 16–18. Complete the following statements.
    The three figures shown have the same, or nearly the same
    ___?___. The figure with the greatest area is the ___?___.

_____   _____

LESSON MASTER

**14-8
B**

Vocabulary

1. What does *isoperimetric* mean?

_____

_____

Properties Objective H: Apply the Isoperimetric Theorems and the Isoperimetric Inequality to determine which figures have the greatest or least area or perimeter.

2. Consider the figures below.

(a)    (b)    (c)   (d)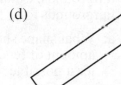

    a. For which figure is the ratio $\frac{\text{area}}{\text{perimeter}}$ greatest?

_____

    b. For which figure is the ratio $\frac{\text{perimeter}}{\text{area}}$ greatest?

_____

3. Consider all figures with an area of 15 ft².

    a. Which has the least perimeter?

_____

    b. What is the perimeter of the figure in Part **a**?

_____

4. Consider all figures with a perimeter of 28 meters.

    a. Which has the greatest area?

_____

    b. What is the area of the figure in Part **a**?

_____

5. A circle and a regular octagon both have the same perimeter. Which figure has the least area?

_____

6. Of all pentagons with a perimeter of 60 cm, which has the greatest area?

_____

7. A triangle has sides of 4.3 m, 7 m, and 9.6 m. What would be the greatest possible area of a figure with the same perimeter?

_____

8. Let A be the area of a figure with perimeter 16. Give the range of possible values for A.

_____

Uses Objective K: Apply the Isoperimetric Theorems and the Isoperimetric Inequality in real situations.

9. An amusement park is going to build an island surrounded by a canal 1.5 miles long.

 a. What shape should the island be so that it has the greatest possible area? _____

 b. What is the area of the island in Part **a**? _____

10. Sunnybrook County is annexing land for new fairgrounds. County officials want the area of the fairgrounds to be 5.5 million ft².

 a. What shape should the fairgrounds be so the amount of fencing on its perimeter is the least possible? _____

 b. What is the perimeter of the fairgrounds in Part **a**? _____

 c. If a rectangular fairgrounds is desired, what shape should it be? _____

 d. What is the perimeter of the rectangle in Part **c**? _____

Review Objectives A, B, and D, Chapter 10

In 11–13, a figure is given. a. Find its surface area. b. Find its volume.

11.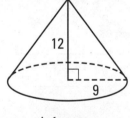

right cone

12.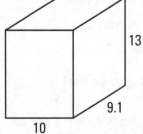

rectangular prism

13.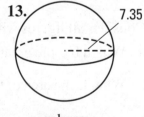

sphere

 a. _____   a. _____   a. _____

 b. _____   b. _____   b. _____

14. Examine your answers to Questions 11–13. What do you notice?

_____

_____

LESSON MASTER 14-9 B

Properties Objective H: Apply the Isoperimetric Theorems and the Isoperimetric Inequality to determine which figures have the greatest or least surface area or volume.

1. Consider the figures below.

(a) 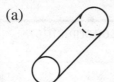 (b) 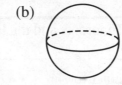 (c) 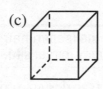 (d)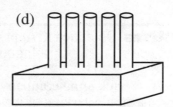

   a. For which figure is the ratio $\dfrac{\text{surface area}}{\text{volume}}$ greatest? _____

   b. For which figure is the ratio $\dfrac{\text{volume}}{\text{surface area}}$ greatest? _____

2. Consider all figures with a surface area of 210 ft^2.

   a. Which has the greatest volume? _____

   b. What is the volume of the figure in Part **a**? _____

3. Consider all figures with a volume of 800 cm^3.

   a. Which has the least surface area? _____

   b. What is the surface area of the figure in Part **a**? _____

4. a. What is the volume of the right square pyramid at the right? _____

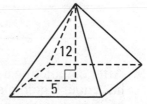

   b. What figure with the same volume has the least surface area? _____

   c. Find the surface area of the figure in Part **b**. _____

   d. What is the surface area of the right square pyramid? _____

   e. What figure with the same surface area has the greatest volume? _____

   f. Find the volume of the figure in Part **e**? _____

5. A cylinder with equal height and diameter has the same volume as a sphere. Which has less surface area?

_____

6. Of all rectangular prisms with a volume of 300 mm³, which has the least surface area?

_____

Uses Objective K: Apply the Isoperimetric Theorems and the Isoperimetric Inequality in real situations.

---

7. A packaging company is to design a container for a single serving of ice cream with volume of 15 in³. Find the surface area of each possible container.

   a. a cube

   _____

   b. a sphere

   _____

   c. a right cone with height 3.5 in.

   _____

   d. a box with a square face 1.5 in. by 1.5 in.

   _____

   e. a right cylinder with diameter 3.5 in.

   _____

8. **a.** Which of the containers in Question 7 has the least surface area?

   _____

   b. Which container would you choose for the ice cream? Why?

   _____

   _____

   _____

9. After completing a big project, a jewelry designer has enough gold plating left to cover a surface area of 35 mm² with a particular thickness of gold.

   a. What is the shape of the object with the greatest volume that could be plated?

   _____

   b. What is the volume of the shape in Part **a**?

   _____

   c. What would be the volume of the largest cube possible that could be plated with gold?

   _____

   d. Why might a jeweler be interested in the volume of the object to be plated?

   _____

   _____

LESSON MASTER 1-1 B — Questions on SPUR Objectives

Vocabulary

1. a. The tiny dots that make images on television screens, computer monitors, and calculator displays are called ___?___.

   pixels

   b. What is a *matrix*?

   a rectangular arrangement of pixels in rows and columns

   c. What does it mean if computer screen A has better *resolution* than computer screen B?

   Computer screen A has more pixels per square inch, resulting in a sharper image.

Skills Objective A: Draw discrete lines.

In 2–4, match the phrase with the diagram.

2. vertical discrete line ___**b**___

3. oblique discrete line ___**c**___

4. horizontal discrete line ___**a**___

a. • • • • • •

b.

c.

5. Draw two oblique discrete lines that intersect in a point.

   Sample:

6. Draw a horizontal discrete line and a vertical discrete line that cross but do not have a point in common

   Sample.

1 ►

► **LESSON MASTER 1-1B** page 2

Properties Objective F: Given a property of points and lines, tell whether it is true in discrete geometry.

In 7–9, tell whether the statement is *true* or *false* in discrete geometry.

7. A point is a dot. **true**

8. A line has no thickness. **false**

9. Two crossing lines intersect in a point. **false**

Uses Objective J: Use discrete geometry to model real-world situations.

10. Use the matrices at the right to create your initials.

    Sample initials are given.

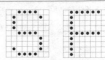

11. Use Seurat's technique of drawing with dots to draw a flower.

    Sample:

12. Draw a picture of a sign formed by light bulbs. Use a message that you might see on such a sign.

    Sample: SALE

2

LESSON MASTER 1-2 B — Questions on SPUR Objectives

Vocabulary

1. Explain what it means when a number line is *dense*.

   Sample: Between any two points on a number line is another point.

Properties Objective F: Given a property of points and lines, tell whether it is true in synthetic geometry.

In 2–4, tell whether the statement is *true* or *false* in synthetic geometry.

2. A point is a physical dot. **false**

3. A line has no thickness **true**

4. A line extends in two directions. **true**

5. When two points are exact locations, how many lines contain the two points? **one line**

6. Refer to the number line at the right.

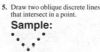

   a. Give a possible coordinate for point Y.

   Sample: -14.3

   b. How many points are there between points X and Z?

   an infinite number

Uses Objective I: Apply the definition of distance to real situations.

7. Timmy placed his foot on a 12-inch ruler. It stretched from the $3\frac{1}{2}$-inch mark to the end of the ruler. How long is Timmy's foot? **$8\frac{1}{2}$ inches**

8. On a vacation, the Ortegas drove at an average speed of 51.5 miles per hour the first day and 63 miles per hour the second day. How much faster was their average speed the second day? **11.5 mph**

3 ►

► **LESSON MASTER 1-2B** page 2

9. From a roll of wax paper, Marcia tore off a piece and saw the imprinted message, "12 feet remaining." Several days later she tore off a piece that read "5 feet remaining." How much wax paper was there between messages? **7 feet**

10. According to the 1995 *Information Please Almanac*, the record high temperature on Earth was recorded at 136° F in Libya in 1922. The record low temperature is –129° F in Antarctica in 1983. How much hotter is the record high than the record low? **265°**

In 11–13, refer to the table of air distances in miles given below.

	Cairo	Hong Kong	London	Rio de Janeiro	San Francisco
Cairo		5061	2181	6146	7364
Hong Kong	5061		5982	11,021	6897
London	2181	5982		5766	5357
Rio de Janeiro	6146	11,021	5766		6621
San Francisco	7364	6897	5357	6621	

11. How much closer is London to Cairo than London is to San Francisco? **3176 mi**

12. Which trip is shorter, London to Hong Kong to San Francisco, or London to Cairo to Rio de Janeiro? **London to Cairo to Rio**

13. If you fly directly from Rio de Janeiro to Hong Kong, how much shorter is the trip than if you fly from Rio de Janeiro to San Francisco and then to Hong Kong? **2497 mi**

Representations Objective K: Determine distance on a number line.

In 14 and 15, refer to the number line at the right.

14. Find each distance.

   a. CD **.5, or $\frac{1}{2}$**   b. AD **4**   c. BC **2**

15. a. If H is on the number line and DH = 10, what are two possible coordinates of H? **12   -8**

   b. If M is on the number line and CM = 6, what are two possible coordinates of M? **7.5   -4.5**

4

LESSON MASTER 1-3 B — Questions on SPUR Objectives

Vocabulary

1. a. Another name for the coordinate plane is ___?___.

the Cartesian plane

b. For whom is the answer in Part **a** named?

René Descartes

2. Give the standard form of an equation for a line.

$Ax + By = C, A \neq 0, B \neq 0$

Properties Objective F: Given a property of points and lines, tell whether it is true in plane coordinate geometry.

In 3–5, tell whether the statement is *true* or *false* in coordinate geometry.

3. A point is a number. — **false**

4. A line is a set of ordered pairs. — **true**

5. A curve is a set of ordered pairs. — **true**

6. Give coordinates for a point on the *x*-axis. — **Sample: (5, 0)**

7. Give coordinates for a point on the *y*-axis. — **Sample: (0, 3)**

Representations Objective L: Graph points and lines in the coordinate plane.

In 8–13, graph the point on the coordinate plane. Label the point with its letter name.

8. $A(4, 1)$ **9.** $B(3, -2)$

10. $C(-5, -5)$ **11.** $D(0, 4)$

12. $E(-4, 0)$ **13.** $F(-2, 2)$

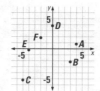

5 ▶

In 14–19, find two points on the line with the given equation. Then graph the line on the coordinate plane.

Sample points are given.

14. $y = -3x$

x	y
0	0
1	-3

15. $y = 2x + 3$

x	y
0	3
1	5

16. $2x + y = 4$

x	y
0	4
1	2

17. $x = -5$

x	y
-5	0
-5	3

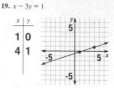

18. $y = 4$

x	y
3	4
-2	4

19. $x - 3y = 1$

x	y
1	0
4	1

In 20–22, tell if the line is *vertical, horizontal,* or *oblique.*

20. $3x + 8y = 22$ — **oblique**

21. $x = 12$ — **vertical**

22. $y = 1550$ — **horizontal**

6

LESSON MASTER 1-4 B — Questions on SPUR Objectives

Skills Objective B: Analyze networks.

1. Consider the network at the right.

a. How many even nodes are there? — **2**

b. How many odd nodes are there? — **4**

c. Is the network traversable? If so, identify a path.

no

2. Consider the network at the right.

a. How many even nodes are there? — **2**

b. How many odd nodes are there? — **2**

c. Is the network traversable? If so, identify a path.

Yes; sample: W X Y Z W X Y Z W Y

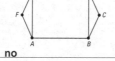

3. Draw a network with 4 nodes and 6 lines.

Sample:

Properties Objective F: Given a property of points and lines, tell whether it is true in graph theory.

In 4–7, tell whether the statement is *true* or *false* in graph theory.

4. A point has a size. — **false**

5. Two points lie on no more than one line. — **false**

6. A line may contain just one point. — **true**

7. A line is dense. — **false**

7 ▶

Uses Objective J: Use graph theory to model real-world situations.

8. The diagram at the right shows the floor plan of a drug store. The heavy lines are the aisles.

a. Model the aisles as a network of nodes and lines.

Sample:

b. Would a customer be able to walk down each aisle exactly one time? Justify your answer.

No; the network has more than 2 odd nodes.

9. At the right is a diagram of World Wonders Amusement Park. The stream through the amusement park is crossed by 5 bridges.

a. Represent the bridges and land masses as a network of nodes and lines.

Sample:

b. Is the network traversable? Justify your answer.

No; the network has more than 2 odd nodes.

c. Suppose another bridge is to be built. Can it be built so the network of 6 bridges is traversable? If so, draw it in the diagram of the amusement park. — **yes**

Sample is given in diagram above.

8

LESSON MASTER **1-5 B** | Questions on SPUR Objectives

Vocabulary

1. In a realistic perspective drawing, vanishing points lie on the ___?___, which is also the horizon line. **vanishing line**

Skills Objective C: Make and analyze perspective drawings.

In 2–5, determine whether the drawing is a perspective drawing. Write *yes* or *no*.

2. **yes**

book

3. **no**
chair

4. **yes**
roll of carpet

5. **no**
building

6. Draw the hidden lines in the cube below.

7. Draw a cube in perspective, showing the hidden lines.
Sample:

---

8. Draw the picture below in perspective.

Sample:

trees on a highway

In 9–12, locate the vanishing point(s) in the drawing.

9.
fence

10.
RICE
box of rice

11.
hed

12.
skyscraper

LESSON MASTER **1-6 B** | Questions on SPUR Objectives

Properties Objective E: Give the dimensions of figures and objects.

In 1–6, give the number of dimensions of the figure or object. Ignore small thicknesses.

1. a number line **1**

2. a cube **3**

3. a point (as a location) **0**

4. a carton **3**

5. a toothpick **1**

6. a sheet of paper **2**

Properties Objective G: Recognize the use of undefined terms.

7. a. Explain *circularity*. **Samples are given for 7 and 9.**
returning to a previously defined word when trying to define a term

b. Explain how defining the word *decay* might lead to circularity.
using "rot" to define "decay," "decompose" to define "rot," and "decay" to define "decompose"

8. Name three undefined geometric terms used in your textbook.
point **line** **plane**

9. Name three undefined algebraic terms or phrases used in your textbook.
number **equal** **set**

10. What is a *figure*? **a set of points**

---

11. What is the *space* of a geometry?
the set of all points in that geometry

In 12–15, write a description of "point" for the type of geometry given.

12. discrete geometry **dot**

13. graph theory **node of a network**

14. synthetic geometry **location**

15. coordinate geometry **ordered pair (x, y)**

In 16–19, label the line with the type of geometry in which it would appear.

16.
graph theory

17.
synthetic geometry

18.
discrete geometry

19.
plane coordinate geometry

LESSON MASTER 1-7 B

Questions on SPUR Objectives

Vocabulary

1. What is a *postulate*?

   an assumption

2. What is a *theorem*?

   a statement which follows from definitions, postulates, or previously proved theorems

3. a. Define *parallel lines*.

   coplanar lines that have no points in common or that are identical

   b. Use symbols to write "line *m* is parallel to line *n*."

   m // n

Properties Objective G: Recognize the use of postulates.

In 4 and 5, complete the statement.

4. The postulates for ___?___ geometry fit both synthetic geometry and coordinate geometry.

   Euclidean

5. Refer to the diagram at the right.

   a. According to the ___?___ Assumption, there is exactly one line through points *M* and *N*.

   Unique Line

   b. In symbols, the name of the line is ___?___

   $\overleftrightarrow{MN}$ **or** $\overleftrightarrow{NM}$

   c. According to the ___?___ Assumption, all the points on the line can be put in one-to-one correspondence with the real numbers with point *M* corresponding to zero and point *N* corresponding to 1.

   Number Line

▶ **LESSON MASTER 1-7B** page 2

6. In the diagram at the right, line *t* is on plane *R*. Plane *R* is in space. Draw two other points on or outside of plane *R*. Use the Dimension Assumption to explain where these points are located.

   Sample: Point A is in plane R but not on line t; point B is in space but not in plane R.

7. Refer to the diagram at the right. Name all the lines that appear to be parallel to line *u*.

   line w, line u

In 8–10, graph the system of two equations on the same grid and tell if the lines are parallel.

8. $\begin{cases} y = x - 1 \\ y = x + 3 \end{cases}$

   yes

9. $\begin{cases} y = 3x \\ y = 3 \end{cases}$

   no

10. $\begin{cases} 2x + y = 3 \\ 4x + 2y = 6 \end{cases}$

    yes

11. Describe a property in discrete geometry that is *not* true in Euclidean Geometry.

    Sample: Two lines can intersect but have no points in common.

12. Describe a property in graph theory that is *not* true in Euclidean Geometry.

    Sample: Two different lines can contain the same two points.

LESSON MASTER 1-8 B

Questions on SPUR Objectives

Vocabulary

1. Points *P* and *Q* are on a number line. The coordinate of point *P* is -3.4 and the coordinate of point *Q* is 7.5. Is a point on the number line with the given coordinate *between P and Q*?

   a. 9 **no**
   b. 5 **yes**
   c. 0 **yes**
   d. -2 **yes**
   e. -3 **yes**
   f. 7 **yes**
   g. -5 **no**
   h. 7.2 **yes**
   i. 7.5 **no**
   j. -3.2 **yes**
   k. 3.5 **yes**
   l. 3.8 **yes**

Skills Objective D: Recognize and use notation for lines, segments, and rays.

2. Draw $\overleftrightarrow{GH}$.

   Samples are given for 2–4.

3. Draw $\overline{JK}$.

4. Draw $\overline{ST}$.

In 5–11, refer to the diagram at the right.

5. Name the line in three different ways.

   Samples: $\overleftrightarrow{UY}, \overleftrightarrow{UX}, \overleftrightarrow{VW}, \overleftrightarrow{VX}, \overleftrightarrow{XY}$

6. In three different ways, name the ray with endpoint *X* that contains point *W*.

   $\overrightarrow{XW}, \overrightarrow{XV}, \overrightarrow{XU}$

7. In two different ways, name the segment with endpoints *X* and *U*.

   $\overline{XU}, \overline{UX}$

8. Name the ray opposite to $\overrightarrow{VU}$.

   Sample: $\overrightarrow{VW}, \overrightarrow{VX}, \overrightarrow{VY}$

9. Is $\overrightarrow{XY}$ the same as $\overrightarrow{YX}$? **no**

10. Is $\overline{XY}$ the same as $\overline{YX}$? **yes**

11. Is $\overrightarrow{WX}$ the same as $\overrightarrow{WX}$? **no**

▶ **LESSON MASTER 1-8B** page 2

Samples are given for 12 and 13.

12. Draw $\overrightarrow{AE}$ with *B* between *A* and *E*.

    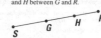

13. Draw $\overrightarrow{RS}$ with *G* between *R* and *S* and *H* between *G* and *R*.

Properties Objective H: Apply the Distance Postulate properties of betweenness.

In 14–19, refer to the diagram at the right. *N* is between *M* and *O*.

14. If *MN* = 8.3 and *NO* = 4.4, what is *MO*?

    12.7

15. If *NO* = 13 and *MO* = 34, what is *MN*? **21**

16. If *NO* = *x*, *MN* = 2*x*, and *MO* = 42, what is *x*? **14**

17. If *MO* = 18, *MN* = 4*y*, and *NO* = 4, what is *y*? **3.5, or $3\frac{1}{2}$**

18. If *M* has coordinate -4 and *O* has coordinate 3, what is the range of coordinates for *N*? **-4 < x < 3**

19. If *M* has coordinate -2, *N* has coordinate 7.6 and *NO* = 5, what is the coordinate of *O*? **12.6**

In 20–23, use the number line at the right. Write an inequality to describe the coordinates of points on the given figure.

20. $\overrightarrow{WY}$ **x ≥ -15**

21. $\overrightarrow{YW}$ **x ≤ 10**

22. $\overline{XY}$ **0 ≤ x ≤ 10**

23. $\overline{WZ}$ **-15 ≤ x ≤ 25**

LESSON MASTER 2-1 B Questions on SPUR Objectives

Vocabulary

1. Define *convex set.*

A convex set is a set in which every segment which connects points of the set lies entirely in the set.

Skills Objective A: Distinguish between convex and nonconvex figures.

In 2–10, tell whether the set is *convex* or *nonconvex.*

2.
convex

3.
convex

4.
nonconvex

5.
nonconvex

6.
nonconvex

7.
nonconvex

8.
convex

9.
nonconvex

10.
nonconvex

In 11 and 12, draw the figure.   **Samples are given.**

11. a nonconvex 6-sided region   12. a convex 5-sided region

▶ **LESSON MASTER 2-1B** *page 2*

13. Draw a segment showing why the set at the right is *not* convex.

14. Explain why Figure 1 is convex, but Figure 2 is nonconvex.

Figure 1   Figure 2

Sample:
In Fig. 1, every segment connecting points of the set is entirely in the set; in Fig. 2, segments connecting points on different sides contain points not in the set.

Review Objective G, Lesson 1-7

In 15–17, complete each statement.

15. Consider the Point-Line-Plane Postulate.

a. Through any two points, there is __?__ .
exactly one line

b. Given a line in a plane, there is at least __?__ .
one point in the plane that is not on the line

c. Given a plane in space, there is at least __?__ .
one point in space that is not in the plane

16. According to the Line Intersection Theorem, two different lines intersect in __?__ .
at most one point

17. By definition, lines *c* and *d* are parallel if and only if __?__ .
they are coplanar and have no points in common or they are identical

---

LESSON MASTER 2-2 B Questions on SPUR Objectives

Vocabulary

In 1 and 2, complete the statements.

1. An if-then statement is also called a ____ **conditional**

2. In an if-then statement,

a. the clause following "if" is called the ____ **antecedent** or the **hypothesis**

b. the clause following "then" is called the ____ **consequent** or the **conclusion**

Skills Objective C: Use and interpret the symbol ⇒.

In 3–6, write in words with   *u* = today is Tuesday;
v = macaroni is served;
w = school lets out early;
x = we will eat at Dorsey's.

3. *u* ⇒ *w*   **If today is Tuesday, then school lets out early.**

4. *u* ⇒ *v*   **If today is Tuesday, then macaroni is served.**

5. *v* ⇒ *x*   **If macaroni is served, then we will eat at Dorsey's.**

6. *w* ⇒ *x*   **If school lets out early, then we will eat at Dorsey's.**

Properties Objective G: Write conditionals.

In 7 and 8, underline the antecedent once and the consequent twice.

7. If you were perfect, then you would not need an eraser.

8. Take the bus if the car won't start.

In 9 and 10, rewrite as a conditional.   **Samples are given.**

9. Any dogs in the park must be on a leash.
If a dog is in the park, then it must be on a leash.

10. Pentagons have five sides.
If a figure is a pentagon, then it has five sides.

▶ **LESSON MASTER 2-2B** *page 2*

Properties Objective H. Evaluate conditionals.

11. Consider the BASIC program at the right.

```
10 INPUT G
20 IF G < 4 THEN PRINT "NONE"
30 END
```

a. Give a value for G which will cause the printer to print "NONE".   **Sample: 3**

b. When Laura ran the program, the computer did not print anything. Explain why this might have happened.
Sample: Laura chose a number greater than or equal to 4.

In 12 and 13, a conjecture is given. Determine whether each example is an *instance* of the conjecture; a *counterexample* to the conjecture; or *neither* an instance nor a counterexample to the conjecture.

12. If *u* > -5, then *u* is positive.

a. *u* = -2   b. *u* = -12   c. *u* = 4
counter-example   **neither**   **instance**

13. If a figure is a convex set, then it is a 6-sided region.

a.   b.   c.
neither   **instance**   **counter-example**

Uses Objective K: Apply properties of conditionals in real situations.

14. An ad said "If you purchase your tickets by 6:00, you pay half." Mr. Yi bought his tickets at 5:30. What happened?
Mr. Yi paid half for the tickets.

15. If you got at least 82% on the last test, your final grade will be an A. You got 89% on the last test. What will happen?
You will get an A for your final grade.

16. a. Rewrite as a conditional: It is always winter when it snows.
Sample: If it snows, then it is winter.

b. Is the conditional in Part a true? Justify your answer.
Sample: No; it might snow in May, which is spring.

LESSON MASTER 2-3 B — Questions on SPUR Objectives

Skills Objective C: Use and interpret the symbol ⇒.

In 1 and 2, write the converse of the given statement.

1. $m \Rightarrow n$ $n \Rightarrow m$ 2. $h \Rightarrow g$ $g \Rightarrow h$

Properties Objective E: Write the converse of a conditional.

In 3 and 4, *multiple choice.* Choose the correct phrase to complete the statement.

(a) is true   (b) is false   (c) may be true or it may be false

3. If a statement is true, its converse __?__.   **c**

4. If a statement is false, its converse __?__.   **c**

In 5–12, a. is the conditional true? If not, give a counterexample. b. Write the converse. c. Is the converse true? If not, give a counterexample.   **Sample counter-examples are given.**

5. If you are in Texas, then you are in Houston.
   a. **False; you could be in Dallas.**
   b. **If you are in Houston, then you are in Texas**
   c. **True**

6. If you are in Nevada, then you are in the United States.
   a. **True**
   b. **If you are in the U.S., then you are in Nevada.**
   c. **False; you could be in Montana.**

7. If it rains, then you will get wet.
   a. **False; you could be indoors.**
   b. **If you get wet, then it is raining.**
   c. **False; you could be in the shower.**

21 ▶

---

8. If the water boils for 3 minutes, then it boils for 180 seconds.
   a. **True**
   b. **If the water boils for 180 seconds, then it boils for 3 minutes.**
   c. **True**

9. You have more than a dollar if you have eleven dimes.
   a. **True**   have eleven dimes.
   b. **If you have more than a dollar, then you**
   c. **False; you could have five quarters.**

10. If $x < 8$, then $x < 10$.
    a. **True**
    b. **If $x < 10$, then $x < 8$.**
    c. **False; x might be 9.**

11. If $y > 2$, then $y < 14$.
    a. **False; y might be 20.**
    b. **If $y < 14$, then $y > 2$.**
    c. **False; y might be 1.**

12. A polygon is an octagon if it has eight sides.
    a. **True**
    b. **If a polygon is an octagon, then it has 8 sides.**
    c. **True**

Uses Objective K: Apply properties of conditionals in real situations.

13. Suppose T. R. West Bank advertises "If you bank with us you'll earn 6%." Last year Joanna's savings earned 6%. Did she bank at T. R. West Bank? Explain your answer.
    Sample: Not necessarily; even though the ad is true, its converse might be false; Joanna could have earned 6% interest at another bank.

22

LESSON MASTER 2-4 B — Questions on SPUR Objectives

Vocabulary

1. Write the definition of *midpoint.*
   The midpoint of a segment $\overline{AB}$ is the point M on $\overline{AB}$ with $AM = MB$.

2. Write the definition of *circle.* **A circle is the set of all points in a plane at a certain distance (its radius) from a certain point (its center).**

Skills Objective C: Use and interpret the symbol ⇔.

In 3–6, write in words with
e = today is Sunday;
f = today is the first day of the week;
g = tomorrow is Monday;
h = yesterday was Saturday.

3. $e \Leftrightarrow g$ **Today is Sunday if and only if tomorrow is Monday.**

4. $e \Leftrightarrow f$ **Today is Sunday if and only if today is the first day of the week.**

5. $f \Leftrightarrow h$ **Today is the first day of the week if and only if yesterday was Saturday.**

6. $g \Leftrightarrow h$ **Tomorrow is Monday if and only if yesterday was Saturday.**

Skills Objective D: Use the definition of midpoint to find lengths of segments.

In 7–9, use the number line at the right.

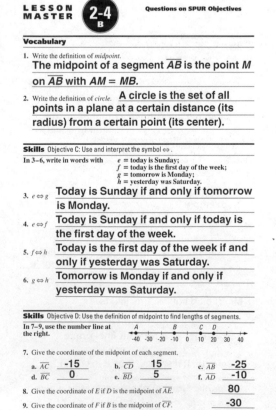

7. Give the coordinate of the midpoint of each segment.
   a. $\overline{AC}$ **-15**   b. $\overline{CD}$ **15**   c. $\overline{AB}$ **-25**
   d. $\overline{BC}$ **0**   e. $\overline{BD}$ **5**   f. $\overline{AD}$ **-10**

8. Give the coordinate of E if D is the midpoint of $\overline{AE}$. **80**

9. Give the coordinate of F if B is the midpoint of $\overline{CF}$. **-30**

23 ▶

In 10–12, S is the midpoint of $\overline{PQ}$.

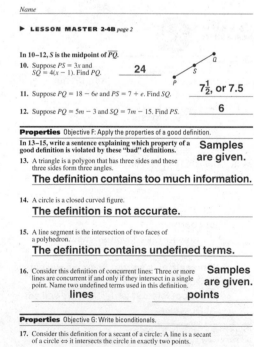

10. Suppose $PS = 3x$ and $SQ = 4(x - 1)$. Find PQ. **24**

11. Suppose $PQ = 18 - 6e$ and $PS = 7 + e$. Find SQ. **$7\frac{1}{2}$, or 7.5**

12. Suppose $PQ = 5m - 3$ and $SQ = 7m - 15$. Find PS. **6**

Properties Objective F: Apply the properties of a good definition.

In 13–15, write a sentence explaining which property of a good definition is violated by these "bad" definitions. **Samples are given.**

13. A triangle is a polygon that has three sides and these three sides form three angles.
    The definition contains too much information.

14. A circle is a closed curved figure.
    The definition is not accurate.

15. A line segment is the intersection of two faces of a polyhedron.
    The definition contains undefined terms.

16. Consider this definition of concurrent lines: Three or more lines are concurrent if and only if they intersect in a single point. Name two undefined terms used in this definition. **Samples are given.**
    lines   **points**

Properties Objective G: Write biconditionals.

17. Consider this definition for a secant of a circle: A line is a secant of a circle ⇔ it intersects the circle in exactly two points.
    a. Write the definition as two conditionals.
    If a line is a secant of a circle, then it intersects the circle in exactly two points. If a line intersects a circle in exactly two points, then it is a secant of the circle.
    b. Underline the conditional in Part a that goes in the direction *characteristics ⇒ term.*

24

LESSON MASTER 2-5 B

Questions on SPUR Objectives

Vocabulary

1. Write the symbol used for each term.
   a. *union*
   $\cup$
   b. *intersection*
   $\cap$
   c. *empty set*
   { } or ϕ

2. Another name for the empty set is the **null set**.

Properties Objective I: Determine the union and intersection of sets.

In 3–9, two sets are given. a. Find $G \cup H$. b. Find $G \cap H$.

3. $G = \{-4, -2, 7, 9\}$; $H = \{-8, -2, 6, 7, 10\}$
   a. **{-8, -4, -2, 6, 7, 9, 10}**
   b. **{-2, 7}**

4. $G = \{3, 5, 9, 15\}$; $H = \{3, 5, 9, 15\}$
   a. **{3, 5, 9, 15}**
   b. **{3, 5, 9, 15}**

5. $G = \{-11, 0, 17, 21, 30\}$; $H = \{-4, -3, 1, 19, 26\}$
   a. **{-11, -4, -3, 0, 1, 17, 19, 21, 26, 30}**
   b. **{ }**

6. $G = \{-5, 0, 5, 10\}$; $H = \{-4, 0, 4\}$
   a. **{-5, -4, 0, 4, 5, 10}**
   b. **{0}**

7. $G = \{ \}$; $H = \{7, 77, 777\}$
   a. **{7, 77, 777}**
   b. **{ }**

8. $G = \{0, 3, 6, 9, 12, 15, 18, \dots\}$; $H = \{0, 6, 12, 18, 24, 30, \dots\}$
   a. **{0, 3, 6, 9, 12, ...}**
   {0, 6, 12, 18, 24, }

9. G = the set of white piano keys; H = the set of black piano keys
   a. **{all piano keys}**
   b. **{ }**

10. Let J = the set of numbers x with $x \geq 4$ and K = the set of numbers x with $x \leq 10$.
    a. Graph J on a number line. 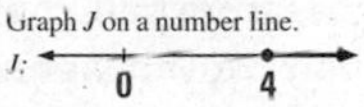
    b. Graph K on a number line. 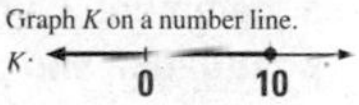
    J: 0 4
    K: 0 10

25 ▶

▶ **LESSON MASTER 2-5B** *page 2*

c. Graph $J \cup K$ on a number line.

0
d. Describe $J \cup K$. **the set of all real numbers**

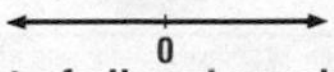

e. Graph $J \cap K$ on a number line.

4 10
f. Describe $J \cap K$. **the set of all real numbers between 4 and 10, inclusive**

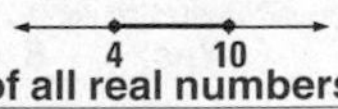

In 11–15, use the diagram at the right. Name the segments or points in each figure.

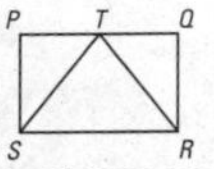

11. $\triangle PTS \cap \triangle QTR$ — **T**
12. $\triangle PTS \cup \triangle QTR$ — **PT, TS, SP, QT, TR, RQ**
13. $\triangle STR \cap PQRS$ — **SR, T**
14. $\triangle STR \cup PQRS$ — **ST, TR, RS, PQ, QR, PS**
15. $\overline{PS} \cap \overline{QR}$ — **{ }**

16. Draw two segments $\overline{EF}$ and $\overline{WX}$ so $\overline{EF} \cap \overline{WX} = M$.
    Sample:

17. Draw two rays $\overrightarrow{NO}$ and $\overrightarrow{YZ}$ so $\overrightarrow{NO} \cup \overrightarrow{YZ} = \overrightarrow{OZ}$.
    Sample:
    Z N Y O

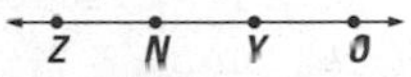

Review Objective A, Lesson 2-1

In 18–20, tell whether the set is *convex* or *nonconvex*.

18.  **nonconvex**
19.  **convex**
20.  **nonconvex**

26

LESSON MASTER 2-6 B

Questions on SPUR Objectives

Vocabulary

1. Define *polygon*.
   A polygon is the union of three or more segments in the same plane such that each segment intersects exactly two others, one at each endpoint.

2. Refer to the polygon at the right. 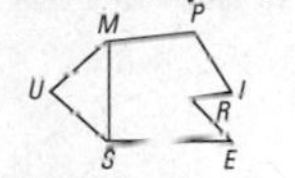
   a. Give two different names for the polygon. **Samples are given.**
   UMPIRES PIRESUM

   b. Name its *vertices*.
   U, M, P, I, R, E, S
   c. Name its *sides*.
   UM, MP, PI, IR, RE, ES, SU
   d. Name two *consecutive* vertices.
   Sample: R, E
   e. Name two consecutive sides.
   Sample: ES, SU
   f. Draw a *diagonal* and identify it.
   Sample: MS

Skills Objective A: Distinguish between convex and nonconvex figures.

3. Draw a convex hexagon.
   Sample:

4. Draw a nonconvex nonagon.
   Sample:

Skills Objective B: Draw and identify polygons.

5. Identify each polygon.
   a. 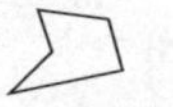 **penta-gon**
   b.  **quadri-lateral**
   c. 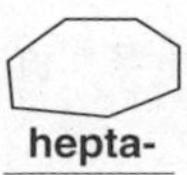 **hepta-gon**
   d.  **deca-gon**

27 ▶

▶ **LESSON MASTER 2-6B** *page 2*

6. *Multiple choice.* Choose the most appropriate drawing.
   (i)  (ii)  (iii) 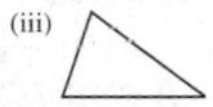
   a. equilateral triangle **ii**
   b. scalene triangle **iii**
   c. isosceles triangle **i**

7. Use the definition of polygon to explain why the figure at the right is *not* a polygon.
   Sample: Some of the segments intersect more than two others.

8. Draw a figure that is the union of five line segments but is not a pentagon. **Sample:**

Uses Objective L: Identify polygons used in the real world.

9. The Math Resource Room has tables shaped like Figure 1 at the right. When group discussion is needed, the tables are put together as shown in Figure 2.
   a. Classify the polygon in Figure 1 by the number of sides. **quadrilateral**
   b. The outer edges of the tables in Figure 2 form what type of polygon? **hexagon**

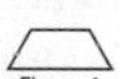

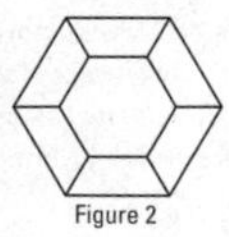

   Figure 1
   Figure 2

Representations Objective N: Draw hierarchies of triangles and polygons.

10. At the right, draw a hierarchy relating the following terms: polygon, figure, isosceles triangle, scalene triangle, hexagon, pentagon, triangle.

    figure
    polygon
    triangle hexagon pentagon
    scalene isosceles
    triangle triangle

28

237

LESSON MASTER 2-7 B

Questions on SPUR Objectives

Properties Objective J: Determine whether a triangle can be formed with sides of three given lengths.

In 1–10, can these numbers be the lengths of the sides of a triangle? Justify your answer.

1. 4, 5, 7   Yes; $4 + 5 > 7, 5 + 7 > 4, 4 + 7 > 5$

2. 4, 5, 9   No; $4 + 5 = 9$

3. 4, 5, 10   No; $4 + 5 < 10$

4. 60, 60, 105   Yes; $60 + 60 > 105, 60 + 105 > 60$

5. 8, 16, 8   No; $8 + 8 = 16$

6. 3, 11, 6   No; $3 + 6 < 11$

7. 9.8, 4.1, 5.9   Yes; $9.8 + 4.1 > 5.9, 4.1 + 5.9 > 9.8, 4.1 + 9.8 > 5.9$

8. .73, .98, 1.66   Yes; $.73 + .98 > 1.66, .73 + 1.66 > .98, .98 + 1.66 > .73$

9. $\frac{3}{4}, \frac{1}{2}, \frac{11}{8}$ No; $\frac{3}{4} + \frac{1}{2} < \frac{11}{8}$

10. $\frac{2}{3}, \frac{2}{3}, 1$ Yes; $\frac{2}{3} + \frac{2}{3} > 1, \frac{2}{3} + 1 > \frac{2}{3}$

11. In $\triangle RST$ at the right, how long can $\overline{ST}$ be? $6 < ST < 18$

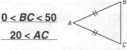

12. In $\triangle ABC$ at the right,

   a. if $AC = 25$ how long can $\overline{BC}$ be? $0 < BC < 50$

   b. if $BC = 40$ how long can $\overline{AC}$ be? $20 < AC$

13. Two sides of a triangle are 15 ft and 22 ft. How long can the third side be?   **between 7 ft and 37 ft**

14. Two sides of a triangle are 7.3 m and 14.6 m. How long can the third side be?   **between 7.3 m and 21.9 m**

► LESSON MASTER 2-7B page 2

In 15–19, thin rods varying in length from 1 in. to 24 in. are arranged to form triangles. Each rod is cut to the nearest whole inch. Two rod lengths are given. a. Find the minimum length of the third rod. b. Find the maximum length of the third rod.

15. 4 in., 6 in.   a. **3 in.**   b. **9 in.**

16. 7 in., 7 in.   a. **1 in.**   b. **13 in.**

17. 2 in., 15 in.   a. **14 in.**   b. **16 in.**

18. 1 in., 1 in.   a. **1 in.**   b. **1 in.**

19. 18 in., 5 in.   a. **14 in.**   b. **22 in.**

Uses Objective M: Apply the Triangle Inequality Postulate in real situations.

20. At a state park, camp headquarters are 4 km from the store. The store is 6 km from the ranger's office. From this information alone, how far is it from the ranger's office to camp headquarters?   **between 2 km and 10 km**

21. *Multiple choice.* Kitchen designers usually plan a kitchen triangle, the triangular path from the stove to the refrigerator to the sink. Plans for a new kitchen place the stove and refrigerator 10 ft apart and the sink and the stove 6 ft apart. Between the sink and the refrigerator, which of these distances are possible? List all choices.   **b, c, d, e**

   (a) 4 ft   (b) 5 ft   (c) 6 ft   (d) 10 ft   (e) 12 ft   (f) 16 ft   (g) 18 ft

Review Objective G, Lesson 1-7

22. What is a *postulate*?   **an assumption**

23. What is a *theorem*?   **a statement which follows from definitions, postulates, and previously proved theorems**

LESSON MASTER 2-8 B

Questions on SPUR Objectives

Vocabulary

1. What is a *conjecture*?   **A conjecture is an educated guess or opinion.**

2. Complete each statement.

   a. A conjecture that is thought to apply to all situations of a particular type is called a **generalization**

   b. A conjecture is **specific** when it refers to a particular situation.

Properties Objective H: Evaluate conjectures.

In 3–6, tell if the conjecture is *specific* or a *generalization*.

3. Los Angeles has a greater population than Seattle.   **specific**

4. The area of quadrilateral *DEFG* is 18 square units.   **specific**

5. The perimeter of $\triangle ABC = AB + BC + AC$.   **generalization**

6. Every person has eight great-grandparents.   **generalization**

In 7–11, a conjecture is given. Determine whether each example is

   (i) an *instance* of the conjecture;

   (ii) a *counterexample* to the conjecture;

   (iii) *neither* an instance nor a counterexample to the conjecture.

7. If $n < 0, n^3 \geq 1$.

   a. $n = -.3$ **ii**   b. $n = 8$ **iii**   c. $n = -2$ **ii**

8. If $x > 0$, then $4 + x > 0$.

   a. $x = 7$ **i**   b. $x = 0$ **iii**   c. $x = -5$ **iii**

9. "i" before "e" except after "c"

   a. receive   **i**   b. tried   **i**   c. fancied   **ii**

► LESSON MASTER 2-8B page 2

10. If $\overline{AB} \cap \overline{CD} = \{ \}$, then $\overleftrightarrow{AB} \parallel \overleftrightarrow{CD}$.

   a.   b.   c.

   i   **iii**   **ii**

11. If $UV = 2(UW)$, then W is the midpoint of $\overline{UV}$.

   a.   b.   c.

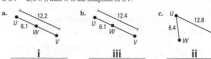

   i   **iii**   **ii**

In 12–15, a conjecture is stated. Draw pictures to help you decide whether you think the conjecture is true or false. If you believe it is false, provide a counterexample.

   Sample counterexamples are given.

12. If the sides of rectangle *ABCD* are twice the lengths of the sides of rectangle *WXYZ*, then the area of rectangle *ABCD* is four times the area of rectangle *WXYZ*.   **true**

13. If the four sides of a quadrilateral are equal in length, then the quadrilateral is a square.   **false**

14. If $A \cup B = 8$, and set B has 8 elements, then set $A = \{ \}$.   **false**

   $A = \{a, b\}, B = \{a, b, c, d, e, f, g, h\}$

15. If the vertices of a triangle are the two endpoints of the diameter of a circle and another point of the circle, then the triangle has a right angle.   **true**

LESSON MASTER 3-1 B

Questions on SPUR Objectives

Vocabulary

1. Define *angle*.

An angle is the union of two rays that have the same endpoint.

2. Define *bisector of an angle*.

$\overrightarrow{VR}$ is the bisector of $\angle PVQ$ if and only if $\overrightarrow{VR}$ (except point V) is in the interior of $\angle PVQ$ and $m\angle PVR = m\angle RVQ$.

Skills Objective A: Draw and analyze drawings of angles.

3. Refer to the drawing at the right.

   a. Name the *vertex* of the angle.

   point S

   b. Name the *sides* of the angle.

   $\overrightarrow{SM}, \overrightarrow{SG}$ (or $\overrightarrow{SW}$)

   c. Give five different names for the angle.

   $\angle S, \angle MSW, \angle MSG, \angle WSM, \angle GSM$

   d. Shade the *interior* of the angle.

   e. Measure the angle with a protractor.   **47**

In 4 and 5, refer to the figure at the right.

Sampleo are given.

4. a. Name two distinct straight angles.

   $\angle HCD$ $\angle HDN$

   b. Name two distinct zero angles.

   $\angle HDC$ $\angle NCD$

5. a. Describe two things you *may* assume from the diagram.

   $H, D, C,$ and N are collinear; $\overleftrightarrow{HN} \cap \overrightarrow{CU} = \{C\}$

   b. Describe two things you *may not* assume from the diagram.

   $HC = CD$; $m\angle NCU = 33$

▶ LESSON MASTER 3-1B page 2

6. Draw and label an $\angle JFD$ with measure 64.

7. Draw and label $\angle 3$ with measure 155.

Samples are given for 6 and 7.

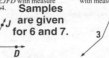

8. Draw the bisector $\overrightarrow{KE}$ of $\angle K$ below.

9. Refer to the figure at the right. Find the measure of each angle.

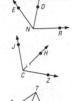

   a. $\angle TVH$ **58**   b. $\angle GVH$ **148**

   c. $\angle GVY$ **90**   d. $\angle GVQ$ **113**

   e. $\angle QVH$ **99**   f. $\angle YVH$ **122**

Skills Objective B: Use algebra to represent and find measures of angles.

10. At the right, $m\angle ENR = 123$, $m\angle END = 2x + 10$, $m\angle DNR = 4x + 5$. Find x and $m\angle END$.

   $x =$ **18** $m\angle END =$ **46**

11. At the right, $\overrightarrow{CH}$ bisects $\angle JCZ$, $m\angle JCH = 4x + 7$, $m\angle JCZ = 10(x - 1)$. Find $m\angle JCZ$.

   110

12. At the right, $m\angle ATG = 4y$, $m\angle GTV = 5(y + 1)$, $m\angle ATV = 8y + 13$.

   a. Write an equation to find y.

   $4y + 5(y + 1) = 8y + 13$

   b. Find the measure of each angle.

   $m\angle ATG = 32$, $m\angle GTV = 45$, $m\angle ATV = 77$

Properties Objective H: Give justifications for conclusions involving angles.

In 13 and 14, refer to Question 12.

13. What property did you use in Part a?   **Angle Addition**

14. Does $\overrightarrow{TG}$ bisect $m\angle ATV$? Justify your answer.

No; by the def. of angle bisector, $m\angle ATG = m\angle VTG$, but $32 \neq 45$.

LESSON MASTER 3-2 B

Questions on SPUR Objectives

Vocabulary

1. Complete each statement for the figure at the right.

   a. $\angle SUG$ is a **central angle**

   b. The "thicker" arc is a **major** arc.

   c. The "thinner" arc is a **minor** arc.

   d. What is the degree measure of the minor arc?   **$m\angle SUG$**

   e. What is the degree measure of the major arc?   **360 – $m\angle SUG$**

2. What are *concentric circles*?   **circles with the same center**

Skills Objective E: Draw rotation images and find magnitudes of rotations.

3. Rotate $\overrightarrow{AB}$ $40°$ about F.

4. Rotate $\triangle HJK$ $-90°$ about D.

5. Rotate $EMST$ $120°$ about E.

6. X is the image of N after a rotation about Z. What is the magnitude of the rotation?

   -98°

▶ LESSON MASTER 3-2B page 2

Skills Objective F: Find the measures of central angles and the degree measure of arcs.

7. Refer to $\odot T$ at the right, in which $m\angle GTD = 45$ and $m\angle WTG = 67$. Find the measure of each arc.

   a. $\overparen{WG}$ **67°**   b. $\overparen{GD}$ **45°**

   c. $\overparen{WD}$ **112°**   d. $\overparen{AGD}$ **225°**

8. Refer to the concentric circles at the right. Suppose $m\angle UOP = 90$ and $m\overparen{RS} = 38°$. Find each measure.

   a. $m\angle ROP$ **52**   b. $m\overparen{XT}$ **142°**

   c. $m\overparen{UP}$ **90°**   d. $m\overparen{XN}$ **90°**

Uses Objective I: Apply angle and arc measures in real situations.

9. At the highest point of the Swinging Canoe ride, $m\angle ABC = 100$. Find the measure of the arc swept as point A travels

   a. to point C.   **100°**

   b. to point D.   **200°**

10. Find the magnitude of the given rotation of a seat on this Ferris wheel.

   a. from position 1 to position 2   **-22.5°**

   b. from position 1 to position 5   **-90°**

   c. from position 1 to position 11   **-225°**

   d. from position 8 to position 16   **-180°**

   e. from position 11 to position 4   **-202.5°**

LESSON MASTER 3-3 B   Questions on SPUR Objectives

Vocabulary

In 1–8, match each term with the appropriate figure.

1. linear pair — **h**
2. obtuse angle — **f**
3. right angle — **b**
4. vertical angles — **e**
5. acute angle — **c**
6. complementary angles — **g**
7. straight angle — **a**
8. non-adjacent supplementary angles — **d**

(a) (b)
(c) (d) 118° 62°
(e) (f)
(g) 40° 50° (h)

Skills Objective A: Draw and analyze drawings of angles.

9. Draw and label a pair of vertical angles ∠1 and ∠2.

Sample:
1 2

10. Draw a linear pair. Label the angles ∠3 and ∠4.

Sample: 4
3

11. Draw and label a pair of adjacent angles ∠5 and ∠6.

Sample: 6
5

12. In the diagram at the right, m∠WVX = 142. Find the measure of each angle.

a. ∠XVY **38**   b. ∠ZVW **38**

W
V X
Z Y

Skills Objective B: Use algebra to represent and find measures of angles.

13. At the right, m∠1 = 4x and m∠2 = 6x + 5. Find each measure.

m∠3 **110**   m∠4 **70**

1 2
3 4

▶ LESSON MASTER 3-3B page 2

14. At the right, m∠8 = 2(3y + 4) and m∠6 = 2(y + 34).

a. Write an equation to find y.

2(3y + 4) = 2(y + 34)

b. Explain how you found the equation in Part a.

By the Vertical Angles Theorem, m∠8 = m∠6.

c. y = **15**   m∠5 = **82**   m∠7 = **82**

8 7
5 6

In 15 and 16, find the measures of both angles.

15. Two angles are complementary. The measure of the larger is 6 less than 3 times the measure of the smaller.   **24**   **66**

16. Two angles are supplementary. The measure of the larger is 54 more than 8 times the measure of the smaller.   **14**   **166**

Uses Objective I: Apply angle measures in real situations.

17. A plane is flying 20° north of west.

a. At the right, draw the path of the plane.

b. How many degrees must the plane turn to change its course to due north?

-70

N
W — — E
S

18. A ladder forms a 73° angle with the level ground. What is the measure of the other angle it forms with the ground?   **107**

19. Refer to the barbecue tool pictured at the right. The range x of possible measures for ∠1 is 24 ≤ x ≤ 170. Find the range of possible measures for each angle.

a. ∠3   **24 ≤ x ≤ 170**

b. ∠4   **10 ≤ x ≤ 156**

1
4 2
3

LESSON MASTER 3-4 B   Questions on SPUR Objectives

Properties Objective G: Recognize and use the postulates of equality and inequality.

In 1–10, choose the statement that illustrates the given property.

1. Substitution Property — **b, i**
2. Addition Property of Equality — **d**
3. Addition Property of Inequality — **j**
4. Equation to Inequality Property — **f**
5. Multiplication Property of Equality — **b, i**
6. Multiplication Property of Inequality — **g**
7. Reflexive Property of Equality — **c**
8. Symmetric Property of Equality — **e**
9. Transitive Property of Equality — **a**
10. Transitive Property of Inequality — **h**

(a) If AB = CD and CD = XY, then AB = XY.
(b) If x = 35.2 + y, then 7x = 7(35.2 + y).
(c) m∠3 = m∠3
(d) If m∠MNO = m∠ABC, then m∠MNO + 90 = m∠ABC + 90.
(e) If 2(UV) = 17, then 17 = 2(UV).
(f) If 14 + 20 = r, then r > 14 and r > 20.
(g) If m∠F < m∠G, then -2(m∠F) > -2(m∠G).
(h) If CY < EF and EF < UR, then CY < UR.
(i) If m∠CD = m∠MN, then 5(m∠CD) = 5(m∠MN).
(j) If m∠P < m∠Q, then m∠P + 45 < m∠Q + 45.

11. a. If m∠FEG + m∠GED = 87 and m∠GED = m∠DEH then what can you conclude about m∠FEG and m∠DEH using the Substitution Property?

m∠FEG + m∠DEH = 87

E H
F G D

b. If m∠FEG = m∠GED, and m∠GED = m∠DEH what can you conclude using the Transitive Property?

m∠FEG = m∠DEH

▶ LESSON MASTER 3-4B page 2

12. a. Use the Distance Postulate to write an equation relating PQ, QR, and PR.

PQ + QR = PR

P
Q R

b. Use the Equation to Inequality Property to write a true statement about PR and QR.   **PR > QR**

c. Is it possible to conclude that QR < PQ?   **no**

13. Suppose m AB = 180 − x. Find m AB if

a. x = 37.   **143°**

b. x = 6d.   **180 − 6d**

c. What property did you use in Parts a and b?   **Substitution**

In 14 and 15, give the properties used in solving the following.

14. 65 = 4r + 17   Given
48 = 4r   **Add. Property of Equality**
12 = r   **Mult. Property of Equality**
r = 12   **Sym. Property of Equality**

15. -5m − 6 < 34   Given
-5m < 40   **Add. Property of Inequality**
m > -8   **Mult. Property of Inequality**

Review Objective D, Lesson 2-4

16. Write the definition of midpoint.

The midpoint of segment AB is the point M on AB such that AM = MB.

In 17 and 18, use the number line at the right. The coordinate of M is 7.

U R M
-8 -6 -4 -2 0 2 4 6 8

17. Give the coordinate of the midpoint of UM.   **0.5, or ½**

18. Give the coordinate of N if M is the midpoint of RN.   **16**

LESSON MASTER 3-5 B

Questions on SPUR Objectives

Name _____

Vocabulary

1. Define *proof.* **Samples are given for 1 and 2.**
A proof of a conditional is a sequence of justified conclusions, starting with the antecedent and ending with the consequent.

2. What is a *justification*?
A justification for a statement is a general property for which the statement is a special case.

Properties Objective H: Give justifications for conclusions involving angles and lines.

In 3–7 *multiple choice.* Choose the correct justification for the conclusion reached.

3. Given: *D* is between *A* and *G.*   **b**
Conclusion: $AD + DG = AG.$
   (a) definition of midpoint
   (b) Distance Postulate
   (c) Addition Property of Equality

4. Given: ∠1 is acute.   **b**
Conclusion: $m\angle 1 < 90.$
   (a) definition of angle
   (b) definition of acute angle
   (c) definition of right angle

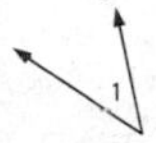

5. Given: ∠D and m∠F are complementary.   **c**
Conclusion: $m\angle D + m\angle F = 90.$
   (a) definition of supplementary angles
   (b) definition of right angle
   (c) definition of complementary angle

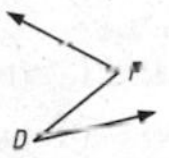

41 ▶

▶ LESSON MASTER 3-5B page 2

Name _____

6. Given: ∠1 and ∠3 are vertical angles.   **b**
Conclusion: $m\angle 1 = m\angle 3.$
   (a) definition of vertical angles
   (b) Vertical Angle Theorem
   (c) Angle Addition Postulate

7. Given: $m\angle OQA = m\angle AQV.$ **a**
Conclusion: $\overrightarrow{QA}$ bisects ∠OQV.
   (a) definition of angle bisector
   (b) definition of adjacent angles
   (c) Angle Addition Postulate

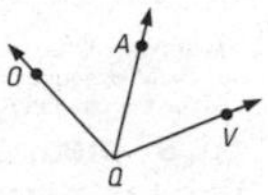

In 8–11, write a justification for each conclusion.

8. Given: ∠7 and ∠8 form a linear pair.
Conclusion: ∠7 and ∠8 are supplementary.
   Linear Pair Theorem

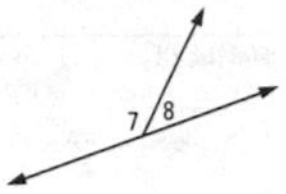

9. Given: △JMH is equilateral.
Conclusion: $JM = MH = JH.$
   definition of equilateral

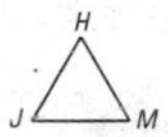

10. Given: ⊙C.
Conclusion: $TC = ZC.$
   definition of circle

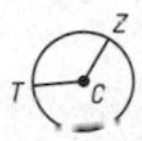

11. Given: $HY = YE.$
Conclusion: Y is the midpoint of HE.
   definition of midpoint

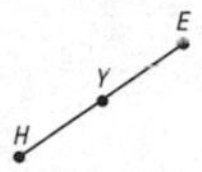

42

LESSON MASTER 3-6 B

Questions on SPUR Objectives

Name _____

Vocabulary

1. Refer to the figure at the right, in which $j \parallel k.$ Complete each statement.
   a. **line g** is a transversal for *j* and *k.*
   b. ∠1 and **∠5** are corresponding angles.
   c. ∠6 and **∠2** are corresponding angles.
   d. ∠4 and **∠8** are corresponding angles.

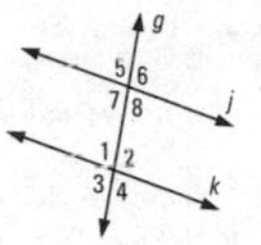

Skills Objective C: Determine measures of angles formed by parallel lines and transversals.

In 2–6, refer to the figure for Item 1 above.

2. If m∠4 = 78, find the measures of every other angle.
$m\angle 1 = m\angle 5 = m\angle 8 = 78; m\angle 2 = m\angle 3 =$
$m\angle 6 = m\angle 7 = 102$

3. If m∠7 = 105, find the measures of every other angle.
$m\angle 2 = m\angle 3 = m\angle 6 = 105; m\angle 1 = m\angle 4 =$
$m\angle 5 = m\angle 8 = 75$

4. If m∠8 = 3u, find the measures of every other angle.
$m\angle 1 = m\angle 4 = m\angle 5 = 3u; m\angle 2 = m\angle 3 =$
$m\angle 6 = m\angle 7 = 180 - 3u$

5. If m∠2 = 2(m∠1), find the measures of every other angle.
$m\angle 1 = m\angle 4 = m\angle 5 = m\angle 8 = 60; m\angle 3 =$
$m\angle 6 = m\angle 7 = 120$

6. If m∠5 = 5(x + 1) and m∠1 = 3x + 31, find the measure of ∠6 and of ∠2.
110   110

Properties Objective H: Give justifications for conclusions involving angles and lines.

7. If $r \parallel s,$ $s \parallel y,$ and $y \parallel e,$ what theorem allows you to conclude that $r \parallel e$?
Transitivity of Parallelism

43 ▶

▶ LESSON MASTER 3-6B page 2

Name _____

8. If line *m* has slope 3.5 and line *f* has slope 3.5, then what theorem allows you to conclude that $m \parallel f$?
Parallel Line and Slopes

In 9–12, refer to the figure at the right. Justify each conclusion.

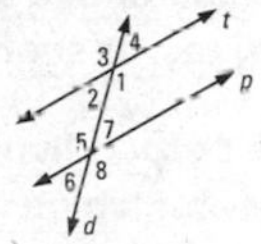

9. ∠4 and ∠1 are supplementary.
Linear Pair Theorem

10. $m\angle 5 = m\angle 8.$
Vertical Angles Theorem

11. If $p \parallel t,$ then $m\angle 5 = m\angle 3.$
Corresponding Angles (b)

12. If $m\angle 4 = m\angle 7,$ then $p \parallel t.$
Corresponding Angles (a)

Representations Objective K: Determine the slope of a line from its equation or given two points on it.

In 13–19, find the slope of the line described.

13. the line containing (3, -5) and (6, 1)   **2**

14. the line containing (u, v) and (a, b), with $u \neq a$ **$\dfrac{b-v}{a-u}$ or $\dfrac{v-b}{u-a}$**

15. the line with equation $y = 3x - 1$ **3**

16. the line with equation $2x + 5y = -20$ **$-\dfrac{2}{5}$**

17. Line *r* at the right   **$-\dfrac{2}{3}$**

18. Line *s* at the right   **0**

19. Line *t* at the right   **undefined**

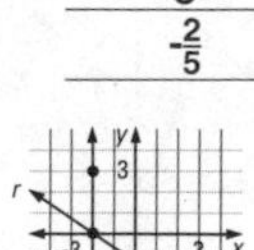

Representations Objective L: Determine the slope of a line parallel to a given line.

20. What is the slope of a line parallel to the line with equation $y = -6x + 5$?   **-6**

21. What is the slope of a line parallel to line *r* shown in the graph for Questions 17–19?   **$-\dfrac{2}{3}$**

44

241

LESSON MASTER 3-7 B — Questions on SPUR Objectives

Vocabulary

1. Define *perpendicular*.

Two lines, rays, or segments are perpendicular if and only if the lines containing them form a 90° angle.

2. Two symbols are used to indicate perpendicularity. Show an example of how each is used and explain what your examples mean.

Samples are given.

"$r \perp s$" means "line r is perpendicular to line s."

This drawing shows that $\vec{BA}$ and $\vec{BC}$ are perpendicular.

Skills Objective C: Determine measures of angles formed by parallel lines, perpendicular lines, and transversals.

3. At the right, $FE \perp FG$ and $m\angle EFG = 4(x + 2)$. Solve for x. **$x = 20.5$**

4. At the right, $m\angle UVR = 54$. Give the measure of each angle.

a. $\angle RVT$ **90**   b. $\angle TVS$ **36**

5. At the right, $m\angle 1 = 2(a + 21)$ and $m\angle 2 = 7a + 6$. Is $QP \perp ON$?

no

6. Given: $a \perp c$ and $m\angle 3 = m\angle 4$.

a. Is $b \perp c$? **yes**

b. Is $a \parallel b$? **yes**

45 ▶

▶ **LESSON MASTER 3-7B** *page 2*

Properties Objective H: Give justifications for conclusions involving angles and lines.

In 7–10, use the diagram at the right.
Given: $WX \parallel MN$, $WX \parallel ZY$, $WX \perp XY$.
Multiple Choice. Choose the correct justification for the conclusion.

7. $MN \parallel ZY$. **d**

8. $ZY \perp XY$. **e**

9. $\angle WXY$ is a right angle. **a**

10. $m\angle WMN = m\angle MZY$. **b**

(a) definition of perpendicular
(b) Corresponding Angles Postulate
(c) Two Perpendiculars Theorem
(d) Transitivity of Parallelism Theorem
(e) Perpendicular to Parallels Theorem
(f) definition of parallel lines

Representations Objective L: Determine the slope of a line perpendicular to a given line.

11. When is the product of the slope of two perpendicular lines not equal to -1? Explain.

Sample: when one line is vertical; the slope of a vertical line is undefined.

In 12 and 13, refer to the graph at the right.

12. Find the slope of any line perpendicular to

a. the x-axis _____   b. the y-axis **0**

c. line e. **-1**   d. line m. **$\frac{1}{2}$**

e. line p. **0**   f. line s. _____

a. and f. undefined

13. Is $m \perp e$? How can you tell without using a protractor?

No; the product of their slopes is -2(1) ≠ -1.

46

LESSON MASTER 3-8 B — Questions on SPUR Objectives

Vocabulary

1. a. What is a *bisector* of a segment?

A bisector of a segment is its midpoint or any line, ray, or segment which intersects it at only its midpoint.

b. What is the *perpendicular bisector* of a segment?

The perpendicular bisector of a segment is a bisector which is also perpendicular to the segment.

2. What are the only tools that may be used in a construction?

unmarked straightedge and compass

3. Complete the following statement. A(n) **algorithm** is a sequence of steps leading to a desired end.

Skills Objective D: Draw parallel lines, perpendicular bisectors, and perpendicular lines.

In 4–6, construct and label the required line.

4. v, the $\perp$ bisector of $\overline{GH}$

5. e, the $\perp$ bisector of $\overline{AB}$

6. line $f \perp$ to y at Q

7. Use the figure at the right. Use the tools of your choice to draw the given line.

a. the line through $C \perp$ to s, with the intersection labeled K

b. the line through $C \parallel$ to s, with the line labeled r

8. In Question 7, state the relationship between r and s. **$r \parallel s$**

47 ▶

▶ **LESSON MASTER 3-8B** *page 2*

Uses Objective J: Apply parallel and perpendicular lines in real situations.

9. a. A bridge is to be built connecting point A on Highway D to Highway H. Draw the shortest bridge possible.

b. Highway Y is to be built parallel to Highway H through point A on Highway D. Draw Highway Y.

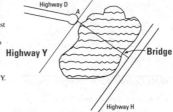

10. a. A new road, Shadow Lane, is to be built perpendicular to Elm Path at its midpoint. Construct and label Shadow Lane.

b. Another new road, Park Crossway, is to be built parallel to Elm Path through the intersection of Shadow Lane and Scenic Drive. Construct and label Park Crossway.

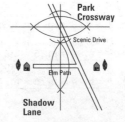

Review Objective L, Lesson 1-3

In 11–16, graph each point on the coordinate plane. Label the point with its letter name.

11. $A = (2, 1)$ 12. $B = (3, -4)$

13. $C = (-4, -4)$ 14. $D = (0, 3)$

15. $E = (-5, 0)$ 16. $F = (2, -2)$

48

LESSON MASTER 4-1 B
Questions on SPUR Objectives

Vocabulary

1. Complete the following definition.

a. For a point P not on a line m, the *reflection image* of P over line m is the point Q if and only if

m is the perpendicular bisector of $\overline{PQ}$

b. For a point P on m, the reflection image of P over line m is

P itself

2. a. Complete this definition: A *transformation* is a correspondence between two sets of points such that

each point in the preimage has a unique image and each point in the image has exactly one preimage

b. What is another name for transformation?   **mapping**

Skills Objective A: Draw figures by applying the definition of reflection image.

3. a. Draw $r_e(H)$.

b. Draw $r_e(K)$.

c. Draw $r_e(J)$.

4. Refer to the figure at the right.

a. $r_a(N) =$ **D**

b. $r_b(N) =$ **S**

c. $r_b(W) =$ **D**

▶ LESSON MASTER 4-1B page 2

5. a. Draw line ℓ so that $r_\ell(T) = U$. Is line ℓ unique? Explain.

Yes; $\overline{TU}$ has exactly one perpendicular bisector.

b. Draw line m so that $r_m(T) = T$. Is line m unique? Explain.

No; an infinite number of lines contain T.

6. Use folding and tracing or a reflecting tool to find the reflection image of the bird over line d.

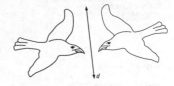

Properties Objective E: Apply the definition of reflection to make conclusions.

In 7–10, *true or false*.

7. If $r_g(X) = X$, then X is on g.   **true**

8. If $r_g(X) = Y$, then $r_g(Y) = X$.   **true**

9. If line u contains the midpoint of $\overline{AB}$, then $r_u(A) = B$.   **false**

10. Every transformation is a reflection.   **false**

Representations Objective K: Find coordinates of reflection images of points over the coordinate axes.

In 11–16, give the coordinates of each image.

11. $r_{x\text{-axis}}(3, -5)$ **(3, 5)**

12. $r_{y\text{-axis}}(3, -5)$ **(-3, -5)**

13. $r_{x\text{-axis}}(0, 6)$ **(0, -6)**

14. $r_{y\text{-axis}}(0, 0)$ **(0, 0)**

15. $r_{x\text{-axis}}(a, b)$ **(a, -b)**

16. $r_{y\text{-axis}}(c, d)$ **(-c, d)**

LESSON MASTER 4-2 B
Questions on SPUR Objectives

Skills Objective A: Draw figures by applying the definition of reflection image.
Objective B: Draw reflection images of segments, angles, and polygons over a given line.

1. Draw $r_j(\overline{GH})$.

2. Draw $r_k(\triangle XYZ)$.

3. Draw $r_{\overline{AB}}(ABCDE)$.

4. Draw $r_m(W)$.

5. Draw a so $r_a(\angle RST) = \angle R'S'T'$.

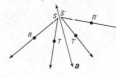

6. Draw b so $r_b(EKHG) = CKOF$.

7. At the right, draw and label a figure showing $r_c(RQTS) = RWTY$.

Sample:

▶ LESSON MASTER 4-2B page 2

Properties Objective E: Apply properties of reflections to make conclusions.

8. List four properties preserved by every reflection.

collinearity, betweenness, distance, angle measure

9. List a property *not* preserved by reflections.   **orientation**

10. Use the figure at the right, where $r_{\overline{GN}}(\triangle RMG) = \triangle BPG$.

a. If $m\angle P = 46$, find $m\angle M$.   **46**

b. If $m\angle BGN = 70$, find $m\angle RGB$.   **140**

c. If $m\angle BNG = 58$, find $m\angle RNE$.   **122**

d. Find $m\angle GOR$.   **90**

e. If $RB = 18$, find RO.   **9**

f. If $RM = 16.4$, find BP.   **16.4**

Representations Objective K: Find coordinates of reflection images of points over the coordinate axes.

11. a. Let $EFGH = r_{x\text{-axis}}(ABCD)$. Give the coordinates of $EFGH$.

$E = (6, -7)$ **$F = (6, -2)$**

$G = (4, 0)$ **$H = (-1, -4)$**

b. Let $JKLM = r_{y\text{-axis}}(ABCD)$. Give the coordinates of $JKLM$.

$J = (-6, 7)$ **$K = (-6, 2)$**

$L = (-4, 0)$ **$M = (1, 4)$**

LESSON MASTER 4-3 B

Questions on SPUR Objectives

Uses Objective I: Use reflections to find a path from an object to a particular point.

1. Ball *B* is rolling toward a wall without spin. Draw the rest of the path showing how the ball will bounce off the wall. Mark any congruent angles made by this path.

2. Draw the path to bounce ball *N* off the wall and hit ball *M*. Mark any congruent angles made by this path.

3. Refer to the miniature golf hole at the right.

   a. Is there a direct path from the golf ball *G* to the hole *H*? How do you know?

   No; *GH* intersects the sides of the course.

   b. Draw a path from *G* to *H* with a bounce off wall *a*.

   c. Draw a path from *G* to *H* with a bounce off wall *b*.

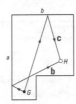

---

4. Refer to the miniature golf hole at the right.

   a. Draw a path from *G* to the hole at *H* with a bounce off one wall.

   b. Draw a path from *G* to the hole at *H* with a bounce off two walls.

   Sample paths are given.

5. Refer to the miniature golf hole at the right. Draw a path from *G* to the hole at *H*.

   A sample path is given.

6. Refer to the diagram at the right. A laser beam sent from point *D* is to be reflected off line *m* and then line *n* in such a way that it finally passes through point *E*. Draw the path of the laser beam.

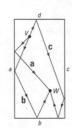

7. Refer to the billiard table at the right. Draw a path from ball *V* to ball *W* such that ball *V*

   a. bounces off wall *a*.

   b. bounces off wall *a* and then wall *b*.

   c. bounces off three walls.

   Sample is given.

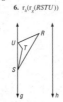

LESSON MASTER 4-4 B

Questions on SPUR Objectives

Vocabulary

1. Define *composite* of two transformations S and T.

   the transformation that maps each point *P* onto T(S(*P*))

2. a. Define *translation*.

   the composite of two reflections over parallel lines

   b. What is the *magnitude* of the translation?

   the distance between a point and its image

   c. What is the *direction* of the translation?

   the direction from the preimage to the image

Skills Objective D: Draw or identify images of figures under composites of two reflections.

In 3 and 4, use reflections to draw the image of the figure under the indicated composite.

3. $r_u \circ r_v(\Delta ABC)$

4. $r_p \circ r_q(DEFG)$

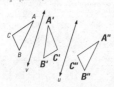

In 5 and 6, use the Two-Reflection Theorem for Translations to draw the indicated image.

5. $r_n(r_m(\Delta HJK))$

6. $r_h(r_g(RSTU))$

Properties Objective F: Apply properties of reflections to obtain properties of translations.
Objective G: Apply the Two-Reflection Theorem for Translations.

7. List five properties preserved by every translation.

   collinearity, betweenness, distance, angle measure, orientation

In 8–12, in the figure at the right, $p \parallel q$, $r_p(ABCD) = A'B'C'D'$, and $r_q(A'B'C'D') = A''B''C''D''$.

8. If $AB = 8$, find $A''B''$. **8**

9. If $m\angle B = 124$, then name two other angles with measure 124. **∠*B'* ∠*B''***

10. State a relationship between $\overline{CC''}$ and *p*. **$p \perp \overline{CC''}$**

11. If $DD'' = 25$, then find the distance between *p* and *q*. **12.5**

12. If $DD'' = 25$, then give three other distances equal to 25. ***AA'' BB'' CC''***

GEOMETRY © Scott, Foresman and Company

LESSON MASTER **4-5** **B** Questions on SPUR Objectives

Vocabulary

1. a. Define *rotation*.
   the composite of two reflections over intersecting lines

   b. Where is the *center* of the rotation?
   at the point of intersection of the two lines

Skills Objective D: Draw or identify images of figures under composites of two reflections.

In 2 and 3, draw the indicated image.

2. $r_u \circ r_k(\Delta ABC)$

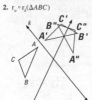

3. $r_c(r_d(WXYZ))$

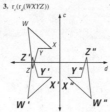

4. Draw $r_{y\text{-axis}} \circ r_{x\text{-axis}}(\Delta PQR)$.
   Label the image $\Delta P''Q''R''$.

   a. Give the coordinates of P, Q, and R.
   $P = (0, 3)$
   $Q = (-6, 2)$ **$R = (-4, -2)$**

   b. Give the coordinates of P'', Q'', and R''.
   $P'' = (0, -3)$
   $Q'' = (6, -2)$ **$R'' = (4, 2)$**

   c. What is the image of (a, b) under this rotation? (Hint: Examine your answers in Parts a and b.)
   $(-a, -b)$

Properties Objective F: Apply properties of reflections to obtain properties of rotations.
Objective G: Apply the Two-Reflection Theorem for Rotations.

5. List five properties preserved by every rotation.
   collinearity, betweenness, distance, angle measure, orientation

6. Refer to the diagram at the right. Is $\Delta C'D'E'$ the image of ΔCDE

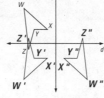

   a. under a rotation? Why or why not?
   No; the orientation is not preserved.

   b. under a reflection? Why or why not?
   Yes; the orientation is reversed.

7. A figure has been rotated -77°. Give the measure of the acute angle formed by the two lines of reflection that define this rotation.
   38.5

8. At the right, $A''B''C''D''$ is the image of $ABCD$ under a rotation, and $m\angle NMD = 47$.

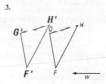

   a. Name the center of the rotation.
   M

   b. What is the direction of the rotation?
   clockwise

   c. What is the magnitude of the rotation?
   -94°

   d. What is the magnitude of the rotation that maps $A''B''C''D''$ onto $ABCD$?
   94°

   e. Find $m\angle CMC''$.
   94

   f. If $m\angle ABC = 110$, then find $\angle A''B''C''$.
   110

9. Can the composite of two reflections ever be both a rotation and a translation? Why or why not?
   Yes; if the two lines of reflection coincide, then the composite is a rotation of 0° and a translation of zero.

LESSON MASTER **4-6** **B** Questions on SPUR Objectives

Vocabulary

1. Define *vector* **a quantity that can be characterized by its direction and magnitude**

Skills Objective C: Draw translation images of figures.

In 2–5, draw and label the image of the figure under the translation described by the indicated vector.

2.

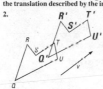

3.

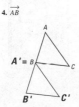

4. $\overrightarrow{AB}$

5. $\overrightarrow{MK}$

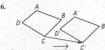

In 6 and 7, draw and name a vector for each translation.

6.

Sample: $\overrightarrow{CC'}$

7.

Sample: $\overrightarrow{QQ'}$

Representations Objective K: Find coordinates of translation images of points over the coordinate axes.

8. A vector has the ordered-pair description $(-6, 14)$.

   a. Name its horizontal component.
   -6

   b. Name its vertical component.
   14

   c. Describe, in words, the translation with this vector.
   A point is translated 6 units left and 14 units up with this vector.

9. Find the image of each point under the translation with vector $(3, 0)$.

   a. $(5, -6)$ **$(8, -6)$** b. (m, n) **$(m + 3, n)$**

10. Give an ordered-pair description for each vector.

    a. a vector to translate a point 7 units left and 5 units up
    $(-7, 5)$

    b. a vector to translate a point 6 units down and 2.4 units left
    $(-2.4, -6)$

    c. a vector to translate a point 12 units up
    $(0, 12)$

    d. a vector that translates $(4, 8)$ to $(-2, 16)$
    $(-6, 8)$

11. The image of point P under a translation by vector $(20, -44)$ is $(10, -50)$. What are the coordinates of P?
    $(-10, -6)$

12. a. Draw and label the image $Q'S'R'H'$ of $QSRH$ under the translation with vector $(-6, -1)$.

    b. Draw and label the image $Q*S*R*H*$ of $QSRH$ under the translation with vector $(3, 0)$.

Top-left sheet

LESSON MASTER **4-7** **B**   Questions on SPUR Objectives

Vocabulary

1. Define *isometry*.
   a reflection or a composite of reflections

2. Complete the following definition. A *glide reflection* is the composite of a reflection and a translation such that the
   line of reflection and the
   direction of the translation are parallel.

Skills Objective C: Draw glide-reflection images of figures.

3. Draw G(△XYZ) where G = T ∘ r_a, and T is determined by v̄.

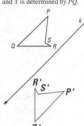

4. Draw G(S) where G − r_m ∘ T, and T is determined by w̄.

5. Draw G(PQRS) where G = T ∘ r_k, and T is determined by PQ⃗.

6. △D′E′F′ is the image of △DEF under a glide reflection. If line *n* is the line of reflection, draw a translation vector.

   Sample:

   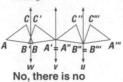

61 ▶

Top-right sheet

7. Draw H(△JKL) where H = T ∘ r_y-axis, and T is the translation with vector (5, -4).

Properties Objective F: Apply properties of reflections to obtain properties of glide reflections.

8. *True or false.* The composite of an odd number of reflections reverses orientation.   **true**

9. Draw three parallel lines, *u*, *v*, and *w*; and △ABC. Then draw r_u ∘ r_v ∘ r_w(△ABC). Is r_u ∘ r_v ∘ r_w a glide reflection? Explain your reasoning.

   No, there is no translation with positive magnitude.

10. Draw line *a* and lines *b* and *c* each perpendicular to *a*. Then draw △XYZ and r_c ∘ r_b ∘ r_a (△XYZ). Is r_c ∘ r_b ∘ r_a a glide reflection? Explain your reasoning.

    Yes; r_b ∘ r_c is a translation perpendicular to *c* and *b*, so it is parallel to *a*.

Uses Objective H: Determine the isometry which maps one figure onto another.

In 11–14, name the type of isometry that maps one letter onto the other.

11. K K   **translation**

12. F   **rotation**

13. ℛ   **glide reflection**

14. N   **reflection**

62

Bottom-left sheet

LESSON MASTER **4-8** **B**   Questions on SPUR Objectives

Vocabulary

1. Define *congruent figures*.
   Two figures F and G are congruent if and only if G is the image of F under an isometry.

2. Complete the following statements.
   a. If two congruent figures have the same orientation, then they are __?__ congruent.   **directly**
   b. If two congruent figures have opposite orientation, then they are __?__ congruent.   **oppositely**

3. Complete the statement: A congruence transformation is another term for __?__ .   **isometry**

Uses Objective J: Use congruence in real situations.

In 4–9, tell whether the performed task involves the concept of congruence. Explain why or why not.   **Sample explanations are given.**

4. growing a tomato plant
   No; the plant changes in size and shape.

5. transplanting a tomato plant
   Yes; the plant's size and shape do not change.

6. photocopying a printed sheet at 100%
   Yes; the copy has the same size and shape as the original.

7. photocopying a printed sheet at 50%
   No; the copy is smaller than the original.

63 ▶

Bottom-right sheet

8. smashing a watch
   No; the watch's shape is changed, and it is split into pieces.

9. replacing the battery in a watch
   Yes; the shape and size of the watch remain the same.

10. Describe a task different from those in Questions 4–9 that involves the concept of congruence.
    Sample: reprinting a photograph

11. Describe a task different from those in Questions 4–9 that does *not* involve the concept of congruence.
    Sample: enlarging a photograph

12. a. Before cutting, Pattern Piece A is pinned onto fabric that has been folded into two thicknesses. Explain why this is done.
       Sample: This gives two congruent pieces with opposite orientation.

    PATTERN PIECE A

    BLOUSE FRONT

    b. What does this have to do with congruence?
       Sample: The pieces have to be congruent in order to form the garment.

Review Objective G, Lesson 3-4

In 13–15, choose the statement that illustrates the given property.

13. Reflexive Property of Equality   **b**

14. Symmetric Property of Equality   **c**

15. Transitive Property of equality   **a**

(a) If m∠E = m∠A, and m∠A = m∠T, then m∠E = m∠T.

(b) RS = RS

(c) If 4(m AB) = 180, then 180 = 4(m AB).

64

LESSON MASTER 5-1 B

Questions on SPUR Objectives

Vocabulary

1. Below, $\triangle FTE = S(\triangle UDR)$. Match the corresponding parts.

a. $\overline{RD}$ **v**		(i) $\angle TEF$
b. $\angle T$ **iv**		(ii) $\angle U$
c. $\overline{UD}$ **iii**		(iii) $\overline{FT}$
d. $\overline{FE}$ **vi**		(iv) $\angle D$
e. $\angle DRU$ **i**		(v) $\overline{ET}$
f. $\angle F$ **ii**		(vi) $\overline{UR}$

Skills Objective A: Identify and determine measures of parts of congruent figures.

2. At the right, $r_h(\triangle BOC) = \triangle VMX$, $VM = 12$, $VX = 6$, $XM = 8$, $m\angle X = 117$, $m\angle M = 27$, $m\angle V = 36$.

   a. Which side of $\triangle BOC$ has length 6? **$\overline{BC}$**

   b. Which angle of $\triangle BOC$ has measure 36? **$\angle B$**

3. $r_b \circ r_a(TQGI) = EZJN$, $GI = 43$, $IT = 33$, $TQ = 27$, $QG = 44$, $m\angle Q = 71$, $m\angle G = 81$, $m\angle I = 68$, $m\angle T = 140$.

   a. Which side of $EZJN$ has length 44? **$\overline{ZJ}$**

   b. Which angle of $EZJN$ has measure 71? **$\angle Z$**

65 ▶

▶ **LESSON MASTER 5-1B** *page 2*

Properties Objective E: Make and justify conclusions about congruent figures.

4. $\triangle ASK \cong \triangle WHY$. **Sample:**

   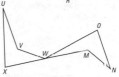

   a. At the right, draw a diagram for this situation. Mark the congruent parts.

   b. List six pairs of congruent parts.

$\angle A \cong \angle W$	**$\angle S \cong \angle H$**	**$\angle K \cong \angle Y$**
$\overline{AS} \cong \overline{WH}$	**$\overline{SK} \cong \overline{HY}$**	**$\overline{AK} \cong \overline{WY}$**

5. Assume the triangles at the right are congruent. Write an appropriate congruence statement with the vertices in the correct order.

   Sample: $\triangle GNR \cong \triangle GDR$

6. $T(UVWX) = WMNO$, and T is an isometry.

   a. Explain why $UVWX \cong WMNO$.

   definition
   of congruent
   figures

   b. Name four properties preserved by T.

   angle measure, betweenness,
   collinearity, distance

   c. Which length is equal to OM? **XV**

7. At the right, $\triangle ABC \cong \triangle SEH$. If $BC = 9$, can you conclude that $SH = 9$? Why or why not?

   No; BC and SH are not
   corresponding parts, and
   we do not know AC.

66

LESSON MASTER 5-2 B

Questions on SPUR Objectives

Skills Objective A: Identify and determine measures of parts of congruent figures.

1. At the right, draw and label a segment $\overline{FG}$ such that $\overline{FG} \cong \overline{AB}$.

2. At the right, draw and label an angle $\angle X$ such that $\angle X \cong \angle U$.

3. At the right, $\overline{HJ}$ and $\overline{IK}$ bisect each other, $\overline{HJ} \cong \overline{IK}$. If $HJ = 18 + 4e$, find each length.

   a. IK **$18 + 4e$**

   b. HG **$9 + 2e$**

   c. GI **$9 + 2e$**

4. At the right, $\angle PYA \cong \angle XYM$. If $m\angle XYA = 24$, find $m\angle PYM$.
   24

67 ▶

▶ **LESSON MASTER 5-2B** *page 2*

5. At the right, $\overleftrightarrow{NK}$ bisects $\angle DOC$ and $\angle BOT$, $\angle DOC \cong \angle BOT$, and $m\angle BOK = 31$. Find the measure of each angle.

   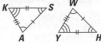

   a. $\angle NOC$ **31**

   b. $\angle DOC$ **62**

   c. $\angle DON$ **31**

   d. $\angle TOC$ **118**

Properties Objective E: Make and justify conclusions about congruent figures.

In 6–8, choose the statement that illustrates the given property.

6. Reflexive Property of Congruence **b**

7. Symmetric Property of Congruence **a**

8. Transitive Property of Congruence **c**

(a) If $\angle PQR \cong \angle XYX$, then $\angle XYZ \cong \angle PQR$.

(b) $\overline{AB} \cong \overline{AB}$

(c) If $m\angle M \cong m\angle W$, and $m\angle W \cong m\angle G$, then $m\angle M \cong m\angle G$.

9. a. *Multiple choice.* Which phrase below may be substituted for $\overline{UN} \cong \overline{TE}$. **iii**

   (i) $UN \cong TE$ (ii) $\overline{UN} = \overline{TE}$ (iii) $UN = TE$

   b. Which theorem justifies Part a?
   Segment Congruence Theorem

10. a. *Multiple choice.* Which phrase below may be substituted for $m\angle JKE = m\angle DSR$? **ii**

    (i) $m\angle JKE \cong m\angle DSR$ (ii) $\angle JKE \cong \angle DSR$ (iii) $\angle JKE = \angle DSR$

    b. Which theorem justifies Part a?
    Angle Congruence Theorem

68

Name _____

LESSON MASTER 5-3 B

Questions on SPUR Objectives

Properties Objective E: Make and justify conclusions about congruent figures.

In 1–5, *multiple choice.* Choose the justification which allows you to make the given conclusion.

1. If $EFGH \cong ABCD$, then $\overline{EF} \cong \overline{AB}$.   **c**
   (a) Segment Congruence Theorem
   (b) definition of midpoint
   (c) CPCF Theorem
   (d) definition of congruence

2. If $\angle X \cong \angle A$, then $m\angle X = m\angle A$.   **a**
   (a) Angle Congruence Theorem
   (b) definition of angle bisector
   (c) Angle Measure Postulate
   (d) Corresponding Angles Postulate

3. If H is the midpoint of DU, then $\overline{DH} \cong \overline{HU}$.   **b**
   (a) Segment Congruence Theorem
   (b) definition of midpoint
   (c) CPCF Theorem
   (d) definition of congruence

4. If $r_m(\triangle RDO) = \triangle YTM$, then $\triangle RDO \cong \triangle YTM$.   **a**
   (a) definition of congruence
   (b) Reflexive Property of Congruence
   (c) CPCF Theorem
   (d) definition of reflection

5. If $\angle 4$ and $\angle 7$ are vertical angles, then $\angle 4 \cong \angle 7$.   **b**
   (a) definition of vertical angles
   (b) Vertical Angles Theorem
   (c) Angle Congruence Theorem
   (d) definition of congruence

69 ▶

Name _____

▶ **LESSON MASTER 5-3B** *page 2*

In 6–11, $r_{\overleftrightarrow{OM}}(\triangle OMU) = \triangle OMD$. Provide a justification for each conclusion.

6. $\triangle OMU \cong \triangle OMD$
   definition of congruence

7. $\overleftrightarrow{OM}$ is the perpendicular bisector of UD.
   definition of reflection

8. $OD = OU$ **CPCF Theorem**

9. $r_{\overleftrightarrow{OM}}(O) = O$ **definition of reflection**

10. $\angle U \cong \angle D$ **CPCF Theorem**

11. $\overline{OM} \cong \overline{OM}$ **Reflexive Prop. of Congruence**

12. In the diagram at the right, A, B, and C are on $\odot O$, and $\overline{OB}$ bisects $\angle AOC$. List three conclusions you can deduce and justify each conclusion.
   Samples are given.

   a. $OA = OB$ **definition of circle**
   b. $\angle AOB \cong \angle COB$ **def. of angle bisector**
   c. $m\angle AOB + m\angle BOC = m\angle AOC$ **Angle Add. Prop.**

13. Write a proof for the following.
   Given: $\angle 3 \cong \angle 8$.
   To prove: $m \parallel n$.

   By the definition of corresponding angles, $\angle 3$ and $\angle 8$ are corresponding angles. Since $\angle 3 \cong \angle 8$, $m \parallel n$ by the Corresponding Angles Postulate.

70

Name _____

LESSON MASTER 5-4 B

Questions on SPUR Objectives

Vocabulary

1. Refer to the diagram at the right.
   a. Name an *interior angle.* $\angle 7, \angle 8, \angle 4, \angle 3$
   b. Name an *exterior angle.* $\angle 6, \angle 5, \angle 1, \angle 2$
   c. Name a pair of *alternate interior angles.* $\angle 7$ and $\angle 3$, $\angle 8$ and $\angle 4$
   d. Name a pair of *alternate exterior angles.* $\angle 6$ and $\angle 2$, $\angle 5$ and $\angle 1$

Skills Objective B: Construct equilateral triangles and the circle through three noncollinear points.

2. Construct an equilateral triangle with side $\overline{VR}$. **Sample:**

3. Construct the circle which passes through the points given.
   Sample:

Skills Objective C: Find angle measures using properties of alternate interior angles.

In 4 and 5, use the figure at the right in which $p \parallel q$.

4. If $m\angle 6 = 57$, find the measures of the other angles.
   $m\angle 1 = m\angle 3 = m\angle 8 = 57$;
   $m\angle 2 = m\angle 4 = m\angle 5 = m\angle 7 = 123$

5. If $m\angle 7 = 5x$, find each of the following.
   a. $m\angle 2$ ___ $5x$ b. $m\angle 5$ ___ $5x$ c. $m\angle 6$ ___ $180 - 5x$

71 ▶

Name _____

▶ **LESSON MASTER 5-4B** *page 2*

In 6 and 7, use the figure at the right in which $s \parallel t$.

6. If $m\angle 3 = 4x + 2$ and $m\angle 8 = 3x + 20$, find x and $m\angle 3$.
   $x =$ **18** $m\angle 3$ **74**

7. If $m\angle 6 = 54n - 5$ and $m\angle 8 = 20n$, find
   a. n. **2.5**   b. $m\angle 6$. **130**   c. $m\angle 8$. **50**

Properties Objective F: Write proofs using the Transitive Properties of Equality or Congruence. **Sample proofs are given.**

In 8–10, complete the proof by writing the argument.

8. Given: $\angle 1 \cong \angle A$.
   To prove: $\angle 2 \cong \angle A$.

Conclusions	Justifications
0. $\angle 1 \cong \angle A$	Given
1. $\angle 2 \cong \angle 1$	Vertical Angles Thm.
2. $\angle 2 \cong \angle A$	Trans. Prop. of Congr.

9. Given: B and C on $\odot Q$; C is the midpoint of $\overline{QE}$.
   To prove: $BQ = EC$.

Conclusions	Justifications
1. $QC = CE$	def. of midpoint
2. $BQ = QC$	def. of circle
3. $BQ = EC$	Trans. Prop. of Equality

10. Given: $\triangle GHK$ is equilateral; $r_{\overleftrightarrow{KH}}(GH) = JH$.
    To prove: $\overline{KG} \cong \overline{JH}$.

    Since $\triangle GHK$ is equilateral, $\overline{KG} \cong \overline{GH}$ by definition. $\overline{GH} \cong \overline{JH}$ by definition of congruence. Hence, $\overline{KG} \cong \overline{JH}$ by Trans. Prop. of Congruence.

Uses Objective I: Use theorems on alternate interior angles in real situations.

11. Is the sign on the street light parallel to the ground if $m\angle 1 = 74$ and $m\angle 2 = 76$? Justify your answer.
    No; if the sign were parallel to the ground, $m\angle 1 = m\angle 2$; but $m\angle 1 \neq m\angle 2$, so they are not parallel.

    PARK BLVD.

72

248

LESSON MASTER 5-5 B

Questions on SPUR Objectives

Skills Objective C: Find lengths using properties of perpendicular bisectors.

1. w is the $\perp$ bisector of $\overline{RS}$.

   a. Mark two pairs of congruent segments.
   b. Suppose $RJ = 8d$, $KS = 3d + 1$, and $JS = 24$. Find d, RJ and RK.

   $d = 3$ $RJ = 24$ $RK = 10$

2. $\overrightarrow{DV}$ is the $\perp$ bisector of $\overline{UH}$. $UD = 6a + 1$, $DH = 4a + 15$, and $VH = 7a$. Find UV.

   $UV = 49$

3. At the right, $Q = (-5, 0)$ and $G = (5, 0)$.
   a. Give an equation for the $\perp$ bisector of $\overline{QG}$.

   $x = 0$
   b. $QA = \sqrt{34}$. Find GA. $GA = \sqrt{34}$
   c. Draw a segment whose length is equal to MQ.   **Sample is given.**

Properties Objective G: Write proof arguments using properties of reflection.

In 4 and 5, supply the justification for each step of the proof.

4. Given: $r_b(H) = T$.
   To prove: $TH = YT$.

   0. $r_b(H) = T$ **Given**
   1. $r_b(Y) = Y$ **def. of reflection**
   2. $YH = YT$ **Refl. preserve distance**

73 ▶

---

5. Given: $\overleftrightarrow{AB}$ is the $\perp$ bisector of $\overline{MN}$.
   To prove: $\angle MAB \cong \angle NAB$.

   1. $r_{\overleftrightarrow{AB}}(M) = N$ **def. of reflection**
   2. $r_{\overleftrightarrow{AB}}(A) = A; r_{\overleftrightarrow{AB}}(B) = B$ **def. of reflection**
   3. $r_{\overleftrightarrow{AB}}(\angle MAB) = \angle NAB$ **Figure Refl. Thm.**
   4. $\angle MAB \cong \angle NAB$ **def. of congruence**

Sample proofs are given for 6 and 7.

In 6 and 7, refer to the diagram at the right. Complete the proof by writing an argument.

6. Given: $\overleftrightarrow{MO}$ is the $\perp$ bisector of $\overline{EK}$.
   To prove: $\triangle MED \cong \triangle MKD$.

Since $\overline{MO}$ is the $\perp$ bisector of $\overline{EK}$ (Given), $r_{\overleftrightarrow{MO}}(M) = M$, $r_{\overleftrightarrow{MO}}(D) = D$, and $r_{\overleftrightarrow{MO}}(E) = K$ by the def. of reflection. Then $r_{\overleftrightarrow{MO}}(\triangle MED) = \triangle MKD$ by the Figure Refl. Thm., and $\triangle MED \cong \triangle MKD$ by the def. of congruence.

7. Given: $r_{\overleftrightarrow{MO}}(E) = K$.
   To prove: $\overline{DE} \cong \overline{DK}$.

Conclusions   Justifications
0. $r_{\overleftrightarrow{MO}}(E) = K$ **Given**
1. $r_{\overleftrightarrow{MO}}(D) = D$ **def. of reflection**
2. $\overline{DE} \cong \overline{DK}$ **Reflections preserve distance.**

Uses Objective I: Use the Perpendicular Bisector Theorem in real situations.

8. Do you think that the two diagonal braces on the fence are equal in length? Explain your reasoning.

Yes; the center post appears to be the $\perp$ bisector of the lower horiz. board, so any point on the center post is the same distance from the endpoints of the board.

74

LESSON MASTER 5-6 B

Questions on SPUR Objectives

Vocabulary

1. What is an *auxiliary figure*?

a segment, line, or other figure added to a given figure.

Properties Objective H: Tell whether auxiliary figures are uniquely determined.

In 2–8, tell if the figure described is unique. If not, tell whether there is *more than one figure* or *no figure* satisfying the description.

2. midpoint of $\overline{UV}$
unique

3. bisector of $\overline{MN}$
not unique; more than one figure

4. diagonal $\overline{AC}$ bisecting $\angle A$
not unique; no figure

5. point R between P and Q
not unique; more than one figure

6. line parallel to $\overline{ZY}$ through W
unique

7. line through H and K perpendicular to m
not unique; no figure

8. perpendicular bisector of $\overline{RT}$
unique

75 ▶

---

9. A student wished to draw as an auxiliary figure line u parallel to two given lines e and r. Explain if this is possible. Use a diagram if you wish.

Sample: No; $u \parallel e$ or $u \parallel r$ but not both, unless $e \parallel r$.

Culture Objective J: Know the history and impact of postulates relating to parallel lines on the development of geometry.

In 10–12, complete the statements.

10. In Euclidean geometry, through a point not on a given line, there is (are) exactly ___?___ line(s) parallel to the given line.   **one**

11. In most non-Euclidean geometries, through a point not on a line there are either no lines parallel to the given line or ___?___ line(s) parallel to the given line.   **more than one**

12. According to the fifth postulate in Euclid's *Elements*, if $m\angle 1 + m\angle 2 < 180$, then lines ℓ and m ___?___.

intersect on the same side of the transversal that $\angle 1$ and $\angle 2$ are located.

13. Have mathematicians been able to prove Euclid's fifth postulate from Euclid's other postulates?   **no**

14. In which branch of science have non-Euclidean geometries been useful?   **physics**

Samples are given for 16 and 17.

Review Objective A, Lesson 3-3

In 15–18, draw each type of angle, and give the measure of the angle you drew.

15. right angle   16. acute angle   17. obtuse angle   18. straight angle
   90   **36**   **105**   **180**

76

Top-left quarter

Name _____

LESSON MASTER **5-7 B**   Questions on SPUR Objectives

Skills Objective D: Use the Triangle-, Quadrilateral-, and Polygon-Sum Theorems to determine angle measures.

In 1–9, find the sum of the measures of the interior angles of each figure.

1. isosceles triangle — **180**

2. rectangle — **360**

3. pentagon — **540**

4. octagon — **1080**

5. quadrilateral — **360**

6. scalene triangle — **180**

7. nonagon — **1260**

8. 15-gon — **2340**

9. hexagon — **720**

10. In △ABC, m∠ABC = 40 and m∠B = 111. Find m∠C. — **29**

11. In △QRS, m∠Q = m∠S, and m∠R = 2x. Find m∠Q. — **90 − x**

12. In quadrilateral EFGH, m∠E = 90, m∠G = 104, and m∠H = 123. Find m∠F. — **43**

13. In hexagon UVWXYZ, m∠U = m∠V = m∠W, m∠X = 158, m∠Y = 107, and m∠Z = 83. Find m∠U. — **124**

14. The measures of the angles of a triangle are in the extended ratio 4:5:11. Find the measure of the smallest angle. — **36**

77 ▶

Top-right quarter

▶ **LESSON MASTER 5-7B** *page 2*

15. Refer to Figure 1 at the right. Find m∠SVE. — **136**

16. Refer to Figure 2 at the right. Solve for x. — **x = 16**

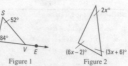

Figure 1   Figure 2

17. Find the measure of each angle of the hexagon pictured at the right.

∠A **90** ∠B **127** ∠C **81**

∠E **160** ∠F **110**

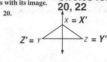
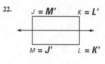

Culture Objective J: Know the history and impact of postulates relating to parallel lines on the development of geometry.

18. Does the Triangle-Sum Theorem hold for △NEQ on the earth's surface as pictured at the right? Explain. **Sample: The theorem is valid in Euclidean geometry; but in △NEQ, the sum of the angle measure > 180.**

Review Objective B, Lesson 4-2

In 19–22, draw the reflection image of each polygon over the line. Circle each polygon that coincides with its image. **Circles for 20, 22**

19.   20.

21.   22.

78

Bottom-left quarter

Name _____

LESSON MASTER **6-1 B**   Questions on SPUR Objectives

Vocabulary

1. Suppose figure Q is *reflection-symmetric*. What does this mean?

There is a line *m*, the line of reflection, such that r$_m$(Q) = Q.

Skills Objective A: Locate symmetry lines of geometric figures.

In 2–7, draw the symmetry line(s), if any, for the figure.

2.   3.   4.

5.   6.    7.

Properties Objective E: Apply properties of symmetry to assert and justify conclusions about symmetric figures.

In 8–13, *true or false.*

8. If r$_m$(∠X) = ∠X, then m is the bisector of ∠X. — **true**

9. A circle has exactly two symmetry lines. — **false**

10. A symmetry line for $\overline{AB}$ is $\overleftrightarrow{AB}$. — **true**

11. If r$_r$(△RST) = △XYZ, then r$_r$(△XYZ) = △RST. — **true**

12. A line is not a reflection-symmetric figure. — **false**

13. Every triangle has at least one symmetry line. — **false**

79 ▶

Bottom-right quarter

▶ **LESSON MASTER 6-1B** *page 2*

14. *a* and *b* are symmetry lines for the polygon at the right.

   a. Name three angles congruent to ∠T. **∠P, ∠R, ∠V**

   b. How is *a* related to ∠PQR? **a bisects ∠PQR**

   c. r$_b$(PQRSTUVW) = ___?___ . **VUTSRQPW**

   d. Name all the segments congruent to $\overline{VW}$. **$\overline{PW}$, $\overline{RS}$, $\overline{TS}$**

Uses Objective I: Locate and draw symmetry lines in real-world designs.

In 15–19, draw the symmetry line(s), if any, for the design.

15. Flag of Israel   16. Flag of Sweden   17. Flag of Japan

18.   19.

20. Is the drawing at the right reflection-symmetric? Explain why or why not. **No; the pull chain is not centered.**

80

GEOMETRY © Scott, Foresman and Company

250

LESSON MASTER 6-2 B
Questions on SPUR Objectives

Vocabulary

1. What is a *corollary*?
   A theorem that follows immediately from another theorem

2. Refer to the isosceles triangle at the right.

   a. Identify the *vertex angle*. **∠R**
   b. Identify the *base angles*. **∠P, ∠Q**
   c. Identify the *base*. **PQ̄**

Skills Objective A: Locate symmetry lines of geometric figures.
Objective B: Draw polygons satisfying various conditions.

3. Draw an isosceles triangle with a vertex angle of 36°. Then draw the symmetry line for the triangle.

4. Draw an isosceles triangle with a base angle of 36°. Then draw the symmetry line for the triangle.

5. Draw a triangle with three symmetry lines. Show the symmetry lines.

Skills Objective C: Apply the theorems about isosceles triangles to find angle measures and segment lengths.

In 6–8, find the indicated measures in each triangle.

6.
   a. m∠N **39**
   b. m∠G **102**
   c. DG **18**

7.
   a. m∠K **73**
   b. JK **14**
   c. m∠B **73**

8.
   a. m∠S **77**
   b. m∠SBW **90**
   c. TS **5.2**

---

9. At the right, △YPQ is isosceles with base PQ̄.

   a. If m∠P = 10x and m∠Y = 52x, find the measure of each angle in △YPQ.
   ∠P **25**   ∠Q **25**   ∠Y **130**

   b. If YQ = 5y + 6, QP = 12y + 1.2, and YP = 10y − 11, find the length of each side of △YPQ.
   YQ̄ **23**   QP̄ **42**   YP̄ **23**

Properties Objective F: Know the properties of various types of triangles.

10. At the right, △URA is isosceles with base UR̄, and AG bisects ∠UAR. Name all pairs of congruent angles and segments.
    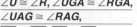
    ∠U ≅ ∠R, ∠UGA ≅ ∠RGA,
    ∠UAG ≅ ∠RAG,
    UG ≅ RG, UA ≅ RA

Properties Objective H: Write proofs using properties of isosceles triangles.

In 11 and 12, complete the proof by giving the argument.

Sample proofs are given.

11. Given: Points S and T are on ⊙O.
    To prove: ∠S ≅ ∠T.

Conclusions	Justifications
1. OS̄ ≅ OT̄	def. of circle
2. △OST is isosceles.	def. of isosceles △
3. ∠S ≅ ∠T	Isos. △ Base ∠s Thm.

12. Given: △FGH is isosceles with symmetry line m
    To prove: ∠1 ≅ ∠2.
    By the Isosceles Triangle Symmetry Theorem, m bisects ∠GFH, so ∠3 ≅ ∠2. Since ∠1 and ∠3 are vertical angles, ∠1 ≅ ∠3. Thus, by the Transitive Property of Congruence, ∠1 ≅ ∠2.

LESSON MASTER 6-3 B
Questions on SPUR Objectives

Skills Objective B: Draw polygons satisfying various conditions.

Samples are given.

1. Draw a parallelogram that is not a rectangle.

2. Draw a rhombus that is not a square.

3. Draw an isosceles trapezoid that is not a parallelogram.

Skills Objective D: Apply theorems about quadrilaterals to find angle measures and segment lengths.

4. In quadrilateral ABCD at the right, find each length and angle measure.

   AD **4y**   CD **x**   m∠D **90**   m∠C **90**

Properties Objective G: Know the properties of the seven special types of quadrilaterals.

In 5–7, classify the quadrilateral based only upon the markings given. Give the most specific name.

5.
   rectangle

6.
   kite

7.
   rhombus

8. Square FOUR is drawn at the right.

   a. Is FOUR also a kite? Why or why not?
   Yes; it has 2 distinct pairs of consecutive sides congruent.
   b. Is FOUR also a trapezoid? Why or why not?
   Yes; it has at least 1 pair of parallel sides.

Properties Objective H: Write proofs using properties of quadrilaterals.

9. Supply justifications for the conclusions in the argument written below.
   Given: r_m(△TEG) = △TEV.
   To prove: TGEV is a kite.

Conclusions	Justifications
0. r_m(△TEG) = △TEV	**Given**
1. △TEG ≅ △TEV	**def. of congruence**
2. TG ≅ TV, EG ≅ EV	**CPCF Theorem**
3. TGEV is a kite.	**definition of kite**

10. Complete the proof by giving the argument.
    Given: m∠1 = m∠B = m∠D.
    To prove: ABCD is a parallelogram.

Sample: Since m∠1 = m∠B, AB // DC because AIA ≅ ⟹ // lines. Since m∠1 = m∠D, AD // BC because corr. ∠s ≅ ⟹ // lines. So ABCD is a parallelogram by definition.

Representations Objective K: Draw and apply hierarchies of polygons.

11. Complete the hierarchy for the seven special types of quadrilaterals. Then answer *true* or *false* for the following statements.
    a. Every rhombus is a kite. **true**
    b. No quadrilateral is both a kite and a trapezoid. **false**
    c. No quadrilateral is both a rectangle and a rhombus. **false**

quadrilateral
kite   trap.
parallel-ogram   isos. trap.
rhombus   rectangle
square

LESSON MASTER 6-4 B

Questions on SPUR Objectives

Skills Objective A: Locate symmetry lines of kites and rhombuses.
Objective D: Apply theorems about kites and rhombuses to find angle measures and segment lengths.

1. Draw the symmetry line(s) for kite *QRST* and mark all right angles and all congruent angles and segments.

2. Draw the symmetry line(s) for rhombus *ABCD* and mark all right angles and all congruent angles and segments.

3. At the right, *M* and *Z* are the ends of kite *MGZX*, m∠2 = 46, and m∠*GZX* = 64. Find each measure.

   a. m∠7 __46__   b. m∠1 __90__

   c. m∠3 __44__   d. m∠5 __32__

   e. m∠4 __58__   f. m∠6 __32__   g. m∠*ZGM* __102__

4. In rhombus *UMNJ*, *UH* = 14 and m∠*UMH* = 31.

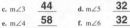

   a. Give as many segment lengths as possible.
   HN = 14

   b. Give as many angle measures as possible.
   m∠NMH = m∠UJH = m∠NJH = 31;
   m∠UHM = m∠NHM = m∠UHJ = m∠NHJ = 90;
   m∠MUH = m∠MNH = m∠JUH = m∠JNH = 59

   c. Give as many pairs of parallel segments as possible.
   UJ // MN, UM // JN

   d. Give as many isosceles triangles as possible.
   △JUM, △UMN, △MNJ, △NJU

   e. Which triangles are congruent?
   △JUM ≅ △MNJ, △UMN ≅ △NJU, △UHM ≅
   △NHM ≅ △UHJ ≅ △NHJ

▶ **LESSON MASTER 6-4B** *page 2*

5. In rhombus *REJD*, m∠*DRE* = 82. Find each measure.

   a. m∠*DRA* __41__   b. m∠*RDA* __49__

   c. m∠*DJA* __41__   d. m∠*DJE* __82__

Properties Objective G: Know the properties of the seven special types of quadrilaterals.

6. How many symmetry diagonals does a kite have? __1__

7. How many symmetry diagonals does a rhombus have? __2__

Properties Objective H: Write proofs using properties of triangles and quadrilaterals.

8. Supply justifications for the conclusions in the argument written below.

   Given: ⊙*O* and ⊙*Q* with points *B*, *C*, and *Q* on ⊙*O*.
   To prove: *QCOB* is a kite.

Conclusions	Justifications
1. $\overline{OB} \cong \overline{OC}$; $\overline{QB} \cong \overline{QC}$	**definition of circle**
2. *QCOB* is a kite.	**definition of kite**

9. Complete the proof by writing the argument.

   Given: $\overline{FW}$ and $\overline{SK}$ are ⊥ bisectors of each other.
   To prove: *SFKW* is a rhombus.

Sample: Because $\overline{FW}$ and $\overline{SK}$ are ⊥ bisectors of each other, SF = SW, KF = KW, FS = FK, and WS = WK by the ⊥ Bisector Theorem. By the Transitive Property of Equality, SF = SW = KW = KF. Hence, SFKW is a rhombus by definition.

86

LESSON MASTER 6-5 B

Questions on SPUR Objectives

Skills Objective A: Locate symmetry lines of geometric figures.

In 1–4, draw the symmetry line(s), if any, for the trapezoid.

1.   2.

3.   4.

Skills Objective D: Apply theorems about quadrilaterals to find angle measures and segment lengths.

5. $\overline{RS}$ and $\overline{JK}$ are the bases of trapezoid *JKSR*, m∠*K* = 133 and m∠*S* = 61. Find m∠*J* and m∠*S*.

   m∠*J* __119__   m∠*S* __47__

6. $\overleftrightarrow{MN}$ is a symmetry line for trapezoid *ABCD*, m∠*D* = 74, *AB* = 28, *AD* = 12, and *DC* = 34.6. Find each measure.

   a. m∠*C* __74__   b. m∠*A* __106__

   c. *BC* __12__   d. *MB* __14__

   e. *DN* __17.3__   f. m∠*AMN* __90__

7. In rectangle *EFGH*, m∠*F* = 2(6t + 3). Solve for *t*.
   t = 7

8. In *UVWX*, m∠*U* = 5x + 13, m∠*X* = 129 − 3x, m∠*W* = 64 − x, and m∠*V* = 8x − 17. Find the measure of each angle in *UVWX*.

   ∠*U* __108__   ∠*V* __135__

   ∠*W* __45__   ∠*X* __72__

▶ **LESSON MASTER 6-5B** *page 2*

Properties Objective G: Know the properties of trapezoids.

9. Do any isosceles trapezoids have more than one symmetry line? Explain why or why not.
   Yes; rectangles have two symmetry lines, and squares have four.

10. Can an isosceles trapezoid have a symmetry diagonal? Explain why or why not.
   Yes; if the trapezoid is a square, it has two symmetry diagonals.

Properties Objective H: Write proofs using properties of trapezoids.

11. Supply justifications for the conclusions in the argument written below.

   Given: $\overleftrightarrow{MN}$ is a symmetry line for isosceles trapezoid *TVHQ*.
   To prove: △*QMH* is an isosceles triangle.

Conclusions	Justifications
1. $\overleftrightarrow{MN}$ is the ⊥ bisector of $\overline{TV}$ and $\overline{QH}$.	**def. of symmetry line**
2. r$_{MN}$(*Q*) = *H*, r$_{MN}$(*M*) = *M*	**def. of reflection**
3. *MQ* = *MH*	**Reflections preserve distance.**
4. △*QMH* is an isosceles triangle.	**def. of isosceles △**

12. Complete the proof by writing the argument.

   Given: $\overline{JP} // \overline{KR}$, and m∠*R* = m∠1.
   To prove: *JK* = *PR*.

Sample: Since // lines ⇒ corr. ∠s ≅, m∠K = m∠1. So m∠R = m∠K by the Transitive Property of Equality. Then, by definition, JPRK is an isosceles trapezoid, and JK = PR by the Isosceles Trapezoid Theorem.

88

252

LESSON MASTER 6-6 B

Questions on SPUR Objectives

Vocabulary

1. Define *rotation-symmetric* figure.

A figure *F* is rotation-symmetric if and only if there is a rotation with magnitude between 0° and 360° such that R(*F*) = *F*.

Skills Objective A: Locate symmetry lines and centers of symmetry of geometric figures.

In 2–7, if the figure has *n*-fold rotation symmetry, find *n*. Then draw and label the center of symmetry point *C*.

2.
n = 4

3.
n = 3

4.
n = 4

5.

6.
n = 2

7.
n = 2

In 8–10, complete each statement.

8. If a figure has 5-fold rotation symmetry, then the least positive magnitude of a rotation that will map the figure onto itself is ___?___.

72°

9. If the least positive magnitude of a rotation that maps a figure onto itself is 60°, then the figure has ___?___-fold rotation symmetry.

6

10. If a rotation of magnitude 90° maps a figure onto itself, then a rotation of magnitude ___?___ will also map the figure onto itself.

180°, 270°

11. Suppose a rotation of magnitude 30° maps a figure onto itself. Give the magnitudes of three other rotations that will map the figure onto itself.

60°, 90°, 120°, 150°, 180°, 210°, 240°, 270°, 300°, 330°

▶ LESSON MASTER 6-6B *page 2*

Samples are given.

12. Draw a figure with 3-fold rotation symmetry that also has reflection symmetry.

13. Draw a figure with 3-fold rotation symmetry that does not have reflection symmetry.

Properties Objective E: Apply properties of symmetry to assert and justify conclusions about symmetric figures.

In 14 and 15, *true* or *false*.

14. If two symmetry lines for a figure intersect at *O*, then the figure has rotation symmetry with center *O*.

true

15. If a figure has 4-fold rotation symmetry, then it is reflection-symmetric.

false

16. If a figure has rotation symmetry, then can the least positive magnitude of a rotation that maps the figure onto itself be 27°? Explain why or why not.

Sample: No; there is no natural number *n* such that 27*n* = 360.

Uses Objective I: Locate and draw symmetry lines in real-world designs.

In 17–19, refer to the design at the right.

17. Does the entire design have reflection symmetry?

no

18. Does the entire design have rotation symmetry?

yes

19. Describe the symmetry in each portion of the design shown below.

a. 6-fold rotation; 6 lines of reflection

b. 3-fold rotation; 3 lines of reflection

LESSON MASTER 6-7 B

Questions on SPUR Objectives

Vocabulary

1. What is a *regular polygon*?

a convex polygon whose sides are all congruent and whose angles are all congruent

Skills Objective A: Locate symmetry lines and centers of symmetry of geometric figures.
Objective B: Draw polygons satisfying various conditions.

In 2–7, draw the figure described. Then draw the symmetry line(s), if any. Finally, draw the center of symmetry, if it exists, and label it *C*.

2. a regular quadrilateral

3. a regular pentagon

4. any polygon that is equilateral, but not regular
Sample:

5. any polygon that is equiangular but not regular
Sample:

6. a regular triangle

7. a regular octagon

Skills Objective C: Apply theorems about isosceles triangles to find angle measures and segment lengths.
Objective D: Apply theorems about regular polygons to find angle measures and segment lengths.

8. Find the measure of one interior angle of a regular

a. pentagon. **108** **b.** heptagon. **128$\frac{4}{7}$** **c.** 16-gon. **157.5**

▶ LESSON MASTER 6-7B *page 2*

9. *J* is the center of regular polygon *ABCDEFGHI*. Find the measures of the angles of △*DEJ*.

m∠*J* = 40, m∠*JDE* = m∠*JED* = 70

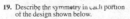

Properties Objective F: Know the properties of the various types of triangles and regular polygons.

10. At the right, *QRSTUVWXYZ* is regular.

a. Name the center of *QRSTUVWXYZ*. **P**

b. How many symmetry lines does *QRSTUVWXYZ* have? **10**

Sample line is given.

c. Are there any symmetry lines that do not contain a vertex of *QRSTUVWXYZ*? If so, draw one. **yes**

d. m∠*ZPQ* = **36**   m∠*PZQ* = **72**   m∠*VPZ* = **144**

Properties Objective H: Write proofs using properties of triangles and quadrilaterals.

11. Complete the proof by supplying the justifications.

Given: *UDTCE* is a regular pentagon.
To prove: ∠1 ≅ ∠2.

Conclusions	Justifications
1. $\overline{UE} \cong \overline{UD}$	**def. of regular polygon**
2. △*UED* is isosceles.	**def. of isosceles △**
3. ∠1 ≅ ∠2	**Isosceles △ theorem**

12. Complete the proof by giving the argument.

Given: *R* is the center of a regular octagon *STKAMHBN*.
To prove: △*RMN* is isosceles.

Sample: By the center of a regular Polygon Thm., *RM* = *RN*. **Thus,** △*RMN* **is isos. by def. of isos. triangle.**

LESSON MASTER 6-8 B — Questions on SPUR Objectives

Vocabulary

1. a. In ⊙A at the right, draw and label a *chord*. Give the name of the chord. __MN__

   b. Name the *minor arc* of the chord. __MN__

Sample:

2. a. When is a tournament called a *round-robin* tournament?
   when each competitor plays each other competitor exactly once

   b. When does a team in a round-robin tournament get a *bye*?
   when a team doesn't play, which happens when there is an odd number of teams

Uses Objective J: Make a schedule for a round-robin tournament.

In 3–10, consider a round-robin tournament for five teams that play once a week.

Samples are given in 3–6.

3. Place the five teams at equal intervals on the circle at the right.

4. Draw a chord and all chords parallel to it. Write the first week's pairings.
   1–2, 5–3

5. Rotate the chords ⅓ of a revolution. Write the pairings for the second week.
   2–3, 1–4

6. Continue until all the teams have played each other. List the remainder of the weeks and the pairings for each week.
   Week 3: 3–4, 5–2; Week 4: 4–5, 1–3;
   Week 5: 5–1, 2–4

▶ LESSON MASTER 6-8B page 2

7. How many weeks are needed? **5 weeks**
8. How many individual games are needed? **10 games**
9. How many byes are needed? **5 byes**
10. How many weeks are needed for six teams? **5 weeks**

In 11–14, consider a round-robin tournament for eight teams that play once a week.

11. In the space below, show the week-by-week pairings. **Sample is given.**

   Week 1: 1–3, 7–4, 6–5, 2–8
   Week 2: 2–4, 1–5, 7–6, 3–8
   Week 3: 3–5, 2–6, 1–7, 4–8
   Week 4: 4–6, 3–7, 2–1, 5–8
   Week 5: 5–7, 4–1, 3–2, 6–8
   Week 6: 6–1, 5–2, 4–3, 7–8
   Week 7: 7–2, 6–3, 5–4, 1–8

12. How many weeks are needed? **7 weeks**
13. How many individual games are needed? **28 games**
14. How many byes are needed? **none**

Review Objective J, Lesson 2-7

In 15–20, can these numbers be the lengths of the sides of a triangle? Justify your answer.

15. 8, 6, 3 **yes; 8 + 6 > 3, 6 + 3 > 8, 8 + 3 > 6**
16. 2, 8, 10 **no; 2 + 8 = 10**
17. 5, 4, 11 **no; 5 + 4 < 11**
18. 40, 40, 86 **no; 40 + 40 < 86**
19. 20, 36, 20 **yes; 20 + 36 > 20, 20 + 20 > 36**
20. 6, 12, 7 **yes; 6 + 12 > 7, 12 + 7 > 6, 6 + 7 > 12**

LESSON MASTER 7-1 B — Questions on SPUR Objectives

Skills Objective A: Draw triangles satisfying certain conditions and determine whether all such triangles are congruent.

In 1–8, use an automatic drawer or other drawing tools. Accurately draw a triangle satisfying the given conditions. Then complete the table on the next page by choosing the correct name for the condition and conjecturing whether all the triangles drawn with these conditions are congruent.

Samples are given.

1. △RST with RS = 4 cm, ST = 6 cm, and RT = 3.5 cm

2. △ABC with m∠A = 44, m∠B = 66, and m∠C = 70

3. △XYZ with XY = 2.5 in., YZ = 1 in., and m∠Y = 105

4. △DEF with DE = 3 cm, DF = 6 cm, and m∠F = 25

5. △OPQ with PQ = 3 in. and m∠Q = 90

6. △UVW with m∠U = 80 and m∠V = 52

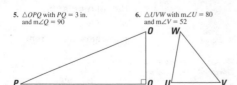

▶ LESSON MASTER 7-1B page 2

7. △GHJ with m∠H = 73, m∠J = 45, and JH = 5 cm

8. △KMN with m∠M = 120, m∠N = 22, and KN = 2.5 in.

Name for given condition	SSS	SSA	SAS	ASA	AAS	SA	AAA	AA
Question which involved this condition	1	4	3	7	8	5	2	6
All triangles with this condition congruent?	Y	N	Y	Y	Y	N	N	N

9. Explain how the AAA condition is similar to the AA condition.
   Sample: Given two angle measures, the third angle measure is determined because the sum of the angle measures is 180.

Review Objective A, Lesson 5-1

10. Refer to the congruent triangles at the right. Correctly complete the following congruence statement. **Sample:**
    △ __VCJ__ ≅ △ __MRF__

11. At the right, △AND is the image of △BUT under an isometry. Mark three pairs of congruent sides and three pairs of congruent angles. **Sample:**

Name _____

LESSON MASTER 7-2 B

Questions on SPUR Objectives

Skills Objective A: Draw triangles satisfying certain conditions and determine whether all such triangles are congruent.

In 1–6, conditions are given. Will all triangles satisfying the same conditions be congruent? Explain your answer.

1. In △JTP, m∠T = 66, m∠P = 51, JP = 3 in.
yes, by AAS Congruence Theorem

2. In △ABC, m∠B = 27, m∠C = 104
no; AA condition is not sufficient.

3. In △ESD, m∠E = 38, ES = 7 cm, DE = 7 cm
yes, by SAS Congruence Theorem

4. In △ORM, OR = 4 cm, OM = 5.4 cm, MR = 8.8 cm
yes, by SSS Congruence Theorem

5. In △HKJ, m∠H = 45, m∠K = 78, HK = 38 mm
yes, by ASA Congruence Theorem

6. In △XYU, UY = 2 in., m∠U = 42, YX = 1 in.
no; SsA condition does not apply.

Properties Objective C: Determine whether triangles are congruent from given information.

In 7–10, use the marked diagram to tell whether the triangles are congruent. If they are congruent, write a congruence statement that indicates corresponding vertices.

7.
yes; △YNM ≅ △ORG

8.
yes; △EWD ≅ △WEG

97 ▶

Name _____

9.
no

10.
yes; △GQP ≅ △BQP

11. Give an additional piece of information that would guarantee that △ZHC ≅ △DMQ
   a. by the SAS Congruence Theorem. **∠H ≅ ∠M**
   b. by the SSS Congruence Theorem. **CZ ≅ QD**

12. a. What additional piece of information would guarantee that △FTD ≅ △CRS? What theorem guarantees the congruence? **Sample: FD ≅ CS; ASA ≅ Thm.**

   b. Give a different piece of information that would guarantee that △FTD ≅ △CRS. What theorem guarantees the congruence? **Sample: DT ≅ SR; AAS ≅ Thm.**

Uses Objective I: Use theorems about triangles to explain real situations.

13. Junior Campers are making toy boats from hobby kits. The directions say to cut a canvas sail with the measurements shown. Will all the sails be congruent? Explain why or why not.
yes, by the SAS Congruence Theorem

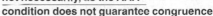

14. Luke ordered a triangular piece of glass with angles of 66°, 66°, and 48° to replace the broken piece in a light fixture. Will the new piece fit? Explain why or why not.
not necessarily, as the AAA condition does not guarantee congruence

98

Name _____

LESSON MASTER 7-3 B

Questions on SPUR Objectives

Properties Objective D: Write proofs that triangles are congruent.
Objective E: Apply the triangle congruence and CPCF theorems to prove that segments or angles are congruent.

In 1 and 2, give a justification for each conclusion.

1. Given: DTFS is a rhombus.
   To prove: △DES ≅ △FET.
   Argument:

Conclusions	Justifications
0. DTFS is a rhombus.	**Given**
1. DS ≅ FT	**def. of rhombus**
2. ST is the ⊥ bisector of FD; FD is the ⊥ bisector of ST.	**Rhombus Diag. Thm.**
3. SE ≅ TE; FE ≅ DE	**def. of bisector**
4. △DES ≅ △FET	**SSS Congruence Thm.**

2. Given: ∠J ≅ ∠K; N is the midpoint of JK.
   To prove: ∠JMN ≅ ∠KMN.
   Argument:

Conclusions	Justifications
0. ∠J ≅ ∠K	**Given**
1. JM ≅ KM	**Isos. △ Base ∠s Conv. Thm.**
2. N is the midpoint of JK.	**Given**
3. JN ≅ KN	**def. of midpoint**
4. △JMN ≅ △KMN	**SAS Congruence Thm.**
5. ∠JMN ≅ ∠KMN	**CPCF Theorem**

99 ▶

Name _____

In 3–6, complete the proof by giving the argument.   **Samples are given.**

3. Given: UQ // VR; UP = RP.
   To prove: △UQP ≅ △RVP.
It is given that UQ // VR and UP = RP. ∠Q ≅ ∠V because // lines ⇒ AIA. ∠QPU ≅ ∠VPR by Vertical Angles Theorem. Finally, △UQP ≅ △RVP by AAS Congruence Theorem.

4. Given: ⊙C.
   To prove: XY ≅ ST.
By definition of circle, CX ≅ CS and CY ≅ CT. ∠XCY ≅ ∠SCT by Vertical Angles Theorem. So △XCY ≅ △SCT by SAS Congruence Theorem, and XY ≅ ST by CPCF Theorem.

5. Given: GH bisects ∠QGR and ∠QHR.
   To prove: GQ ≅ GR.

Conclusions	Justifications
1. ∠QGH ≅ ∠RGH; ∠GHQ ≅ ∠GHR	**def. of bisect**
2. GH ≅ GH	**Reflexive Prop. of ≅**
3. △GHQ ≅ △GHR	**ASA Congruence Thm.**
4. GQ ≅ GR	**CPCF Theorem**

6. Given: Regular pentagon ABCDE.
   To prove: ∠BAC ≅ ∠EAD.

Conclusions	Justifications
1. ∠B ≅ ∠E; AB ≅ AE; BC ≅ ED	**def. of regular polygon**
2. △ABC ≅ △AED	**SAS Congruence Theorem**
3. ∠BAC ≅ ∠EAD	**CPCF Theorem**

100

255

Top-left panel

Name _____

LESSON MASTER **7-4 B**   Questions on SPUR Objectives

Vocabulary

In 1 and 2, redraw the figure separating the pair of overlapping triangles. Label your drawing and mark the shared parts.

1.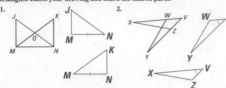

2.

Properties Objective D: Write proofs that triangles are congruent.
Objective E: Apply the triangle congruence and CPCF theorems to prove that segments or angles are congruent.

3. Write a justification for each conclusion.
Given: *GNTP* is an isosceles trapezoid with base angles ∠*GPT* ≅ ∠*NTP*.
To prove: △*GTP* ≅ △*NPT*.
Argument:

Conclusions	Justifications
1. $\overline{GP} \cong \overline{NT}$	**Isosceles Trapezoid Thm.**
2. $\overline{PT} \cong \overline{PT}$	**Reflexive Prop. of Congruence**
3. △*GTP* ≅ △*NPT*	**SAS Congruence Thm.**

In 4–7, complete the proof by giving the argument. **Samples are given.**

4. Given: *DN* = *YN*; *WN* = *FN*.
To prove: ∠*W* ≅ ∠*F*.

Argument: It is given that
DN* = *YN* and *WN* = *FN*. ∠*N* ≅ ∠*N
by the Reflexive Property of
Congruence. Then △*WNY* ≅ △*FND*
by the SAS Congruence Theorem,
and ∠*W* ≅ ∠*F* by the CPCF Theorem.

101 ►

Top-right panel

Name _____

► **LESSON MASTER 7-4B** *page 2*

5. Given: *CDEFGH* is a regular hexagon.
To prove: $\overline{FD} \cong \overline{EG}$.
Argument:

Conclusions	Justifications
1. $\overline{DE} \cong \overline{FG}$; ∠*DEF* ≅ ∠*EFG*	def. of regular polygon
2. $\overline{EF} \cong \overline{FE}$	Reflexive Prop. of ≅
3. △*DEF* ≅ △*EFG*	SAS Congruence Theorem
4. $\overline{FD} \cong \overline{EG}$	CPCF Theorem

6. Given: ⊙*S*; ∠*U* ≅ ∠*K*.
To prove: △*SKT* ≅ △*SUM*.

Argument: By the definition of
circle, $\overline{SK} \cong \overline{SU}$. It is given that
∠*U* ≅ ∠*K*, and ∠*S* ≅ ∠*S* by the
Reflexive Property of Congruence.
Therefore, △*SKT* ≅ △*SUM* by
the ASA Congruence Theorem.

7. Given: *JR* = *MJ*; ∠*RYM* ≅ ∠*MQR*.
To prove: $\overline{QR} \cong \overline{YM}$.

Argument: It is given that
***JR* = *MJ* and ∠*RYM* ≅ ∠*MQR*.**
∠*QJR* ≅ ∠*YJM* by the Vertical Angles
Theorem. So △*QJR* ≅ △*YJM* by the AAS
Congruence Theorem. Thus $\overline{QR} \cong \overline{YM}$
by the CPCF Theorem.

102

Bottom-left panel

Name _____

LESSON MASTER **7-5 B**   Questions on SPUR Objectives

Skills Objective A: Draw triangles satisfying certain conditions and determine whether all such triangles are congruent.

In 1–4, use an automatic drawer or other drawing tools. Accurately draw a triangle satisfying the given conditions. Tell whether all triangles meeting these conditions are congruent. If all triangles meeting these conditions are *not* congruent, show this with a second drawing.

1. △*ABC* with *AC* = 3 cm, *AB* = 2.5 cm, and m∠*C* = 45

no

2. △*RST* with m∠*R* = 90, *RS* = 1.5 in., and *ST* = 2 in.

yes

3. △*MNO* with m∠*O* = 90 and *MO* = 3.5 cm

no

2. △*XYZ* with *XY* = 20 mm, *XZ* = 25 mm, and m∠*Y* = 105

yes

Properties Objective C: Determine whether triangles are congruent from given information.

In 5–7, use the marked diagram to tell whether the triangles are congruent. If they are congruent, justify with a triangle congruence theorem. Otherwise, write *not enough to tell*.

5.

HL ≅
Theorem

6.   *HJ* > *CJ*

not enough
to tell

7.   *GV* > *MV*

SsA ≅
Theorem

103 ►

Bottom-right panel

Name _____

► **LESSON MASTER 7-5B** *page 2*

Properties Objective D: Write proofs that triangles are congruent.
Objective E: Apply the triangle congruence and CPCF theorems to prove that segments or angles are congruent.

In 8 and 9, complete the proof by giving the argument.

8. Given: *GHTC* is an isosceles trapezoid with bases $\overline{GH}$ and $\overline{CT}$; *GM* = *HN*; $\overline{GM} \perp \overline{CT}$; $\overline{HN} \perp \overline{CT}$.   **Samples are given.**
To prove: △*GMC* ≅ △*HNT*.

Argument: By the Isosceles
Trapezoid Theorem, $\overline{GC} \cong \overline{HT}$. Since $\overline{GM} \perp \overline{CT}$
and $\overline{HN} \perp \overline{CT}$, △*GMC* and △*HNT* are right
triangles. It is given that $\overline{GM} \cong \overline{HN}$, so △*GMC* ≅
△*HNT* by the HL Congruence Theorem.

9. Given: $\overline{FN}$ is the ⊥ bisector of $\overline{OE}$; $\overline{ON} \cong \overline{EF}$.
To prove: $\overline{ON} \parallel \overline{EF}$.

Argument: Since $\overline{FN}$ is the ⊥
bisector of $\overline{OE}$, $\overline{OG} \cong \overline{EG}$ by definition and
△*OGN* and △*EFG* are right triangles. It is given
that $\overline{ON} \cong \overline{EF}$, so △*OGN* ≅ △*EGF* by the HL
Congruence Theorem. Therefore, ∠*N* ≅ ∠*F*
by the CPCF Theorem, and $\overline{ON} \parallel \overline{EF}$ because
AIA ≅ ⇒ ∥ lines.

Uses Objective I: Use theorems about triangles to explain real situations.

10. Cables $\overline{AB}$ and $\overline{XY}$ on the suspension bridge pictured at the right are the same length. End supports $\overline{AC}$ and $\overline{XZ}$ are equal in length and are perpendicular to the ground. Explain why the distance from the base of the support to the point where the cable meets the ground is the same on each side of the bridge.

△*ACB* ≅ △*XZY* by the HL Congruence
Theorem, so $\overline{CB} \cong \overline{ZY}$ by the CPCF Theorem.

104

256

Name _____

LESSON MASTER 7-6 B

Questions on SPUR Objectives

Vocabulary

1. a. What is a *tessellation*?
a covering of a plane (with no holes) with non-overlapping congruent regions

b. What is the *fundamental region* of a tessellation?
the non-overlapping congruent regions in a tessellation

Uses Objective J: Draw tessellations of real objects.

2. A brick patio is tiled with rectangular bricks, as shown at the right. The length of each rectangle is twice its width. Draw part of a tessellation that will yield a different rectangular-brick pattern for the patio.
Sample:

Samples are given

In 3–5, draw part of a tessellation using the given figure.

3. equilateral triangles

4. scalene triangles

5. quadrilaterals with no right angles

6. Can a regular octagon be used as a fundamental region for a tessellation? Explain your answer.
No; the measure of each angle in the octagon is 135, and 135 does not divide 360.

105 ►

Name _____

► LESSON MASTER 7-6B page 2

In 7 and 8, the tessellation is a tile pattern found in the Alhambra in Granada, Spain.

7. Shade a possible fundamental region in the tessellation below.

8. Use the fundamental region below to draw part of a tessellation.

9. Doreen is needle-pointing the pattern shown below. Outline a possible fundamental region.

10. Draw part of a tessellation using the figure below as the fundamental region.

106

Name _____

LESSON MASTER 7-7 B

Questions on SPUR Objectives

Properties Objective F: Apply properties of parallelograms.

1. Consider the symmetry of a parallelogram.

a. Does every parallelogram have reflection symmetry? If so, describe the line(s) of reflection.
no

b. Does every parallelogram have rotation symmetry? If so, describe the center and the magnitude(s) of the rotation(s).
Yes; the center is the intersection of the diagonals, and the magnitude is 180°.

2. Refer to parallelogram QRST at the right.

a. If m∠QTS = 102, find as many other angle measures as you can.
m∠SRQ = 102, m∠TQR = m∠RST = 78

b. If m∠STR = 48 and m∠QSR = 40, find as many other angle measures as you can.
m∠QRT = 48, m∠SQT = 40

c. If QT = 12 and QS = 22, find as many other lengths as you can.
SR = 12, QU = SU = 11

d. If UR = 4 and RQ = 7, find as many other lengths as you can.
TS = 7, UT = 4, RT = 8

3. At the right, if AB = 32, BD = 52, and CD = 5x + 2, solve for x.
x = 6

107 ►

Name _____

► LESSON MASTER 7-7B page 2

4. KMNJ is a parallelogram. Solve for

a. a. **114**   **b.** b. **66**

c. x. **8**   **d.** y. **6**

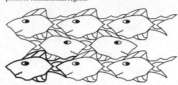

5. a. At the right, draw a parallelogram EFGH with congruent diagonals.   **Sample:**

b. What type of special parallelogram is EFGH?
rectangle

c. Justify your answer to Part b.
Sample: Since EFGH is a parallelogram, $\overline{EH} \cong \overline{FG}$ and $\overline{EF} \cong \overline{HG}$, so △EFG ≅ △FEH ≅ △GHE ≅ △HGF by the SSS ≅ Thm. Then ∠E ≅ ∠F ≅ ∠H ≅ ∠G by the CPCF Thm., and m∠E = m∠F = m∠H = m∠G = 90 by the Quadrilateral-Sum Thm. and EFGH is a rectangle by definition

Uses Objective K: Use theorems about parallelograms to explain real situations.

6. Mrs. Parisi is making draperies for the windows shown at the right. She measured the distance along the left side of the windows from the drapery rod to the floor.

a. What does she know about the distance along the right side of the windows from the drapery rod to the floor?
same as along left side

b. What theorem justifies Part a?
The distance between // lines is constant.

7. Mr. Santiago is sewing a banner for Napleton High School. If the measure of one angle of the parallelogram-shaped piece of fabric in the center is 45, what are the measures of the other three angles?
135, 45, 135

108

257

LESSON MASTER 7-8 B — Questions on SPUR Objectives

Properties Objective G: Determine whether conditions are sufficient for parallelograms.

In 1–10, use the diagram at the right. Tell whether sufficient conditions are given for ABCD to be a parallelogram. If your answer is *yes*, write the sufficient condition.

1. $AB = DC$ — **no**

2. $\angle DAB \cong \angle BCD$ — **no**

3. E is the midpoint of $\overline{BD}$ and $\overline{AC}$. — **yes; diag. bisect each other**

4. $\angle DAB \cong \angle BCD$, $\angle ABC \cong \angle CDA$ — **yes; both pr. opp. ∠s ≅**

5. $AB = BC$, $CD = AD$ — **no**

6. $AB = BD$ — **no**

7. $AB = DC$, $BC = AD$ — **yes; both pr. opp. sides ≅**

8. $\overline{BC} \parallel \overline{AD}$, $\overline{AB} \parallel \overline{DC}$ — **yes; both pr. opp. sides //**

9. $\overline{BC} \parallel \overline{AD}$, $\overline{AB} \cong \overline{DC}$ — **no**

10. $\overline{BC} \parallel \overline{AD}$, $\overline{BC} \cong \overline{AD}$ — **yes; 1 pr. opp. sides // and ≅**

In 11 and 12, a conditional is given. a. Draw an instance of the conditional. b. Tell whether you think the conditional is always true. If it is, explain why you think so. If not, draw a counterexample. **Samples are given.**

11. If three sides of a quadrilateral are congruent, then the quadrilateral is a parallelogram.

a.   b. **not always true**

12. If a quadrilateral has two pairs of consecutive angles that are supplementary, then the quadrilateral is a parallelogram.

a.   b. **not always true**

▶ **LESSON MASTER 7-8B** page 2

13. Provide the argument for the proof.
Given: $\triangle RQP \cong \triangle SPQ$.
To prove: $QSPR$ is a parallelogram.

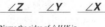

Sample: Since $\triangle RQP \cong \triangle SPQ$, $\overline{RQ} \cong \overline{SP}$ and $\overline{RP} \cong \overline{SQ}$ by the CPCF Theorem. Therefore, $QSPR$ is a parallelogram by the Sufficient Conditions Theorem, Part b.

Uses Objective K: Use theorems about parallelograms to explain real situations.

14. The log tool of a fireplace set pivots at A, B, C, and D; and $AB = BC = CD = DA$.

a. Explain why $ABCD$ is always a parallelogram.
Both pairs of opposite sides are congruent.

b. As $\angle B$ gets smaller, what happens to $\angle D$ and $\angle BAD$? Explain your answer.
$\angle D$ gets smaller because $\angle D \cong \angle B$. $\angle BAD$ gets larger because m$\angle BAD$ + m$\angle B$ = 180.

c. If the handles are pushed closer together, does the opening for the logs increase or decrease in size? Explain your answer.
Decrease; $\angle BAD$ and $\angle DCB$ grow smaller, so the opening, determined by the angle vertical to $\angle DCB$, grows smaller.

15. A Girl Scout tied a knot in a piece of rope and then tied four more knots 8 ft, 14 ft, 22 ft, and 28 ft from the first knot. She drove a spike into the ground through each of the first four knots, keeping the rope tight between the spikes and bringing the last knot to meet the first. Did the rope form a parallelogram? Explain why or why not.

Yes; one pair of opposite sides measure 8 ft, the other 6 ft; these are sufficient conditions.

LESSON MASTER 7-9 B — Questions on SPUR Objectives

Skills Objective B: Determine measures of angles in polygons using exterior angles.

1. Draw an exterior angle at each vertex of $\triangle EFG$ below. Then give the sum of the measures of the angles you drew. **Sample:**

360

2. Draw an exterior angle at each vertex of $WXYZ$ below. Then give the sum of the measures of the angles you drew. **Sample:**

360

In 3–11, find the value of the variable(s).

3. $n = 116$

4. $e = 30$

5. $x = 45$

6. $g = 111$

7. $y = 7$

8. $a = 135$, $b = 45$

9. $d = 128$

10. $p = 69$

11. $k = 163$

▶ **LESSON MASTER 7-9B** page 2

Properties Objective H: From given information, deduce which sides or angles of triangles are smallest or largest.

12. a. Which angle measure is greater, m$\angle 1$ or m$\angle 2$? **$\angle 2$**

b. What theorem justifies your answer to Part a?
Exterior Angle Inequality

13. Name the angles in $\triangle XYZ$ in order from smallest to largest.
$\angle Z$ $\angle Y$ $\angle X$

14. Name the sides of $\triangle HJK$ in order from smallest to largest.
HJ HK KJ

15. In $\triangle PQR$,
a. find x. **$x = 46$**
b. find m$\angle PRQ$. **84**
c. tell which side of $\triangle PQR$ is longest. **PQ**

16. a. In $\triangle ABC$, which angle has the greater measure, $\angle A$ or $\angle B$? **$\angle A$**
b. Can you tell from the given information if m$\angle C$ is less than m$\angle B$? Why or why not?
No; AB can be greater than, equal to, or less than AC.

Review Objective G, Lesson 6-3

In 17–21, for each term, complete the following definition: A quadrilateral is a (given term) if and only if ___?___. **Samples are given.**

17. rhombus — **all 4 sides congruent**
18. rectangle — **it has 4 right angles**
19. square — **it has 4 sides ≅ and 4 right angles**
20. trapezoid — **it has at least 1 pair of parallel sides**
21. kite — **2 distinct prs. of consecutive sides ≅**

LESSON MASTER 8-1 B

Questions on SPUR Objectives

Skills Objective A: Calculate perimeters of parallelograms, kites, and equilateral polygons given appropriate lengths and vice versa.

In 1–9, give the perimeter of each figure.

1. a rectangle with length 8 cm and width 2.5 cm — **21 cm**

2. an equilateral triangle with one side of length 15 in. — **45 in.**

3. a square-shaped region $\frac{1}{4}$ yard on a side — **1 yard**

4. a regular hexagon with one side of length 16 mm — **96 mm**

5. a parallelogram with one side of length 12 and the adjacent side half as long — **36 units**

6. a regular octagon with side $(y + 7)$ — **(8y + 56) units**

7. an equilateral pentagon with side length $(4a + 13)$ — **(20a + 65) units**

8. a rectangle with one dimension $n + 2$ and the other dimension $2n - 1$ — **(6n + 2) units**

9. a kite with the length of a shorter side $4m$ and the length of a longer side 5 more than twice the length of a shorter side — **(24m + 10) un.**

10. The perimeter of an equilateral triangle is 13.5 m. Find the length of a side. — **4.5 m**

11. The perimeter of a parallelogram is 48, with the length of a shorter side 10. Find the length of a longer side. — **14 units**

12. The perimeter of a rhombus is 34 mm. What is the length of a side? — **$8\frac{1}{2}$, or 8.5, mm**

13. The longer sides of a rectangle are 3 times as long as the shorter sides. If the perimeter is 100 feet, what are the dimensions of the rectangle? — **12.5 ft, 37.5 ft**

14. The perimeter of a regular hexagon is $84h + 12$. What is the length of a side? — **(14h + 2) units**

15. Pictured at the right is kite *KITE*. If its perimeter is 72 cm, what are the lengths of its sides? — **24 cm, 12 cm**

▶ **LESSON MASTER 8-1B** *page 2*

16. The perimeter of a kite is 120 inches, and the length of one side is 18 inches. Is this enough information to find the lengths of the other three sides of the kite? If so, find the lengths. If not, tell why not.

Yes; the longer sides measure 42 inches, and the other short side measures 18 inches.

Uses Objective H: Apply perimeter formulas for parallelograms, kites, and equilateral polygons to real-world situations.

17. The Parthenon in Athens, Greece, was completed in 432 B.C. It is about 69.5 m long and 30.9 m wide. Find its perimeter. — **200.8 m**

18. The Pentagon, outside Washington, D.C., is shaped like a regular pentagon with each side 921 feet long. Find the perimeter. — **4605 feet**

19. The base of the Great Pyramid of Khufu, near Cairo, Egypt, is shaped like a square. If the perimeter is about 922.4 m, find the length of a side. — **230.6 m**

20. The Taj Mahal in Agra, India, is octagonal, with a perimeter of 212 m. Four sides each measure about 44.5 m, and the remaining sides are each the same length. Find the length of a remaining side. — **8.5 m**

21. A stockade fence is to be supported at 6-foot intervals by vertical posts. If the area to be fenced is a rectangle 54 feet by 72 feet, how many posts will be needed? — **42 posts**

22. Sue Ling wishes to sew braid trim 3 inches from the edges of a 72-in. × 108-in. table cloth. How many yards of trim will she need? — **$9\frac{1}{3}$ yards**

23. The molding for an ornate gold picture frame with outside dimensions of 5 inches and 7 inches costs $12. At this rate, what will the same molding cost for a frame whose outside dimensions are 3 times as long? — **$36**

24. For an outdoor display, Jose wishes to outline a large 6-pointed star with small lights. The sides of each point are $3\frac{1}{2}$ feet long, and he plans to place the lights 4 inches apart. How many lights will he need? — **126 lights**

LESSON MASTER 8-2 B

Questions on SPUR Objectives

Skills Objective C: Calculate areas of squares and rectangles given relevant lengths of sides and vice versa.

1. Rectangle *ABCD* is 25 mm wide and 40 mm long.
   a. Find Area (*ABCD*) in square millimeters. — **1000 mm²**
   b. Find Area (*ABCD*) in square centimeters. — **10 cm²**

2. Find the area of a square with side length 14 cm. — **196 cm²**

3. A rectangle has a perimeter of 36 and a shorter side measures 8. Find the area of the rectangle. — **80 units²**

4. The perimeter of a square is $16s + 24$. Find its area. — **$(16s^2 + 48s + 36)$ units²**

5. The area of a rectangle is 99 cm². One dimension is 22 cm. What is the other? — **4.5 cm**

6. The area of a square is 324 square centimeters. Find the length of a side. — **18 cm**

7. The length of a rectangle is 3 times its width. If its area is 108 square feet, find its dimensions. — **6 ft, 18 ft**

Properties Objective G: Relate various formulas for area.

8. Explain how the formula for the area of a square can be derived from the formula for the area of a rectangle. — **Sample: The area formula for a rectangle is $A = bh$. In a square $b = h = s$, so its area is $A = s^2$.**

9. Find the area of the shaded region in the figure at the right. — **125 units²**

10. Given a square with side length s, how many times as great is the area of a square whose side is 3 times s? — **9 times**

11. How does the area of a rectangle change if its width is doubled and its length is halved? — **remains same**

12. How does the area of a rectangle change if its width is doubled and its length is tripled? — **is 6 times as great**

▶ **LESSON MASTER 8-2B** *page 2*

Uses Objective I: Apply formulas for areas of squares and rectangles to real-world situations.

13. The width of a soccer field can vary from about 46 m to about 91 m, while the length can vary from about 91 m to about 119 m. What is the range for possible areas for a soccer field? — **4186 m² to 10,829 m²**

14. A room measures 15 feet by 21 feet.
    a. How many square tiles 9 inches on a side will be needed to cover the floor? — **560 tiles**
    b. What will be the total cost, excluding tax, for the tiles if they are priced at 79¢ each? — **$442.40**

15. Rolls of sod measure 18 in. by 6 ft. How many rolls will be needed for a football field $53\frac{1}{3}$ yd by 120 yd? — **6400 rolls**

16. What will be the total cost, without tax, to carpet a 12-ft × 18-ft living room if the cost per yd² is $18.95 plus $6.50 per yd² for padding and installation? — **$610.80**

17. Cathy has 60 feet of chain link to make a rectangular pen for her dog Daisy.
    a. Find the dimensions of the largest pen she can make. — **15 ft, 15 ft**
    b. What is the area of that pen? — **225 ft²**

Representations Objective K: Determine the areas of polygons on a coordinate plane.

18. Find the perimeter and the area of *MONKEY*.
    perimeter — **40 units**
    area — **76 units²**

19. Find the perimeter and the area of the quadrilateral with vertices (-2, -3), (-2, 5), (4, 5), and (4, -3).
    perimeter — **28 units**   area — **48 units²**

20. A floor plan for a doll-house living room is shown on the grid at the right. If the unit of measure is centimeters, find the area of its floor. — **1350 cm²**

LESSON MASTER 8-3 B

Questions on SPUR Objectives

Vocabulary

1. The area of a region is the __?__ of the estimates made using finer and finer grids. **limit**

2. Define *lattice point*.
a point whose coordinates are integers

3. In the area formula $A = (I + \frac{1}{2}B) \times U$, what does each variable represent?
   a. A **area**
   b. I **number of inside squares**
   c. B **number of boundary squares**
   d. U **area of a single square**

Skills Objective B: Describe or apply a method for determining the area of an irregularly shaped region.

In 4–6, estimate the area of the irregular region. The side length of one small square is given. **Estimates may vary.**

4. 10 in. **2100 in²**   5. .5 km **4.25 km²**   6. 40 m **25,600 m²**

7. Estimate the area of the figure at the right.
   a. Use the left-hand grid. **20 in²**
   b. Use the right-hand grid. **32 in²**

side of squares = 1 in.   side of squares = $\frac{1}{2}$ in.

   c. Which answer is more accurate? Justify your answer.
   b; the finer the grid, the better the estimate

In 8–13, estimate the area of the state or country. The side length of a small square is given in miles. **Actual areas are given.**

8. 7 mi. RHODE ISLAND
1213 mi²

9.  125 mi. TEXAS
266,874 mi²

10.  48 mi. NEW YORK
49,112 mi²

11.  42 mi. AUSTRIA
32,376 mi²

12.  40 mi. WISCONSIN
56,145 mi²

13.  210 mi. MEXICO
756,066 mi²

14. What are the approximate dimensions in feet of a square lot with an area of a half acre? (640 acres = 1 square mile, 1 mile = 5280 feet) **≈ 148′, ≈ 148′**

LESSON MASTER 8-4 B

Questions on SPUR Objectives

Vocabulary

1. Define *altitude of a triangle*.
the perpendicular segment from a vertex to the line containing the opposite side

2. The length of an altitude is also called the **height**

Skills Objective C: Calculate areas of triangles given relevant lengths of sides and vice versa.

In 3–5, find the area of △*BUG*.

3.
G 5 12 13 B U
30 units²

4.
B D G U
DU = 8 cm
DG = 6 cm
BD = 12 cm
72 cm²

5.
U 3y G 2y D 16 B
Area (△DUB) = 80 ft²
48 ft²

6. If Area (△*LON*) = 150 units², find *IN*.
15 units

L 8 I 12 O N

7. The two legs of a right triangle measure 8 cm and 25 cm. Find the area of the triangle. **100 cm²**

8. The area of a right triangle is 36 in². If the length of one leg is 6 in., what is the length of the other leg? **12 in.**

Properties Objective G: Relate various formulas for area.

9. a. Give a formula for the area of kite *KITE* at the right. **Sample:**
$A =$ Area (△KIT) + Area (△KET)

K I T E

   b. If *KT* = 36 and *IE* = 24, find Area (*KITE*). **432 units²**

10. Given △*ABC* and △*DEF* with *AB* = *DE*, m∠*C* = 80 and m∠*F* = 120, can Area △*ABC* = Area △*DEF*? Why or why not?
No; altitude from ∠C is longer than one from ∠F.

Uses Objective I: Apply formulas for areas of triangles to real-world situations.

11. The flag of Antigua shown at the right is a rectangle 3 feet high and $4\frac{1}{2}$ feet wide. The two solid-colored red triangles are congruent. How much material is needed for each red triangle?
$3\frac{3}{8}$ ft²

12. The rectangular Congo flag pictured at the right is 225 cm wide and 150 cm high. What percent of the flag is the yellow stripe which is enclosed by the red and the green isosceles triangles?
$33\frac{1}{3}$%

13. The roof sections of the hexagonal gazebo at the right are shaped like congruent isosceles triangles.
   a. What is the total area of the roof?
   300 ft²

10′ 10′

   b. What will be the approximate cost for roof shingles if the price is $12.99 per bundle and 3 bundles cover 100 square feet?
   $116.91

Representations Objective K: Determine the areas of triangles on a coordinate plane.

14. A triangle has vertices (-5, 7), (4, 7), and (1, 2).
   a. Draw the triangle on the grid at the right.
   b. Find the area of the triangle.
   $22\frac{1}{2}$ units²

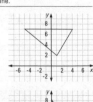

15. The three sides of a triangle are on the x-axis, the y-axis, and the line with equation $8x + 5y = 40$.
   a. Draw the triangle on the grid at the right.
   b. Find the area of the triangle.
   20 units²

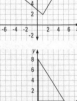

LESSON MASTER 8-5 B

Questions on SPUR Objectives

Vocabulary

1. Define *altitude of a trapezoid*.

any segment from one base perpendicular to the other

Skills Objective C: Calculate areas of trapezoids and parallelograms given relevant lengths of sides and vice versa.

In 2–6, use the information in the drawing to find the area of the trapezoid.

2.

$6y^4$ units²

3.

180 units²

4.

272 units²

5.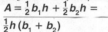

128 units²

6.

41.58 units²

7. A rhombus has a perimeter of 84 cm and an area of 252 cm². Find the length of the altitude.

12 cm

8. An isosceles trapezoid has an area of 144 in². Its altitude measures 9 in. Give a possible combination of lengths for the bases of the trapezoid.

Sample: 20 in., 12 in.

Properties Objective G: Relate various formulas for area.

9. How is the formula for the area of a trapezoid derived from the triangle area formula? Draw a diagram to illustrate your explanation.

$A = \frac{1}{2}b_1h + \frac{1}{2}b_2h = \frac{1}{2}h(b_1 + b_2)$

---

10. How is the formula for the area of a parallelogram related to the formula for the area of a trapezoid? **Sample:**

The area formula for a trap. is $A = \frac{1}{2}h(b_1 + b_2)$.

In a parallelogram, $b_1 = b_2$, so its area is bh.

Skills Objective I: Apply formulas for areas of trapezoids and parallelograms to real-world situations.

In 11 and 12, use the diagrams to estimate the area of the state. Dimensions are given in miles.

11.

≈ 70,350 mi²

12.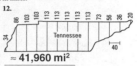

≈ 41,960 mi²

13. The tables in a pre-school classroom are shaped like isosceles trapezoids as shown at the right.

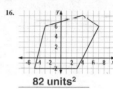

a. If two of these tables are placed with their longer bases aligned, what shape is formed? **hexagon**

b. What is the area of the two tables in Part a? **36 ft²**

14. Suppose four tables like those in Question 13 are put together with their sides matched and their longer bases on the perimeter.

a. What shape is formed by the perimeter? **square**

b. What is the area of the figure in Part a? **81 ft²**

Representations Objective K: Determine the areas of trapezoids and parallelograms on a coordinate plane.

In 15 and 16, find the area of the region.

15.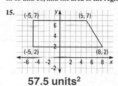

57.5 units²

16. **82 units²**

LESSON MASTER 8-6 B

Questions on SPUR Objectives

Vocabulary

1. State the *Pythagorean Theorem*.

In any right triangle with legs of lengths a and b and hypotenuse of length c, $a^2 + b^2 = c^2$.

2. State the *Pythagorean Converse Theorem*.

If a triangle has sides of lengths a, b, and c and $a^2 + b^2 = c^2$, then the triangle is a right triangle.

Skills Objective D: Apply the Pythagorean Theorem to calculate lengths and areas in right triangles and other figures.

In 3–5, a triangle is given. a. Find the length of the missing side. b. Find the area.

5a. $\sqrt{25m^2 + 36n^2}$ un.

3.

a. **12 units**
b. **30 units²**

4.

a. **25 units**
b. **84 units²**

5.

a. **15 mn un.²**

6. Find the perimeter and the area of a rhombus with diagonals measuring 20 in. and 32 in.

perimeter **$8\sqrt{89} ≈ 75.47$ in.**   area **320 in²**

Skills Objective E: Apply the Pythagorean Converse Theorem.

In 7–9, could the numbers be the lengths of sides of a right triangle?

7. 4, 5, 7 **no**   8. 9, 40, 41 **yes**   9. 20, 21, 29 **yes**

10. Find the perimeter and the area of a right triangle with a hypotenuse of 25 mm and one side 7 mm long.

perimeter **56 mm**   area **84 mm²**

11. Given $A = (5, 2)$ and $B = (8, 2)$, give possible integer coordinates for C such that $BC = \sqrt{34}$.

Samples: (5, 7), (5, -3), (8, 7), (8, -3)

Uses Objective H: Apply the Pythagorean Theorem to real-world situations.

12. The minute hand of Big Ben is 14 feet long and the hour hand is 9 feet long. What is the distance between the tips of the hands at 3:00 P.M.? **≈ 16.64 ft**

13. The north-south distance from South Bend, Indiana, to Indianapolis is about 140 miles. Richmond is about 73 miles due east of Indianapolis. What is the distance between South Bend and Richmond "as the crow flies"? **≈ 157.89 mi**

14. Four guy wires are to be placed from the top of a 40-meter-tall radio tower to points 12 meters from the center of the base of the tower. What is the total length of wire needed? **≈ 167.04 m**

15. The top of a tree broken by a storm just touches the ground 12 feet from the base of the tree. If the tree had been 36 feet tall, how much is still standing? **≈ 16 ft**

16. The glass for a window is 7.5 feet wide. About how high must a doorway be in order for a contractor to get the glass through the door if the doorway is 3 feet wide? **≈ 6.87 ft**

17. Barney wants to use felt to cover the top of a regular-hexagonal game table. Each side is 3 feet long.

a. What is the area to be covered? **≈ 23.38 ft²**

b. Felt comes 72 inches wide. Can Barney cover the table top without having a seam in the felt? **yes**

18. How much ribbon is needed to wrap the package as shown below?

≈ 70 in.

19. Find the length of wire needed to brace the two poles shown below.

≈ 28 ft

Culture Objective L: Identify cultures in which the Pythagorean Theorem is known to have been studied.

In 20 and 21, *true or false*.

20. In Japan, the Pythagorean Theorem is called "The Theorem of Three Triangles." **false**

21. Leonardo Da Vinci gave a proof of the Pythagorean Theorem. **true**

LESSON MASTER 8-7 B

Questions on SPUR Objectives

Vocabulary

1. a. Define *circumference*.   **the perimeter of a circle**

   b. Define *pi*.   **the ratio of circumference to diameter of a circle**

Skills Objective F: Calculate lengths and measures of arcs and the circumference of a circle given measures of relevant lengths and angles and vice versa.

2. *Multiple choice.* Which expression shows the exact circumference of a circle with a radius of 30 cm?   **c**

   (a) 30π cm   (b) 188.5 cm   (c) 60π cm   (d) 15π cm

3. Give the circumference of a circle with a diameter of 23 m.

   a. exactly.   **23π m**   b. to the nearest meter.   **72 m**

In 4–7, the circumference of a circle is given. Find the desired length.

4. 242π, radius   **121 units**   5. 8.75 ft, diameter   **≈ 2.79 ft**

6. 22π mm, diameter   **22 mm**   7. $17y$, radius   **≈ 2.7y units**

In 8–10, find the diameter of the circle with the given arc measure and length.

8. 60°, 16π cm   **96 cm**   9. 45°, 12 in.   **≈ 30.6 in.**   10. 135°, 6π **16 un.**

11. In the circle below, $CB = 8$ and $AB = 6$. Find m AB.

   ≈ 43°

12. In the circle below, how much longer is CD than $\overarc{CD}$?

   ≈ 1.88 units

13. By how much is the circumference of a circle with the given diameter increased if the radius is increased by 1 meter?

   a. 20 meters   **≈ 6.28 m**   b. 2000 meters   **≈ 6.28 m**

Uses Objective J: Apply formulas for the circumference of a circle to real situations.

14. The sizes of many flower bulbs are given by circumference. Find the diameter for each bulb with the given measure.

   a. tulip, 12 cm   **≈ 3.8 cm**   b. crocus, 8 cm   **≈ 2.5 cm**

   c. amaryllis, 34 cm   **≈ 10.8 cm**

15. In center-point irrigation, a long pipe describes a circle as it rotates to water a field. What is the circumference of the circle described by an irrigation pipe $\frac{1}{4}$ mile long?   **≈ 1.6 mi**

16. A track for automobile racing is shown at the right. Each end portion is a half-circle with diameter .477 mi, and the two side sections are straight-line segments with length .5 mi.

   a. What is the total length of the track?   **≈ 2.5 mi**

   b. How many laps must a car make to travel 500 miles?   **200 laps**

17. Kitty is making cone-shaped cardboard party hats by cutting sections out of circles with 6-in. radii as shown at the right. How much trim will she need to go around the curved edge of each hat?   **≈ 23.6 in.**

18. The *bore* of a tree is the diameter of its trunk. How much greater is the circumference of a tree with a 3-inch bore than the circumference of a tree with a 2-inch bore?   **≈ 3.1 in.**

19. Erik plans to use 6-in. board to make a round table 24 in. in diameter as shown at the right. He will use two 24-in. boards for the middle of the table. What is the minimum length for each outer board?   **≈ 20.8 in.**

20. How many times must Pedro ride around a 70-meter-diameter circular track in order to cover 1 kilometer?   **≈ 4.6 times**

21. In a half mile, how many more wheel revolutions are made by a 20″ child's bike than by a 26″ adult's bike?   **≈ 116 rev.**

LESSON MASTER 8-8 B

Questions on SPUR Objectives

Skills Objective F: Calculate the area of a circle given measures of relevant lengths and angles and vice versa.

In 1–3, estimate to the nearest tenth the area of the circle described.

1. a radius of 8 inches   **201.1 in²**

2. a circumference of 24π units   **452.4 units²**

3. a diameter of $4\sqrt{3}$ cm   **37.7 cm²**

4. The area of a circle is 12.96π square units. Find its diameter.   **7.2 units**

5. The area of a circle is 50 square inches. Find its radius.   **≈ 3.99 in.**

6. Find the area of a semi-circle with diameter 26 m.   **≈ 265.5 m**

7. In $\odot$ O at the right, find the area of the region bounded by $\overline{OA}$, $\overline{OB}$, and AB.

   ≈ 134 units²

Properties Objective G: Relate various formulas for area.

8. Which has greater area, a circle with diameter of 6 feet or an equilateral triangle with a side of 6 feet? Justify your answer.

   Circle; the circle has area ≈ 28.2 ft², while the triangle has area ≈ 15.6 ft².

In 9 and 10, find the area of the shaded region.

9.

   ≈ 84.8 m²

10.

   ≈ 72.7 units²

Properties Objective J: Apply formulas for the area of a circle to real situations.

11. The free-throw circle and rectangular lane of a basketball court are shown at the right. In high-school and college, the lane is 12 feet wide, while in professional basketball the lane is 16 feet wide. Find the total area of the region on

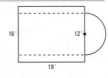

   a. a high school/college court.   **≈ 284.5 ft²**

   b. a professional court.   **≈ 360.5 ft²**

12. Suppose a radio station can transmit within a 100-km radius from its broadcast tower. What is the area of the transmission region?   **≈ 31,416 km²**

13. Another radio station claims that it can reach people in an area of 25,000 square kilometers. What is the radius of its transmission area?   **≈ 89 km**

14. Find the area of the region that can be watered by a center-point irrigation system with a $\frac{1}{4}$-mile pipe

   a. in square miles.   **≈ .20 mi²**

   b. in square feet.   **≈ 5,473,911 ft²**

   c. in acres.   **≈ 125.7 acres**

15. The usable portion of a CD has an outer radius of 5.7 cm and an inner radius of 2.3 cm. Find the area of the usable portion of the CD.   **≈ 85.45 cm²**

16. A window in the shape of a half circle is to be installed over a door frame which is 40 inches wide. What is the area of the glass needed for the window?   **≈ 628.3 in²**

17. A circular drop-leaf table is shown at the right. Find the area of

   a. the table with leaves up (as pictured).   **≈ 3.14 m²**

   b. the table with leaves down (a square).   **2 m²**   c. one leaf.   **≈ .29 m²**

LESSON MASTER 9-1 B

Questions on SPUR Objectives

Vocabulary

1. What is *solid geometry*?

the study of 3-dimensional
figures

Properties Objective F: Apply the properties of planes.

In 2–5, *true* or *false*. Justify your answer by stating the
appropriate assumption from the Point-Line-Plane Postulate.

2. There are at least two different planes containing ∠*DEF*.

**False; Unique Plane Assumption: Through
three noncollinear points, there is exactly
one plane.**

3. If point *A* is on planes *M* and *N*, then *M* ∩ *N* is a line.

**True; Intersecting Planes Assumption: If
two different planes have a point in
common, then their intersection is a line.**

4. Given plane *E*, there is at least one point in space *not* in *E*.

**True; Dimension Assumption(2); Given a
plane in space, there is at least one point
in space that is not in the plane.**

5. If points *S* and *T* lie in plane *Z*, then
$\overline{ST}$ may not lie in plane *Z*.

**False; Flat Plane Assumption: If two
points lie in a plane, the line containing
them lies in the plane.**

129 ▶

▶ **LESSON MASTER 9-1B** *page 2*

In 6–10, match the situation with the assumption it most
closely illustrates.

(a) Unique Line Assumption   (b) Number Line Assumption
(c) Dimension Assumption   (d) Flat Plane Assumption
(e) Unique Plane Assumption   (f) Intersecting Planes Assumption

6. The glass panels in a revolving door meet
along the center post.   **f**

7. A tricycle offers a stable ride.   **e**

8. A ruler might show inches or centimeters.   **b**

9. There is only one straight route from Train
Station A to Train Station B.   **a**

10. The line joining two points on a sheet of
cardboard is on the cardboard.   **d**

In 11–14, tell if the figure must be contained in exactly one plane.

11.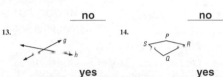

12.

no   **no**

13.

14.

yes   **yes**

Review Objective C: Lessons 3-6 and 3-7

In 15 and 16, refer to the diagram at
the right.

15. Is *u* // *v*? Justify your answer.
**yes; Two Perpendiculars
Theorem**

16. Solve for *x*. Justify your answer. **x = 32; // lines
⇒ corresponding angles ≅**

130

LESSON MASTER 9-2 B

Questions on SPUR Objectives

Vocabulary

1. When is a line perpendicular to a plane?

**when it is perpendicular to every line in
the plane containing the intersection of the
plane and the given line**

2. Define *parallel planes*.
**planes that have no points in common
or are identical**

3. Define *skew lines*.
**lines in space that are not coplanar
and do not intersect**

Skills Objective A: Draw common 3-dimensional shapes.

In 4–9, draw the figure.   **Samples are given.**

4. two parallel planes

5. a line perpendicular to a plane

6. a line intersecting a plane at a
45° angle

7. a dihedral angle

8. two intersecting planes that are
not perpendicular

9. a line parallel to a plane

131 ▶

▶ **LESSON MASTER 9-2B** *page 2*

Properties Objective F: Apply the properties of planes.

10. a. At the right, *m* and *n* are in plane *D*. *a* ⊥ *m*
and *a* ⊥ *n*. Is *a* ⊥ *D*? Explain your answer.

**Yes; if a line is ⊥ to two
different lines in space at
the same point, it is ⊥ to the
plane containing the lines.**

b. Is *a* perpendicular to any other lines in *D*?
Explain your answer. **Yes; since a is ⊥ to
the plane, it is ⊥ to every line in the plane
that intersects a by def. of line ⊥ to a plane.**

c. Is *m* ⊥ *n*? Explain your answer.
**No; m and n intersect but are not
necessarily perpendicular.**

d. Why can't you apply the Two Perpendiculars Theorem
from Chapter 3 to conclude that *m* // *n*?
**The Two Perpendiculars Theorem
applies to lines in the same plane.**

11. Provide the argument for the proof.

Given: $\overline{GE}$ ⊥ plane *S* at *E*; *E* is the
midpoint of $\overline{XY}$; *X*, *E*, and *Y*
are in plane *S*.
To prove: △*GXE* ≅ △*GYE*.

**Sample: Since $\overline{GE}$ ⊥ S, $\overline{GE}$ ⊥ $\overline{XY}$ by
definition of a line ⊥ to a plane. Since
E is the midpoint of $\overline{XY}$, $\overline{GE}$ is the ⊥ bisector
of $\overline{XY}$. So, $\overline{EX}$ ≅ $\overline{EY}$ and $\overline{GX}$ ≅ $\overline{GY}$ by the ⊥
Bisector Thm. $\overline{GE}$ ≅ $\overline{GE}$ by the Reflexive
Prop. of Congruence. Thus, △GXE ≅ △GYE
by the SSS Congruence Thm.**

132

263

LESSON MASTER 9-3 B — Questions on SPUR Objectives

Vocabulary

1. a. Define *cylinder*. **the surface of a cylindric solid whose base is a circle**

   b. Define *prism*. **the surface of a cylindric solid whose base is a polygon**

In 2–5, refer to the prism at the right.

2. a. How many edges are there? **15**

   b. Name any two edges. **AB, CH**

3. a. How many vertices are there? **10**

   b. Name any two vertices. **E, F**

Samples are given for 2b, 3b, 4b.

4. a. How many faces are there? **7**

   b. Name two lateral faces. **AEJF, CDIH**

   c. Name faces in two parallel planes. **ABCDE, FGHIJ**

5. What type of prism is this? **pentagonal prism**

6. What is the difference between a 3-dimensional surface and a solid? **A surface is a boundary of a 3-dimensional figure, while a solid is the union of such a boundary and the region it encloses.**

Skills Objective A: Draw prisms and cylinders.

In 7–12, sketch the indicated surface. **Samples are given.**

7. a cube   8. a right cylinder   9. an oblique cylinder

---

10. a right rectangular prism   11. a right triangular prism   12. a regular hexagonal prism

Skills Objective D: Given appropriate lengths, calculate areas and lengths in prisms and cylinders.

13. Refer to the box at the right.

   a. Name all segments with length 14. **VR, US, XP, WQ**

   b. Find XV. **10 units**

   c. Find XR to the nearest tenth. **17.2 units**

14. Refer to the oblique cylinder at the right.

   a. Find its height. **12 units**

   b. Find the area of its base. **$16\pi \approx 50.2$ units^2**

Uses Objective H: Recognize prisms and cylinders in the real world.

In 15–18, tell which 3-dimensional figure most resembles the real-world object. Be as specific as you can.

15. the top story of the house pictured at the right **right triangular prism**

16. the front door of the house pictured at the right **right rectangular prism**

17. the cabinet pictured at the right **regular hexagonal prism**

18. the lamp shade pictured at the right **right cylinder**

LESSON MASTER 9-4 B — Questions on SPUR Objectives

Vocabulary

1. a. Define *cone*. **the surface of a conic solid whose base is a circle**

   b. Define *pyramid*. **the surface of a conic solid whose base is a polygon**

In 2–5, refer to the pyramid at the right.

2. a. Name its base. **QRSTUV**

   b. Name its vertex. **P**

3. a. Name its base edges. **QR, RS, ST, TU, UV, VQ**

   b. Name its lateral edges. **PQ, PR, PS, PT, PU, PV**

4. a. How many faces are there? **7**

   b. How many lateral faces are there? **6**

   c. Name any two lateral faces. **Sample: △PRS, △PST**

5. What type of pyramid is this? **hexagonal pyramid**

In 6–8, refer to the cone at the right.

6. a. Name its base. **⊙F**

   b. Name its vertex. **M**

7. a. Name a lateral edge. **MH, MN**

   b. Name its axis. **↔MF**

8. What type of cone is this? **oblique cone**

Skills Objective A: Draw pyramids and cones.

In 9–11, sketch the indicated surface. **Samples are given.**

9. a right cone   10. a right square pyramid   11. a truncated cone

Skills Objective D: Given appropriate lengths, calculate areas and lengths in pyramids and cones.

12. Refer to the regular triangular pyramid with base S at the right.

   a. Find the perimeter of its base. **18 units**

   b. Find its slant height. **≈ 9.5 units**

13. Refer to the truncated regular square pyramid at the right.

   a. What is the ratio of the lengths of the base edges? **$\frac{3}{5}$**

   b. What is the ratio of the areas of its bases? **$\frac{9}{25}$**

14. Refer to the cone at the right.

   a. Find its altitude. **≈ 16.0 units**

   b. Find the area of its base. **$529\pi \approx 1661.9$ un.^{2}**

Uses Objective H: Recognize pyramids and cones in the real world.

In 15–18, tell which 3-dimensional figure most resembles the real-world object. Be as specific as you can.

15. a teepee **right cone**

16. a soft-drink cup **truncated right cone**

17. Egyptian pyramid **regular square pyramid**

18. a cow bell **truncated rectangular pyramid**

LESSON MASTER 9-5 B — Questions on SPUR Objectives

Vocabulary

1. Define *sphere*.
the set of points in space at a certain distance from a point

2. Define *plane section*.
the intersection of a plane with a 3-dimensional figure

Skills Objective A: Draw spheres.
Objective B: Draw plane sections of common 3-dimensional shapes.

3. Use the sphere pictured at the right.   **Samples for 3b, 3c, 3d**
   a. Draw and label Q, the center of the sphere.
   b. Draw and label $\overline{QR}$, a radius not in $\odot Q$.
   c. Draw and label $\odot G$, a great circle different from $\odot Q$.
   d. Draw and label $\odot S$, a small circle.

In 4–6, sketch the plane section and describe its shape.

4. parallel to the base of a regular pentagonal prism
reg. pentagon

5. neither parallel to nor intersecting the bases of an oblique cylinder
ellipse

6. perpendicular to the base of a right cone but not through the vertex
(1 branch) hyperbola

Skills Objective D: Given appropriate lengths, calculate areas and lengths in spheres.

7. The diameter of a sphere is 16 in. What is the area of a great circle of the sphere?
$64\pi \approx 201.1$ in.^{2}

▶ LESSON MASTER 9-5B page 2

8. Refer to the right prism pictured at the right. A plane section is formed when a plane cuts through the prism and is parallel to the bases. What is the area of the plane section?
≈ 18.0 units^2

9. Refer to the cone pictured at the right. A plane section is formed when a plane cuts through the center of the base and is perpendicular to the base. What is the area of the plane section?
≈ 4848 units^2

Uses Objective H: Recognize 3-dimensional figures in the real world.

In 10–12, tell which 3-dimensional figure and what kind of plane section are most representative of the situation.

10. cutting a tomato in half
sphere; circle

11. cutting off a piece of pipe
right cylinder; circle

12. making an oblique cut through a pencil
regular hexagonal prism; non-regular hexagon or right cylinder; ellipse

Review Objective A, Lesson 6-1

In 13–18, draw the symmetry line(s), if any, for the figure.

13.

14.

15.

16.

17.

18.

LESSON MASTER 9-6 B — Questions on SPUR Objectives

Vocabulary

1. Define *reflection image in space*.
For a point P which is not on plane M, the reflection image of P over M is the point Q if and only if M is the $\perp$ bisector of $\overline{PQ}$. For a point P on plane M, the reflection image of P over M is P itself.

2. When are two 3-dimensional figures congruent?
When one is the image of the other under a reflection or a composite of reflections

3. When is a 3-dimensional figure reflection-symmetric?
When there is a plane M such that for figure F $r_M(F) = F$

Properties Objective G: Determine symmetry planes in 3-dimensional figures.

In 4–12, a 3-dimensional figure is given. a. Tell if the figure has bilateral symmetry. b. If so, give the number of symmetry planes.

4.
oblique cone
a. **yes**
b. **1**

5.
football
a. **yes**
b. **infinite number**

6.
mixing bowl
a. **yes**
b. **infinite number**

▶ LESSON MASTER 9-6B page 2

7.
regular pentagonal prism
a. **yes**
b. **6**

8.
triangular pyramid
a. **no**
b. **0**

9.
pliers
a. **no**
b. **0**

10.
bird
a. **yes**
b. **1**

11.
truncated right cone
a. **yes**
b. **infinite number**

12.
cube
a. **yes**
b. **9**

13. Draw a prism with exactly one plane of symmetry.
Sample:
right scalene triangular prism

14. Draw a pyramid with exactly four planes of symmetry.
Sample:
right square pyramid

15. Draw a real-world object with an infinite number of symmetry planes.
Sample:
flower pot

Name _____

LESSON MASTER **9-7** B
Questions on SPUR Objectives

Skills Objective C: Give views of a figure from the top, sides, or front.

In 1–4, a figure is given. Sketch views of the figure from the given direction. a. top b. front c. right side d. bottom

1.
right cylinder

a.   b.

c. d.

2.
stairs

a.   b.

c. d.

3.
truncated
square pyramid

a. b.

c. d.

4.
HISTORY
GEOMETRY
BIOLOGY II books

a. b.

c. d.

141 ▶

Name _____

▶ **LESSON MASTER 9-7B** page 2

Skills Objective E: From 2-dimensional views of a figure determine the 3-dimensional figure.

In 5–8, name a surface with the views shown.

5.
top   front   side
truncated right cone

6.
top   front   side
right cone

7.
top   front   side
right square pyramid

8.
top   front   side
right rectangular prism

9. A building is made of congruent prefabricated boxes. Three views of the building are given.

front   left side   top

a. How tall in stories is the building? **4 stories**

b. How long in sections is the building from front to back? **2 sections**

c. At the right, sketch a possible shape of the building.

Sample:

142

Name _____

LESSON MASTER **9-8** B
Questions on SPUR Objectives

Vocabulary

1. Define *polyhedron*.
   a 3-dimensional surface which is the union of polygonal regions and has no holes

2. Define *regular polyhedron*.
   a convex polyhedron in which all faces are congruent regular polygons and the same number of edges intersect at each vertex

3. List the regular polyhedra. For each one describe the faces and tell how many faces it has.
   tetrahedron, equilateral triangles, 4 faces
   cube, squares, 6 faces
   octahedron, equilateral triangles, 8 faces
   dodecahedron, regular pentagons, 12 faces
   icosahedron, equilateral triangles, 20 faces

Representations Objective J: Make a surface from a net and vice versa.

In 4–7, sketch the surface that can be made from each net.

4.

5.
$\frac{4}{3}d$

143 ▶

Name _____

▶ **LESSON MASTER 9-8B** page 2

6.

7.

8. Draw a net for a right cylinder whose height is equal to the diameter of a base.

Sample:

d πd d
d

9. Draw a net for a regular triangular prism.

Sample:

10. Draw two different nets for a cube.

Sample:

11. Draw a net for a regular tetrahedron.

Sample:

144

GEOMETRY © Scott, Foresman and Company

266

Name _____

LESSON MASTER 9-9 B

Questions on SPUR Objectives

Uses Objective I: Apply the Four-Color Theorem to maps.

1. a. State the *Four-Color Theorem*.

Suppose regions which share a border of some length must have different colors. Then any map of regions on a plane or sphere can be colored so that only four colors are needed.

b. In what year was the Four-Color Theorem proved?   **1976**

In 2 and 3, color each map using as few colors as possible.

Samples are given.

2.

3.

4. Draw a map with seven regions that can be colored with only <u>two</u> colors.

Sample:

5. Draw a map with seven regions that requires <u>four</u> colors to be colored.

Sample:

6. At the right is a map of some of the central states in the United States. Color it using the least number of colors.

145 ▶

Name _____

7. At the left is a map of Mexico and Central America. Color it using exactly three colors. Then label as many countries as you can.

Sample:

- Mexico
- Belize
- Honduras
- Nicaragua
- Guatemala
- El Salvador
- Panama
- Costa Rica

Representations Objective K: Interpret maps of the world.

8. How is a Mercator-projection map made?

by projecting the surface of the earth onto the lateral edge of a cylinder

9. a. Name a property that is not preserved on a Mercator-projection map.

distance, area

b. Name a property that is preserved on a Mercator-projection map.

collinearity, betweenness

10. Describe two problems with using a map of the world that is made up of gores.

Sample: Different parts of a country may be on different gores; the shape tears easily and is not convenient to use.

146

Name _____

LESSON MASTER 10-1 B

Questions on SPUR Objectives

Vocabulary

1. What is the difference between the *surface area* and the *lateral area* of a 3-dimensional figure?

Surface area is the total area of all surfaces of the figure, while lateral area is the total area of only the lateral surfaces.

Skills Objective A: Calculate lateral areas and surface areas of cylinders and prisms from appropriate lengths, and vice versa.

In 2–9, a figure is described. **a.** Give its lateral area.
b. Give its surface area.

2. a box with length 12 in., width 7 in., and height 8 in.

a. **304 in²**

b. **472 in²**

3. a right cylinder with base radius 5 cm and height 8.5 cm

a. **$85\pi \approx 267.0$ cm²**

b. **$135\pi \approx 424.1$ cm²**

4. a right pentagonal prism with base area 72 mm², base perimeter 32 mm, and height 35 mm

a. **1120 mm²**

b. **1264 mm²**

5. a right cylinder with base circumference 18π ft and height 10 ft

a. **$180\pi \approx 565.5$ ft²**

b. **$342\pi \approx 1074.4$ ft²**

6. a cube with edge 3 yd

a. **36 yd²**

b. **54 yd²**

7. a cube with edge *e*

a. **$4e^2$ units²**

b. **$6e^2$ units²**

8.

right cylinder

a. **$20\pi x^2 \approx 62.8x^2$ units²**

b. **$28\pi x^2 \approx 88.0x^2$ units²**

9.

right triangle prism

a. **600 in²**

b. **660 in²**

147 ▶

Name _____

In 10 and 11, a net for a 3-dimensional figure is shown. **a.** Give the lateral area of the figure.
b. Give the surface area of the figure.

10.

a. **$57\pi \approx 179.1$ in²**

b. **$75\pi \approx 235.6$ in²**

11.

a. **630 ft²**

b. **738 ft²**

Uses Objective H: Apply formulas for lateral and surface area of prisms and cylinders to real situations.

12. A section of concrete sewer pipe is 4 ft in diameter and 8 ft long. Find the lateral area of the pipe.

$32\pi \approx 100.5$ ft²

13. A wooden toy box measures .75 m by .6 m by .5 m. Find the surface area of the toy box.

2.25 m²

14. Refrigerated biscuit dough comes in a cylindrical can with diameter 2.5 in. and height 8 in. The bases are aluminum and the lateral face is cardboard.

a. How many square inches of aluminum are used?

$3.125\pi \approx 9.8$ in²

b. How many square inches of cardboard are used?

$20\pi \approx 62.8$ in²

15. Pipe organs often have large wooden pipes shaped like long, narrow boxes without bases. One of the largest organ pipes, in Liverpool Cathedral, England, is about 36 ft long, 2 ft 9 in. wide, and 3 ft 2 in. deep. Find its lateral area.

426 ft²

148

267

LESSON MASTER 10-2 B — Questions on SPUR Objectives

Skills Objective B: Calculate lateral areas and surface areas of pyramids and cones from appropriate, lengths, and vice versa.

In 1–8, a figure is described. a. Give its lateral area.
b. Give its surface area.

1. a regular square pyramid with slant height of 2 yd and base edge of 1 yd
   a. **4 yd²**
   b. **5 yd²**

2. a right cone with radius 6 cm and slant height of 9 cm
   a. **54π ≈ 169.6 cm²**
   b. **90π ≈ 282.7 cm²**

3. a regular square pyramid with slant height of 5 in. and base area of 49 in²
   a. **70 in²**
   b. **119 in²**

4. a right cone with circumference of base 14π ft and slant height of 8 ft
   a. **56π ≈ 175.9 ft²**
   b. **105π ≈ 329.9 ft²**

5. a regular square pyramid with slant height of t and base edge of u
   a. **2tu units²**
   b. **2tu + u² units²**

6. a right cone with radius j and slant height of $2j$
   a. **2πj² ≈ 6.3j² units²**
   b. **3πj² ≈ 9.4j² units²**

7.

regular triangular pyramid slant height 13, base edge 10, altitude of base 5√3
   a. **195 units²**
   b. **195 + 25√3 units²**

8.

right cone
   a. **16π√65 ≈ 405.3 un²**
   b. **(16√65 + 64)π ≈ 606.3 units²**

▶ LESSON MASTER 10-2B page 2

9. Find the lateral area of a regular hexagonal pyramid with a slant height of 9 and a base edge of 8. **216 units²**

10. The slant height of a regular square pyramid is 20 mm and its lateral area is 560 mm². What is the length of a base edge? **14 mm**

11. Pictured at the right are a right cone and regular square pyramid.

   a. Find the slant height of each. **10 units, 10 units**
   b. Find the lateral area of each. **60π units², 240 units²**
   c. What is the ratio of the lateral area of the cone to the lateral area of the pyramid? **π/4**
   d. Find the surface area of each. **96π units², 384 units²**
   e. What is the ratio of the surface area of the cone to the surface area of the pyramid? **π/4**

Uses Objective H: Apply formulas for lateral and surface area of pyramids and cones to real situations.

12. A paper weight is shaped like a regular square pyramid with a base edge of 8 cm and a height of 6.5 cm. Find its surface area. **≈ 168 cm²**

13. A clown's hat is in the shape of a right cone with a radius 3.5 in. and a height 10 in. Find its lateral area. **≈ 116 in²**

14. A watch crystal, shown at the right, is shaped like the lateral sides of a regular pyramid having a 12-sided base. If the slant height is 17 mm and the perimeter of the base is 96 mm, what is its lateral area? **816 mm²**

15. Paper covers for ice-cream cones are made of heavy paper. Cone A has a radius of 1 in. and a slant height of 4 in. Cone B has a radius of 1.25 in. and a slant height of 3.5 in. Which cone contains more paper? **cone B**

LESSON MASTER 10-3 B — Questions on SPUR Objectives

Vocabulary

1. A glass bottle is filled with sand.
   a. Is the volume of the bottle better represented by the amount of glass or the amount of sand? **sand**
   b. Is the surface area of the bottle better represented by the amount of glass or the amount of sand? **glass**

Skills Objective A: Calculate volumes of rectangular prisms from appropriate lengths, and vice versa.

In 2–7, give the volume of the boxes with the given dimensions.

2. 6 cm, 11 cm, 8 cm
   528 cm³

3. 2.4 in., 6 in., 6 in.
   86.4 in³

4. ⅔ yd, ½ yd, 2¾ yd
   11/12 yd³

5. 11 mm, 11 mm, 11 mm
   1331 mm³

6. x, $2x$, $3x$
   6x³ units³

7. 5 in., 5 ft, 5 yd
   54,000 in³

8. Refer to the boxes at the right.

   a. Find the surface area of each box.
   184 units², 184 units²
   b. Find the volume of each box.
   160 units³, 112 units³
   c. Study your answers in Parts a and b. What do you notice?
   Surface areas are equal, but volumes are not.

9. Refer to the boxes at the right.
   a. Find the surface area of each box.
   216 units², 300 units²
   b. Find the volume of each box.
   216 units³, 216 units³
   c. Study your answers in Parts a and b. What do you notice?
   Volumes are equal, but surface areas are not.

▶ LESSON MASTER 10-3B page 2

10. The volume of a box is 624 units³. Two of the dimensions are 6 units and 13 units. Find the third dimension. **8 units**

Skills Objective C: Calculate cube roots.

In 11–16, give the cube root of the number. Round inexact answers to the nearest tenth.

11. 512 **8**
12. 117.649 **4.9**
13. 7000 **19.1**
14. 0.14887 **.5**
15. 45 **3.6**
16. 100 **4.6**

17. Find the length of the edge of a cube whose volume is 4,096 m³. **16 m**

18. The volume of a cube is about 614 ft³. What is the area of a face, to the nearest tenth? **72.2 ft²**

Uses Objective I: Apply formulas for volumes of rectangular prisms to real situations.

19. A carton contains 16 ounces of cream. How many cubic inches is this? **≈ 29 in³**

20. Which holds more, a metal foot locker 26 in. by 14 in. by 12 in., or a carton 22 in. by 16 in. by 13 in.? **carton**

21. The inside dimensions of a freezer are 32 in. by 28 in. by 60 in. Find its volume in cubic feet. **≈ 31 ft³**

22. The dimensions of each brick at the right are 2 in., 3.5 in., and 8 in.

   a. Find the volume of a single brick. **56 in³**
   b. Find the total volume of the 2 steps shown. **16,128 in³**
   c. How many gallons of water would be displaced if the steps shown were built totally submerged into a pond? **≈ 70 gal.**

268

LESSON MASTER 10-4 B

Questions on SPUR Objectives

Properties Objective E: Determine what happens to the surface area and volume of a figure when its dimensions are multiplied by some number(s).

1. A box has a volume of 450 m³.

   a. If one dimension of the box is doubled, what is the volume of the larger box? **900 m³**

   b. If two dimensions of the box are doubled, what is the volume of the larger box? **1800 m³**

   c. If all three dimensions of the box are doubled, what is the volume of the larger box? **3600 m³**

2. A box has a volume of 200 ft³.

   a. If one dimension of the box is multiplied by 5, what is the volume of the larger box? **1000 ft³**

   b. If one dimension of the box is multiplied by 5 and another dimension is doubled, what is the volume of the larger box? **2000 ft³**

   c. If one dimension of the box is multiplied by 5, another dimension is doubled, and the third dimension is tripled, what is the volume of the larger box? **6000 ft³**

3. What happens to the volume of a box if all three dimensions are

   a. tripled? **It is multiplied by 27.**

   b. multiplied by 5? **It is multiplied by 125.**

   c. multiplied by $\frac{1}{2}$? **It is multiplied by $\frac{1}{8}$.**

   d. multiplied by k? **It is multiplied by k^3.**

4. A box has dimensions ℓ, w, and h. If the dimensions are changed as indicated, give the volume of the new box.

   a. Just the length is multiplied by 4. **$4\,\ell wh$**

   b. Its length is multiplied by 3, its width by 6, and its height by 10. **$180\,\ell wh$**

   c. Five is added to each dimension. **$(\ell + 5)(w + 5)(h + 5)$ or $\ell wh + 5wh + 5\ell h + 5\ell w + 25h + 25w + 25\ell + 125$**

▶ LESSON MASTER 10-4B page 2

Representations Objective J: Represent products of two (or three) numbers or expressions as areas of rectangles (or volumes of boxes), and vice versa.

In 5–10, a diagram is shown. a. Write the multiplication of polynomials represented by the diagram. b. Find the product of the polynomials.

5.

   a. **$(m + r)(m + n)$**

   b. **$m^2 + mn + mr + nr$**

6.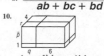

   a. **$(x + 4)(y + 2)$**

   b. **$xy + 2x + 4y + 8$**

7.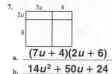

   a. **$(7u + 4)(2u + 6)$**

   b. **$14u^2 + 50u + 24$**

8.

   a. **$(a + b)(a + c + d)$**

   b. **$a^2 + ac + ad + ab + bc + bd$**

9.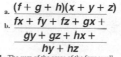

   a. **$(f + g + h)(x + y + z)$**

   b. **$fx + fy + fz + gx + gy + gz + hx + hy + hz$**

10.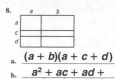

    a. **$(r + 4)(p + 1)(q + 6)$**

    b. **$rpq + rq + 4pq + 4q + 6rp + 6r + 24p + 24$**

11. The sum of the areas of the four small rectangles at the right is $x^2 + 7x + 6$. If the length of the largest rectangle is $x + 6$, what is the width? **$x + 1$**

12. a. Draw a diagram that models $(x + 2)(x + 7)$.

    b. Give the product. **$x^2 + 9x + 14$**

LESSON MASTER 10-5 B

Questions on SPUR Objectives

Skills Objective A: Calculate volumes of cylinders and prisms from appropriate length, and vice versa.

In 1–5, calculate the volume of the figure with the specified dimensions.

1. **$441\pi \approx$ 1385.4 units³**

2. **400 units³**

3. **$3025\pi \approx$ 9503.3 units³**

4. circumference 25π mm **$1250\pi \approx$ 3927.0 mm³**

5. **216 units³**

6. What is the area of the base of a prism that has a volume of 140 m³ and a height of 7 m? **20 m²**

7. What is the radius of a cylinder that has a volume of 108π ft³ and a height of 3 ft? **6 ft**

8. What is the volume of a regular hexagonal prism with a base area of $24\sqrt{3}$ cm² and a height of 12 cm? **$288\sqrt{3}$ cm³**

9. What is the length of a base edge of an oblique square prism with a height of 42 in. and a volume of 168 in³? **2 in.**

10. A square prism and a cylinder have the same height of 13 mm and the same volume of 832 mm³. Which is greater, the base edge of the prism or the diameter of the base of the cylinder? **diameter**

▶ LESSON MASTER 10-5B page 2

Properties Objective G: Know the conditions under which Cavalieri's Principle can be applied.

11. *Multiple choice.* List all of the rectangular prisms below that may be paired with the one at the right under Cavalieri's Principle. **a, b**

(a)   (b)   (c)   (d)

Uses Objective I: Apply formulas for volumes of prisms and cylinders to real situations.

12. In terms of volume, list the cans at the right in order from the smallest to largest. **II   I   III**

13. Find the volume of the flower tray at the right. Its end pieces are shaped like isosceles trapezoids. **2640 in³, or ≈ 1.5 ft³**

14. How many gallons of oil can be stored in a cylindric tank 8 feet long with a 5-foot diameter? (1 cubic foot = 7.5 gallons) **≈ 1178 gal.**

15. Find the total weight of 30 steel rods shaped like regular hexagonal prisms with 3-inch sides and 20 feet long. The density of steel is 490 pounds per cubic foot. **≈ 47,740 lb**

LESSON MASTER 10-6 B

Questions on SPUR Objectives

Properties Objective F: Develop formulas for specific figures from more general formulas.

1. a. What is the special formula for the volume of a cylinder?

   $V = \pi r^2 h$

   b. Explain how the formula in Part **a** was derived from the basic formula for the volume of a cylindric surface.

   Substitute πr^2 for B in the formula $V = Bh$.

2. a. What is the special formula for the surface area of a right cone?

   $S.A. = \pi r\ell + \pi r^2$

   b. Explain how the formula in Part **a** was derived from the basic formula for the lateral area of a right conical surface.

   Use $S.A. = L.A. + B$. For L.A., use $\frac{1}{2}\ell p$ and substitute $2\pi r$ for p and simplify. For B, substitute πr^2.

In 3–8, write a specific lateral-area formula for each figure.

3.

   right cylinder

   L.A. $= 2\pi rh$

4.

   regular triangular prism

   L.A. $= 3sh$

5.

   right square prism

   L.A. $= 4sh$

► **LESSON MASTER 10-6B** page 2

6.

   regular pentagonal pyramid

   L.A. $= \frac{5}{2}s\ell$

7.

   regular square pyramid

   L.A. $= 2s\ell$

8.

   cube

   L.A. $= 4e^2$

In 9–11, give a formula for each measure.

9.

   surface area of the right cone

   S.A. $= 3\pi kp + \pi k^2$

10.

    lateral area of right cylinder

    L.A. $= 4\pi m^2$

11.

    volume of right cylinder

    V $= \frac{\pi}{4}d^2h$

Review Objective A, Lesson 10-1; Objective B, Lesson 10-2

In 12–14, a figure is shown. a. Give its lateral area. b. Give its surface area.

12.

    right cylinder

    a. **180π ft²**

    b. **342π ft²**

13.

    regular square pyramid

    a. **260 units²**

    b. **360 units²**

14.

    right cone

    a. **32√13π units²**

    b. **32π(2+√13)units²**

LESSON MASTER 10-7 B

Questions on SPUR Objectives

Skills Objective B: Calculate volumes of pyramids and cones from appropriate lengths, and vice versa.

In 1–9, find the volume of the figure.

1.

   triangular pyramid

   200 units³

2.

   right cone

   324π ≈ 1017.9 units³

3.

   rectangular pyramid

   12,693$\frac{1}{3}$ ft³

4.

   right square pyramid

   $\frac{512}{3}$√33 units³

5.

   cone with circumference of base 36π

   2808π ≈ 8821.6 units³

6.

   octagonal pyramid with base area of 180

   540 units³

7.

   triangular pyramid

   294 mm³

8.

   trapezoidal pyramid

   216 units³

9.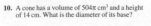

   right cone

   $\frac{4}{3}$π ≈ 4.2 in³

10. A cone has a volume of 504π cm³ and a height of 14 cm. What is the diameter of its base?

    12 cm

► **LESSON MASTER 10-7B** page 2

11. A square pyramid has a base edge of 8.2 m and a volume of 3362 m³. What is its height?

    150 m

12. A hexagonal pyramid has a height of 15 in. and a volume of 720√3 in³. What is the area of the base?

    144√3 in²

13. Pictured at the right is a square pyramid sitting on a box. What is the ratio of the volume of the pyramid to the volume of the box?

    1 to 3

Uses Objective I: Apply formulas for volumes of pyramids and cones to real situations.

14. Determine the volume of a cone-shaped coffee filter that has a diameter of 4 in. and a height of 4 in.

    $\frac{16}{3}$π ≈ 16.8 in³

15. Mr. Hong needs to calculate the volume of his garage to determine which exhaust fan he should buy. If the overall height of the garage is 17 ft, find the volume, ignoring wall and roof thicknesses.

    5390 ft³

16. A *wall pocket* is a vase that hangs on the wall. Find the volume of one that is half of a right cone with diameter 17 cm and height 22 cm.

    ≈ 832 cm³

17. What is the total volume of the silo pictured below?

    28 π ≈ 88 m³

18. Which of the candles pictured below contains more wax?

    II

270

LESSON MASTER 10-8 B — Questions on SPUR Objectives

Skills Objective D: Calculate the volume of a sphere from appropriate lengths, and vice versa.

1. Refer to the sphere and the cylinder containing two cones shown at the right.

   a. Inside the cylinder, shade the space that has the same volume as the sphere.

   b. Complete the following. Given a cylinder with radius r and height 2r containing two cones each with radius r and height r, the volume of a sphere with radius r is equal to the volume of __?__ minus the volume of __?__.

   the cylinder   **two cones**

In 2–4, draw the sphere with the given dimension. Then find its volume.

2. radius = 18 mm

   7776π ≈ 24,429.0 mm³

3. radius = 1.5 cm

   4.5π ≈ 14.1 cm³

4. diameter = 1 in.

   $\frac{1}{6}$π ≈ .5 in³

5. The radius of a sphere is 26 in.

   a. Find the volume of the sphere to the nearest cubic inch.

   73,622 in³

   b. Find the volume of the sphere to the nearest tenth of a cubic foot.

   42.6 ft³

6. The circumference of a great circle of a sphere is 28π cm. What is its volume?

   $\frac{10,976}{3}$π ≈ 11,494 cm³

In 7–10, give the radius of the sphere with the given volume. Round inexact answers to the nearest tenth.

7. $\frac{32}{3}$π cubic units

   2 units

8. 288π in³

   6 in.

9. 52 ft³

   2.3 ft

10. 1262 m³

   6.7 m

Properties Objective E: Determine what happens to the volume of a sphere when its dimensions are multiplied by some number(s).

11. Refer to the sphere at the right. What would happen to its volume

   a. if the radius were doubled?   **It is multiplied by 8.**

   b. if the radius were tripled?   **It is multiplied by 27.**

   c. if the radius were multiplied by ten?   **It is multiplied by 1000.**

   d. if the radius were halved?   **It is multiplied by $\frac{1}{8}$.**

   e. if the radius were multiplied by k?   **It is multiplied by k^3.**

Uses Objective I: Apply the formula for volume of a sphere to real situations.

12. Find the volume of each ball.

   a. tennis ball, 6.4 cm in diameter   **≈ 137 cm³**

   b. table-tennis ball, 3.8 cm in diameter   **≈ 29 cm³**

   c. baseball, 23.5 cm in circumference   **≈ 219 cm³**

13. How many ounces of water are displaced if 120 glass marbles are dropped into a 20-gallon aquarium, and the diameter of each marble is $\frac{1}{2}$ in.?   **≈ 4.35 oz.**

14. The diameter of an inflatable beach ball is 16 in. If a person blowing it up exhales 120 cubic inches of carbon dioxide with each breath, how many breaths will it take to fill the ball?   **≈ 18 breaths**

LESSON MASTER 10-9 B — Questions on SPUR Objectives

Skills Objective D: Calculate the surface area of a sphere from appropriate lengths, and vice versa.

1. Refer to the sphere with great circle G shown at the right. What is the ratio of the surface area of the sphere to the area of ⊙G?

   4 to 1

In 2–9, find the surface area of a sphere with the given dimension.

2. radius = 7

   196π ≈ 615.8 units²

3. radius = 18 mm

   1296π ≈ 4071.5 mm²

4. diameter = 38 cm

   1444π ≈ 4536.5 cm²

5. diameter = 5

   25π ≈ 78.5 units²

6. circumference of great circle = 16π ft

   256π ≈ 804.2 ft²

7. area of great circle ≈ 225π in³

   900π ≈ 2827.4 in²

8. volume = 972π cm³

   324π ≈ 1017.9 cm²

9. volume ≈ 11,500 cubic units

   ≈ 2463 units²

10. The radius of a sphere is 58 in.

   a. Find the surface area of the sphere to the nearest square inch.   **42,273 in²**

   b. Find the surface area of the sphere to the nearest tenth of a square foot.   **293.6 ft²**

11. The surface area of a sphere is 688 cm². What is its radius to the nearest tenth of a centimeter?   **7.4 cm**

Properties Objective E: Determine what happens to the surface area of a sphere when its dimensions are multiplied by some number(s).

12. Refer to the sphere at the right. What would happen to its surface area

   a. if the radius were doubled?   **It is multiplied by 4.**

   b. if the radius were tripled?   **It is multiplied by 9.**

   c. if the radius were multiplied by 10?   **It is multiplied by 100.**

   d. if the radius were halved?   **It is multiplied by $\frac{1}{4}$.**

   e. if the radius were multiplied by k?   **It is multiplied by k^2.**

Uses Objective I: Apply the formula for the surface area of a sphere to real situations.

13. Estimate the surface area of each planet to the nearest million square miles.

   a. Venus, radius ≈ 3750 miles   **177 million mi²**

   b. Mars, radius ≈ 2100 miles   **55 million mi²**

   c. Jupiter, radius ≈ 44,500 miles   **24,885 million mi²**

14. The diameter of a plastic beach ball is 18 in. It is made up of 12 gores, each a different color. How many square inches of plastic are used for each gore?   **≈ 85 in²**

15. The United States launched its first communications satellite, Echo I, in 1960. Find the area of the thin metal that coated this 100-foot diameter balloon.   **≈ 31,416 ft²**

Review Objective C, E, and H, Lessons 2-2 and 2-3

In 16–19 a conditional statement is given.   a. Tell if the conditional is true.   b. tell if its converse is true.

a = I am 16 years old today.   c = I am a teenager.

b = I cannot vote in the next year's   d = I will be 17 in a year.
national election.

16. a ⇒ b   a. **yes**   b. **no**

17. a ⇒ d   a. **yes**   b. **yes**

18. c ⇒ a   a. **no**   b. **yes**

19. b ⇒ c   a. **no**   b. **no**

Name _____

Properties Objective D: Follow the Law of Detachment and the Law of Transitivity to make conclusions.

In 1–5, use both mathematical statements. **a.** What (if anything) can you conclude? **b.** What law(s) of reasoning did you use?

1. (1) If the measure of an angle is between 0 and 90, then the angle is acute.
   (2) m∠X = 62
   a. **∠X is acute.**
   b. **Law of Detachment**

2. (1) If EFGH is a rhombus, it is also a parallelogram.
   (2) EFGH is a parallelogram.
   a. **no conclusion**
   b. _____

3. (1) If b = 12, then c = 20.
   (2) If a = 2b, then b = 12.
   a. **If a = 2b, then c = 20.**
   b. **Law of Transitivity**

4. (1) If Figure A is the image of Figure B under a reflection, Figure A is congruent to Figure B.
   (2) △WXY is the reflection image of △RST.
   a. **△WXY ≅ △RST**
   b. **Law of Detachment**

5. (1) If p > 0 and q > 0, then pq > 0.
   (2) pq > 0
   a. **no conclusion**
   b. _____

Name _____

6. Consider the statements below.
   (1) If a quadrilateral is a rectangle, then it has two lines of symmetry.
   (2) If a figure has two lines of symmetry, then it has rotation symmetry.
   (3) SYMT is a rectangle.
   a. Apply the Law of Transitivity to the first two statements and write a conclusion.
   If a quadrilateral is a rectangle, then it has rotation symmetry.
   b. Apply the Law of Detachment to statement 3 and the statement you wrote in Part a to write a conclusion.
   SYMT has rotation symmetry.

Properties Objective H: Apply the Law of Detachment and the Law of Transitivity in real situations.

In 7–10, using all the given statements, what (if anything) can you conclude?

7. (1) Marty drives to school whenever he has an early chemistry lab.
   (2) Marty has early chemistry labs every Wednesday.
   Marty drives to school every Wednesday.

8. (1) After basketball practice, Jennie goes to the Snack Shack.
   (2) Jennie went to the Snack Shack yesterday.
   no conclusion

9. (1) If Beatriz does well in her next recital, she'll get to be in the orchestra next year.
   (2) If Beatriz plays "Ode to Joy," she is sure to do well.
   (3) Beatriz will play "Ode to Joy."
   Beatriz will get to be in the orchestra next year.

10. (1) City Hall is closed on national holidays.
    (2) Building permits are issued only at City Hall.
    (3) Today is July 4.
    Building permits are not issued today.

Name _____

Properties Objective D: Follow the Law of the Contrapositive to make conclusions.

In 1–5, use both given statements. **a.** What (if anything) can you conclude? **b.** What law(s) of reasoning did you use?

1. (1) If a triangle is equilateral, then it is isosceles.
   (2) △ABC is not isosceles.
   a. **△ABC is not equilateral.**
   b. **Law of the Contrapositive**

2. (1) If Figure 1 is the reflection image of Figure 2, then Figure 1 does not have the same orientation as Figure 2.
   (2) J'K'L'M' has the same orientation as JKLM.
   a. **J'K'L'M' is not the reflection image of JKLM.**
   b. **Law of the Contrapositive**

3. (1) If the measure of an angle is greater than 90, then the angle is obtuse.
   (2) m∠C is not greater than 90.
   a. **no conclusion**
   b. _____

4. (1) If m = 15, then m² = 225.
   (2) m² = 225
   a. **no conclusion**
   b. _____

5. (1) The diagonals of a kite are perpendicular.
   (2) In QRST, QS ⊥ RT.
   a. **no conclusion**
   b. _____

6. Assume the statements below are all true. What final conclusion can you reach using all three statements?
   (1) r ⇒ i   (2) i ⇒ d   (3) not-d
   not-r

Name _____

7. What final conclusion can you reach using all three statements?
   (1) A reflection or composite of reflections is an isometry.
   (2) If a transformation is an isometry, then distance is preserved.
   (3) W is a transformation that does not preserve distance.
   W is not a reflection nor a composite of reflections.

Properties Objective E: Write the converse, inverse, or contrapositive of a conditional.

In 8 and 9, a statement is given. **a.** Write its converse. **b.** Write its inverse. **c.** Write its contrapositive. **d.** Assuming the original statement is true, which of a, b, and c are also true?   **Samples are given for 8a–8c and 9a–9c.**

8. If ∠X and ∠Y are vertical angles, then m∠X = m∠Y.
   a. **If m∠X = m∠Y, ∠X and ∠Y vertical ∠s.**
   b. **If ∠X and ∠Y not vertical ∠s, m∠X ≠ m∠Y.**
   c. **If m∠X ≠ m∠Y, ∠X and ∠Y not vertical ∠s.**
   d. **c (contrapositive)**

9. If you are a teen, you were born after 1975.
   a. **If you were born after '75, you are a teen.**
   b. **If not a teen, you were not born after '75.**
   c. **If not born after '75, you are not a teen.**
   d. **c (contrapositive)**

Properties Objective H: Apply the Law of the Contrapositive in real situations.

In 10 and 11, using both given statements, what (if anything) can you conclude using the laws of logic?

10. (1) If Joe does not get a scholarship, he will not attend Yale.
    (2) Joe will attend Yale.
    Joe will get a scholarship.

11. (1) Today I bought a leather purse.
    (2) If I don't get a raise, I won't buy a leather purse.
    I got a raise.

LESSON MASTER 11-3 B
Questions on SPUR Objectives

Properties Objective D: Follow the Law of Ruling Out Possibilities to make conclusions.

1. Explain the *Law of Ruling Out Possibilities*.
When one or the other of two statements is true, if one is not true the other is true.

In 2 and 3, what can you conclude from the given statements?

2. (1) $x > 19$ or $x \le 19$.
   (2) x is not greater than 19.
   $x \le 19$

3. (1) $\angle U$ is either right or obtuse.
   (2) $m\angle U \ne 90$
   $\angle U$ is obtuse.

In 4–6 use all the given statements. a. What (if anything) can you conclude? b. What law(s) of reasoning did you use?

4. (1) F is either a circle or a sphere.
   (2) A sphere is a 3-dimensional figure.
   (3) F is not a 3-dimensional figure.
   a. F is a circle.
   b. Laws of Contrap. and Ruling Out Poss.

5. (1) b is either even or odd.
   (2) An odd number has an odd square.
   (3) b^2 is not odd.
   a. b is even.
   b. Laws of Contrap. and Ruling Out Poss.

6. (1) N is either a rotation or a translation.
   (2) A rotation is the composite of two reflections over two intersecting lines.
   (3) The two lines of reflection defining transformation N do not intersect.
   a. N is a translation.
   b. Laws of Contrap. and Ruling Out Poss.

169 ▶

▶ **LESSON MASTER 11-3B** page 2

Properties Objective H: Apply the Law of Ruling Out Possibilities in real situations.

In 7–9, using all the given statements, what (if anything) can you conclude using the laws of logic?

7. (1) Mr. Harner gets either a 20% or a 30% discount.
   (2) 30% discounts are not given to store employees.
   (3) Mr. Harner is a store employee.
   Mr. Harner gets a 20% discount.

8. (1) Margaret is a freshman, a sophomore, a junior, or a senior.
   (2) Margaret's grade level does not begin with "s."
   (3) Freshmen may not take U.S. History.
   (4) Margaret is taking U.S. History.
   Margaret is a junior.

9. (1) Elena, Kiyoko, and Douglas are each taking a different science course: Chemistry, Physics, or Biology.
   (2) Kiyoko is not taking Chemistry.
   (3) Douglas is taking either Physics or Biology.
   Elena is taking Chemistry.

10. Make a grid using the clues below to determine who participates in what sport. Ajay, Maxine, Kenny, Lindsey, and Susan each play a different sport. The sports are basketball, soccer, tennis, baseball, and swimming.
    (1) Maxine does not play soccer.
    (2) Susan plays either tennis or she swims.
    (3) Ajay plays either basketball or tennis, or he swims.
    (4) Kenny does not play a sport with a ball.

Sample grid is given.

	Ajay	Lindsey	Susan	Maxine	Kenny		bskt-ball	soc.	ten.	bse-ball	swm.
basketball						A	O	X_3	X	X_3	X
soccer						M	X	X_1	X	O	X
tennis						K	X_4	X_4	X_4	X_4	O
baseball						L	X	O	X	X	X
swimming						S	X_2	X_2	O	X_2	X

170

LESSON MASTER 11-4 B
Questions on SPUR Objectives

Vocabulary

1. What is *direct reasoning*? Using given information known to be true, Laws of Detachment and Transitivity are used to reason from the information to a conclusion.

2. What is *indirect reasoning*? All possibilities other than the one thought to be true are ruled out.

3. What are *contradictory* statements? Statements that cannot both be true at the same time.

Properties Objective D: Follow the Law of Indirect Reasoning to make conclusions.

In 4–6, you are given two statements p and q. Are p and q contradictory? Explain your answer. **Samples are given.**

4. p: $\angle E$ and $\angle F$ are supplementary angles.
   q: $\angle E$ and $\angle F$ are vertical angles.
   No; $\angle E$ and $\angle F$ could be 90° vertical angles.

5. p: $\triangle RST$ is equiangular.
   q: $\triangle RST$ is scalene.
   Yes; if $m\angle R = m\angle S = m\angle T$, then $RS = ST = TR$; but a scalene triangle has no sides of equal length.

6. p: perimeter of square $ABCD = x$ units.
   q: area of square $ABCD = x$ square units.
   No; the length of the side of the square could be 4 units.

171 ▶

▶ **LESSON MASTER 11-4B** page 2

Properties Objective F: Write indirect proofs.

7. Use an indirect argument to prove that a right triangle *cannot* have an obtuse angle.
   Sample: Suppose in $\triangle ABC$, $m\angle A = 90$ and $m\angle B > 90$. Then $m\angle A + m\angle B + m\angle C > 180$, which contradicts the Triangle-Sum Theorem. Therefore, a right triangle cannot have an obtuse angle.

8. Use an indirect argument to prove that $\sqrt{7} \ne \frac{111}{42}$.
   Sample: Suppose $\sqrt{7} = \frac{111}{42}$. Then $7 = \left(\frac{111}{42}\right)^2$. But $= \left(\frac{111}{42}\right)^2 \approx 6.98$. Since $7 \ne 6.98$, $\sqrt{7} \ne \frac{111}{42}$.

9. Finish the proof with an indirect argument.
   Given: In acute triangle UOE, $\overleftrightarrow{DN}$ is the perpendicular bisector of $\overline{EO}$.
   To prove: $\overleftrightarrow{DN}$ is *not* parallel to $\overleftrightarrow{UO}$. **Sample:**
   If $\overleftrightarrow{DN} \parallel \overleftrightarrow{UO}$, $m\angle DNE = m\angle UOE$ because $\parallel$ lines $\Rightarrow$ corr. $\angle$s $\cong$. But $m\angle DNE = 90$, while $m\angle UOE < 90$ by definition. Thus, $\overleftrightarrow{DN}$ is not parallel to $\overleftrightarrow{UO}$.

Properties Objective H: Apply the Law of Indirect Reasoning in real situations.

10. Pam has three coins. They are either all the same, or all different. They may be pennies, nickels, dimes, and quarters. The sum of their values is an odd number. Use an indirect proof to show that Pam has *no* dimes.
    Sample: Suppose Pam has at least one dime. Then if all alike, the possible coins are 3 dimes whose value is even (30¢). If all different, the possible coins are: penny, nickel, dime—even (16¢); penny, dime, quarter—even (36¢); nickel, dime, quarter—even (40¢). Thus, Pam has no dimes.

172

273

Name _____

Properties Objective F: Write indirect proofs involving coordinates.

1. If $V = (-3, 0)$, $M = (0, -4)$, $T = (0, 3)$, and $J = (4, 0)$, use an indirect proof to show that $\overleftrightarrow{VM}$ is *not* parallel to $\overleftrightarrow{TJ}$. **Sample:**
If $\overleftrightarrow{VM} \parallel \overleftrightarrow{TJ}$, then slope of $\overleftrightarrow{VM} =$ slope of $\overleftrightarrow{TJ}$. Slope of $\overleftrightarrow{VM} = \frac{0+4}{-3-0} = -\frac{4}{3}$ and of $\overleftrightarrow{TJ} = \frac{3-0}{0-4} = -\frac{3}{4}$.
Since $-\frac{4}{3} \neq -\frac{3}{4}$, $\overleftrightarrow{VM}$ is not parallel to $\overleftrightarrow{TJ}$.

2. Let $A = (0, 4)$, $B = (6, 0)$, $C = (0, -4)$, and $D = (-6, 0)$. Use an indirect proof to show that $ABCD$ is *not* a square. **Sample:**
If $ABCD$ is a square, $\overline{AB} \perp \overline{BC}$ and slope of $\overline{AB}$ times slope of $\overline{BC} = -1$. Slope of $\overline{AB} = \frac{4-0}{0-6} = -\frac{2}{3}$ and of $\overline{BC} = \frac{0+4}{6-0} = \frac{2}{3}$.
Since $-\frac{2}{3} \cdot \frac{2}{3} \neq -1$, $ABCD$ is not a square.

Properties Objective G: Use coordinate geometry to deduce properties of figures and prove theorems.

3. Given $E = (1, 4)$, $F = (4, 3)$, $G = (-1, -3)$, and $H = (-4, -2)$.
   a. At the right, draw $EFGH$.
   b. Prove that $EFGH$ is a parallelogram. **Sample:**
Slope of $\overline{EF} = \frac{4-3}{1-4} = -\frac{1}{3}$ and of $\overline{GH} = \frac{-3+2}{-1+4} = -\frac{1}{3}$, so $\overline{EF} \parallel \overline{GH}$. Slope of $\overline{EH} = \frac{4+2}{1+4} = \frac{6}{5}$ and of $\overline{FG} = \frac{3+3}{4+1} = \frac{6}{5}$, so $\overline{EH} \parallel \overline{FG}$.
Therefore, by def. $EFGH$ is a parallelogram.

173 ►

Name _____

4. Given $Q = (-4, -4)$, $R = (-1, -5)$, and $S = (1, 1)$.
   a. At the right, draw $\triangle QRS$.
   b. Prove that $\triangle QRS$ is a right triangle. **Sample:**
Slope of $\overline{QR} = \frac{-4+5}{-4+1} = -\frac{1}{3}$ and of $\overline{RS} = \frac{-5-1}{-1-1} = 3$. Since $-\frac{1}{3} \cdot 3 = -1$, $\overline{QR} \perp \overline{RS}$ and $\angle R$ is a right angle. Thus $\triangle QRS$ is a right triangle.

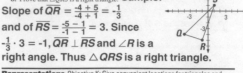

Representations Objective K: Give convenient locations for triangles and quadrilaterals in the coordinate plane.

In 5–8, draw the figure in a convenient location on the coordinate plane. **Samples are given.**

5. a rectangle
6. a kite

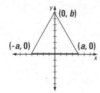

7. an isosceles triangle
8. a square

174

Name _____

Skills Objective A: Determine the length of a segment in the coordinate plane.

In 1–6, find the distance between the given points.

1. $(-6, 1)$ and $(4, 5)$ — $\sqrt{116} \approx 10.77$
2. $(7, 0)$ and $(2, 12)$ — 13
3. $(12, 0)$ and $(26, 0)$ — 14
4. $(-3, -8)$ and $(9, -1)$ — $\sqrt{193} \approx 13.89$
5. $(2.3, 6.1)$ and $(-1.4, 0.3)$ — $\sqrt{47.33} \approx 6.88$
6. $(32, -40)$, and $(51, -16)$ — $\sqrt{937} \approx 30.61$

7. What is the length of a diagonal of rectangle $FNET$ at the right?
$\sqrt{89} \approx 9.43$

$F = (-4, 4)$ $T = (1, 4)$
$N = (-4, -4)$ $E = (1, -4)$

Properties Objective F: Write indirect proofs involving the use of the Distance Formula.

8. Let $A = (-2, 5)$, $B = (3, 6)$, $C = (3, 0)$, and $D = (-2, -1)$.
   a. Draw $ABCD$ at the right.
   b. Use an indirect proof to show that $ABCD$ is *not* a rhombus.

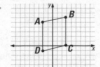

Sample: If $ABCD$ is a rhombus, then $AB = BC$. But $AB = \sqrt{(-2-3)^2 + (5-6)^2} = \sqrt{26}$ and $BC = \sqrt{(3-3)^2 + (6-0)^2} = \sqrt{36}$. Since $\sqrt{26} \neq \sqrt{36}$, $ABCD$ is not a rhombus.

175 ►

Name _____

9. Given $E = (7, 1)$, $F = (-3, 5)$, and $G = (4, 7)$. Use an indirect proof to show that E and F do *not* lie on the circle with center G. **Sample:**
Suppose E and F both lie on the circle with center G. Then $EG = FG$. But $EG = \sqrt{(7-4)^2 + (1-7)^2} = \sqrt{45}$ and $FG = \sqrt{(-3-4)^2 + (5-7)^2} = \sqrt{53}$.
Since $\sqrt{45} \neq \sqrt{53}$, E and F do not both lie on the circle with center G.

Properties Objective G: Use coordinate geometry to deduce properties of figures and prove theorems.

10. Given $GHJK$ as shown at the right. Prove that $GHJK$ is a kite. **Sample:** $GH = \sqrt{(-4-0)^2 + (0-4)^2} = \sqrt{32}$, $JH = \sqrt{(4-0)^2 + (0-4)^2} = \sqrt{32}$, $GK = \sqrt{(0+4)^2 + (2-0)^2} = \sqrt{20}$, and $JK = \sqrt{(4-0)^2 + (0-2)^2} = \sqrt{20}$. So, $GH = JH$ and $GK = JK$ and $GHJK$ is a kite by def.

Uses Objective I: Apply the Distance Formula in real situations.

11. Judd lives 4 blocks north and 6 blocks east of the water tower. Marta lives 2 blocks south and 7 blocks west of the water tower.
   a. Represent this situation on the grid at the right. **Sample is given.**
   b. Find the distance between Judd's and Marta's homes.
   $\sqrt{205} \approx 14.3$ blocks

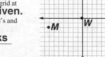

12. Mrs. Kurinsky's car phone works within a 75-mile radius of her office. She made a sales call 26 miles east and 58 miles south of her office. From there, she made a second call by driving 8 miles north and 17 miles west. Then she drove 14 miles west and 3 miles south for lunch at a restaurant. Could Mrs. Kurinsky use her car phone from the parking lot of the restaurant? Explain your answer.
Yes; she is about 53 miles from her office.

176

274

Name _____

Representations Objective J: Graph and write an equation for a circle given its center and radius, and vice versa.

In 1–10, write an equation for the circle satisfying the given conditions.

1.
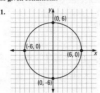

$$x^2 + y^2 = 36$$

2. center (-3, 2)
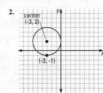

$$(x + 3)^2 + (y - 2)^2 = 9$$

3. radius 15, center (5, -3)
$$(x - 5)^2 + (y + 3)^2 = 225$$

4. radius 3.5, center (2, 0)
$$(x - 2)^2 + y^2 = 12.25$$

5. diameter 22, center (0, 0)
$$x^2 + y^2 = 121$$

6. radius 4, center (-1, -2.8)
$$(x + 1)^2 + (y + 2.8)^2 = 16$$

7. center (2, 5), containing (13, 5)
$$(x - 2)^2 + (y - 5)^2 = 121$$

8. center (-1, 6), containing (2, 1)
$$(x + 1)^2 + (y - 6)^2 = 34$$

9. radius r, center (18, -7)
$$(x - 18)^2 + (y + 7)^2 = r^2$$

10. radius 25, center (h, k)
$$(x - h)^2 + (y - k)^2 = 625$$

11. a. Draw the circle with radius 4 and center at (-2, -3).

b. Give two points on the circle.
Sample: (2, -3), (-2, 1)

c. What is an equation for this circle?
$$(x + 2)^2 + (y + 3)^2 = 16$$

177 ▶

Name _____

12. Which of these points are on the circle with center (-5, 4) and radius 13?   **A, B, C, D**

$A = (8, 4)$ $B = (0, 16)$ $C = (-18, 4)$
$D = (-17, -1)$ $E = (-13, 13)$ $F = (16, 0)$

In 13–18, an equation of a circle is given.   **Samples are given**
a. Determine its center. b. Determine its   **for 13c, 14c, 15c,**
radius. c. Find two points on the circle.   **16c, 17c, 18c.**

13. $(x - 4)^2 + (y - 2)^2 = 196$
a. **(4, 2)**
b. **14**
c. **(4, 16), (-10, 2)**

14. $(x - 8)^2 + (y + 2)^2 = 4$
a. **(8, -2)**
b. **2**
c. **(8, 0), (10, -2)**

15. $(x + 3.8)^2 + (y + 2.2)^2 = 2.89$
a. **(-3.8, -2.2)**
b. **1.7**
c. **(-3.8, -.5), (-2.1, -2.2)**

16. $x^2 + y^2 = 94$
a. **(0, 0)**
b. **$\sqrt{94}$**
c. **$(0, \sqrt{94}), (-\sqrt{94}, 0)$**

17. $x^2 + (y - 8)^2 = 18$
a. **(0, 8)**
b. **$3\sqrt{2}$**
c. **$(0, 8 + 0\sqrt{2}), (3\sqrt{2}, 8)$**

18. $(x + 19)^2 + y^2 = 1$
a. **(-19, 0)**
b. **1**
c. **(-19, 1), (-18, 0)**

Review Objective D, Lesson 2-4.

In 19–21, use the number line at the right.

19. Give the coordinate of the midpoint of each segment.
a. $\overline{AC}$ **-10**   b. $\overline{BD}$ **5**   c. $\overline{AB}$ **$-12\frac{1}{2}$**
d. $\overline{BC}$ **$-2\frac{1}{2}$**   e. $\overline{CD}$ **$7\frac{1}{2}$**   f. $\overline{AD}$ **$-2\frac{1}{2}$**

20. Give the coordinate of E if A is the midpoint of $\overline{BE}$.   **-35**

21. Give the coordinate of F if B is the midpoint of $\overline{DF}$.   **-25**

178

Name _____

Skills Objective A: Determine the coordinates of the midpoint of a segment in the coordinate plane.

In 1–8, determine the coordinates of the midpoint of the segment described.

1. endpoints (-8, 4) and (5, 5)   **(-1.5, 4.5)**
2. endpoints (0, 0) and (-10, -3)   **(-5, -1.5)**
3. endpoints (4, 9) and (19, 9)   **(11.5, 9)**
4. endpoints (2.8, 13) and (-6.6, -4.2)   **(-1.9, -8.6)**
5. $\overline{AB}$ at the right   **(-3, 2)**
6. $\overline{CD}$ at the right   **(0, 0)**
7. $\overline{EF}$ at the right   **(2.5, -.5)**
8. $\overline{FG}$ at the right   **(-4, -5.5)**

9. Find the midpoint of $\overline{PQ}$ given that $P = (-4, -4)$ and that Q is the midpoint of the segment with endpoints (-12, 9) and (6, 0).   **(-3.5, .25)**

Skills Objective B: Apply the Midpoint Connector Theorem.

10. a. In $\triangle XYZ$ at the right, D and E are midpoints of $\overline{XY}$ and $\overline{XZ}$, respectively. If $YZ = \frac{1}{2}$, find $\overline{DE}$.
$\frac{1}{4}$

b. What other relationship exists between $\overline{DE}$ and $\overline{YZ}$?   **$\overline{DE} \parallel \overline{YZ}$**

c. Name an angle congruent to $\angle XDE$. Justify your answer.
$\angle XYZ$; $\parallel$ lines $\Rightarrow$ corr. $\angle$s $\cong$.

179 ▶

Name _____

11. In $\triangle JKM$ at the right, P, Q, and R are midpoints of the sides, as shown. If $JK = 22$, and $PR = 17$, give all other segment lengths that can be found.
$JP = PK = RQ = 11$; $JM = 34$;
$JQ = QM = 17$

Properties Objective G: Use coordinate geometry to deduce properties of figures and prove theorems.

12. Use $ABCD$ pictured at the right. Give an indirect argument to prove that the diagonals of $ABCD$ do *not* bisect each other.
Sample: If the diagonals $\overline{AC}$ and $\overline{BD}$ bisect each other, then the midpoint of $\overline{AC}$ coincides with the midpoint of $\overline{BD}$. Midpoint of $\overline{AC}$ = (0, 0) and midpoint of $\overline{BD}$ = (1, 0). Since (0, 0) ≠ (1, 0), the diagonals of $ABCD$ do not bisect each other.

$A = (0, 4)$, $B = (6, 0)$, $D = (-4, 0)$, $C = (0, -4)$

13. Given $\triangle UVW$ at the right with M and N, the midpoints of $\overline{UW}$ and $\overline{UV}$, respectively. Without using the Midpoint Connector Theorem, prove each statement.
a. $\overline{MN} \parallel \overline{WV}$

$U = (-4, 8)$, $V = (10, 4)$, $W = (-3, -6)$

Sample: $M = (-3.5, 1)$ and $N = (3, 6)$. Slope of $\overline{MN}$ = $\frac{1 - 6}{-3.5 - 3} = \frac{10}{13}$ and of $\overline{WV} = \frac{-6 - 4}{-3 - 10} = \frac{10}{13}$. Since slope of $\overline{MN}$ = slope of $\overline{WV}$, $\overline{MN} \parallel \overline{WV}$.
b. $MN = \frac{1}{2} WV$

Sample: $MN = \sqrt{(-3.5 - 3)^2 + (1 - 6)^2} = \sqrt{67.25}$; $WV = \sqrt{(10 + 3)^2 + (4 + 6)^2} = \sqrt{269}$. $\sqrt{67.25} = \sqrt{67.25(\frac{4}{4})} = \frac{\sqrt{269}}{2}$, so $MN = \frac{1}{2} WV$.

180

275

LESSON MASTER 11-9 B

Vocabulary

1. Complete each statement.

a. Points in space can be located using a __?__ system.
3-dimensional coordinate

b. The three axes of the system in Part **a** are the **x-axis**,
the **y-axis**, and the **z-axis**.

c. (x, y, z), which specifies a point's position, is called __?__.
an ordered triple

Skills Objective C: Plot points, find distances between them, and find coordinates of midpoints in 3-dimensional space.

In 2 and 3, a pair of points is given. **a.** Plot the points.
b. Find the coordinates of the midpoint of the segment joining the points. **c.** Find the distance between the points.

2. $A = (5, 4, 2)$ and $B = (-3, -1, 7)$

a.

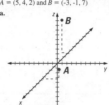

b. **(1, 1.5, 4.5)**

c. **$\sqrt{114} \approx 10.7$**

3. $P = (-6, 3, 0)$ and $Q = (4, -3, -2)$

a.

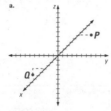

b. **(-1, 0, -1)**

c. **$\sqrt{140} \approx 11.8$**

Uses Objective I: Apply the Box Diagonal Formulas in real situations.

4. A gift box measures 15 cm by 20 cm by 70 cm. Will an umbrella 75 cm long fit in the box? Explain your answer.
No; the length of the diagonal of the box is
$\sqrt{15^2 + 20^2 + 70^2} \approx 74.3$ centimeters.

5. A foot locker measures 2.5 ft by 1.75 ft by 1.5 ft. Will a baseball bat 39 in. long fit in the locker? Explain your answer.
Yes; the length of the diagonal of the locker
is $\sqrt{2.5^2 + 1.75^2 + 1.5^2} \approx 3.40$ ft ≈ 40.8 in.

Representations Objective J: Graph and write an equation for a sphere given its center and radius, and vice versa.

6. A sphere has the equation
$(x + 2)^2 + (y + 4)^2 + (z - 3)^2 = 25$.

a. What is the center of the sphere? **(-2, -4, 3)**

b. What is the radius of the sphere? **5**

c. Give two points on the sphere.
Samples: (-7, -4, 3),
(3, -4, -3)

d. Graph the sphere at the right.

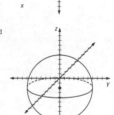

7. Write an equation for the sphere graphed at the right with center (0, 0, -2).
$x^2 + y^2 + (z + 2)^2 = 49$

(0, 0, -9)

LESSON MASTER 12-1 B

Representations Objective G: Perform and analyze size transformations on figures in the coordinate plane.

1. Let $Q = (-3, 4)$, $R = (1, 3)$, $S = (2, -2)$, and $T = (-2, -3)$.

a. Graph $QRST$ at the right.

b. Give the coordinates of Q', R', S', and T', where $Q'R'S'T'$ is the image of $QRST$ under S_2.
$Q' = (-6, 8)$, $R' = (2, 6)$,
$S' = (4, -4)$, $T' = (-4, -6)$

c. Graph $Q'R'S'T'$.

d. What is a relationship between QR and $Q'R'$? **$Q'R' = 2QR$**

e. How are $\overline{QR}$ and $\overline{Q'R'}$ related? **$\overline{QR} \parallel \overline{Q'R'}$**

2. Let $A = (8, -2)$, $B = (0, 0)$, and $C = (-2, 8)$.

a. Graph $\triangle ABC$ at the right.

b. Give the coordinates of A', B', and C', where $\triangle A'B'C' = S_{.75}(\triangle ABC)$.
$A' = (6, -1.5)$, $B' = (0, 0)$
$C' = (-1.5, 6)$

c. Graph $\triangle A'B'C'$.

d. What is a relationship between AC and $A'C'$? **$A'C' = .75AC$**

e. How are $\overline{BC}$ and $\overline{B'C'}$ related? **$\overline{BC} \parallel \overline{B'C'}$**
(or $\overline{BC}$ contains $\overline{B'C'}$)

---

3. Let $H = (-2, -4)$, $K = (1, 3)$, and $W = (4, -4)$, and let $S_{2.5}(\triangle HKW) = H'K'W'$.

a. Give the coordinates of H', K', and W'.
$H' = (-5, -10)$, $K' = (2.5, 7.5)$, $W' = (10, -10)$

b. What is a relationship between HW and $H'W'$? **$H'W' = 2.5 \cdot HW$**

c. Use the Distance Formula to verify your answer to Part **b**.
$HW = \sqrt{(-2-4)^2 + (-4+4)^2} = \sqrt{36} = 6$; $H'W' =$
$\sqrt{(-5-10)^2 + (-10+10)^2} = \sqrt{225} = 15 = 2.5 \cdot HW$

d. How are $\overline{KW}$ and $\overline{K'W'}$ related? **$\overline{KW} \parallel \overline{K'W'}$**

e. Use slopes to verify your answer to Part **d**.
slope of $\overline{KW} = \frac{3+4}{1-4} = -\frac{7}{3}$; slope of $\overline{K'W'} =$
$\frac{7.5 + 10}{2.5 - 10} = -\frac{7}{3}$

f. What is the image of (m, n) under $S_{2.5}$? **$(2.5m, 2.5n)$**

4. Let $E = (a, b)$ and $F = (p, q)$, and let $S_k(EF) = E'F'$.

a. Give the coordinates of $E' = S_k(E)$ and $F' = S_k(F)$.
$E' = (ka, kb)$; $F' = (kp, kq)$

b. How do EF and $E'F'$ compare? **$E'F' = k \cdot EF$**

c. Use the Distance Formula to verify your answer to Part **b**.
$EF = \sqrt{(a - p)^2 + (b - q)^2}$;
$E'F' = \sqrt{(ka - kp)^2 + (kb - kq)^2} =$
$\sqrt{k^2(a - p)^2 + k^2(b - q)^2} = k \cdot EF$

d. How are $\overline{EF}$ and $\overline{E'F'}$ related? **$\overline{EF} \parallel \overline{E'F'}$**

e. Use slopes to verify your answer in Part **d**.
slope of $\overline{EF} = \frac{b - q}{a - p}$; slope of $\overline{E'F'} =$
$\frac{kb - kq}{ka - kp} = \frac{k(b - q)}{k(a - p)} = \frac{b - q}{a - p}$

LESSON MASTER 12-2 B

Questions on SPUR Objectives

Vocabulary

1. Define *size transformation*. **Let O be a point and k be a positive real number. For any point P, let $S(P) = P'$ be the point on $\overrightarrow{OP}$ with $OP' = k \cdot OP$. Then S is the size transformation with center O and magnitude, or size-change factor, k.**

2. When is a size transformation

   a. an expansion? **when $k > 0$**

   b. a contraction? **when $0 < k < 1$**

   c. the identity transformation? **when $k = 1$**

Skills Objective A: Draw size-transformation images of figures.

In 3–6, draw the image of the figure under a size transformation with the designated magnitude and center.

3. magnitude .25, center C

4. magnitude 3, center R

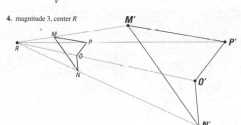

▶ **LESSON MASTER 12-2B** *page 2*

5. magnitude 1.5, center H

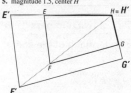

6. magnitude $\frac{3}{5}$, center E

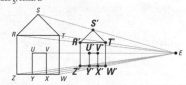

Properties Objective C: Recognize and apply properties of size transformations.

7. At the right, the dashed figure is the image of the solid one under a size transformation S. Use a ruler to locate the center C and determine the magnitude of S.

   $k \approx 1.7$

8. $\triangle A'B'C'$ is a size change image of $\triangle ABC$.

   a. Is the size change a contraction or an expansion?

   contraction

   b. If $AC = 40$ and $A'C' = 24$, what is the magnitude of the size change?

   .6

   c. Use the value in Part **b** to find AB if $A'B' = 21$. **35**

LESSON MASTER 12-3 B

Questions on SPUR Objectives

Skills Objective A: Draw size-transformation images of figures.

In 1–3, draw the image of the figure under a size transformation with the designated magnitude and center.

1. $k = 2.5$, center Z

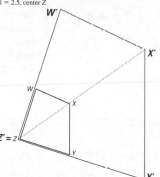

2. $k = .75$, center G

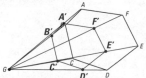

▶ **LESSON MASTER 12-3B** *page 2*

Properties Objective C: Recognize and apply properties of size transformations.

3. Give three properties preserved by size transformations.
   Sample: angle measure, betweenness, collinearity

4. Give a property that is *not* preserved by all size transformations.
   distance

5. At the right, $HUGE$ is the image of $TINY$ under a size transformation with center C. $UH = 18$, $IT = 12$, $IC = 9$, and m$\angle HEG = 144$. Find each of the following.

   a. the magnitude of the size change **1.5**

   b. UI **4.5**

   c. m$\angle TYN$ **144**

6. At the right, $S(\triangle OAB) = \triangle ODC$, $OD = 8$, $DA = 14$, $OB = 16.5$, and $AB = 11$. Find the lengths of as many other segments as you can.
   $OA = 22$, $OC = 6$, $DC = 4$
   $CB = 10.5$

7. Anita designed a campaign sign on her computer and printed it out on a sheet of paper 8.5 in. wide. She took it to a copy store to be made into a poster 18 in. wide.

   a. Find the size change factor of the enlargement. **≈ 2.1**

   b. The lettering on the sign Anita printed is .75 in. tall. About how tall is it on the poster? **≈ 1.6 in.**

   c. If Anita's sign is 11 in. long, what is the minimum length the poster can be so that nothing from the original sign is cut off? **≈ 23.3 in.**

Name _____

LESSON MASTER 12-4 B

Questions on SPUR Objectives

Vocabulary

1. a. What is a *ratio*? **a quotient of two numbers $\frac{m}{n}$, or m/n, where m and n are quantities of the same kind**

b. Give three examples of ratios. **Samples: $\frac{6 \text{ in.}}{7 \text{ in.}}$, $\frac{3 \text{ lb.}}{4 \text{ lb}}$, $\frac{48,000 \text{ people}}{2,000 \text{ people}}$**

2. a. What is a *proportion*? **a statement that two quotients, or ratios, are equal**

b. Give three examples of proportions. **Samples: $\frac{AB}{CD} = \frac{WX}{YZ}$, $\frac{9}{10} = \frac{12}{x}$, $\frac{6m}{DC} = \frac{4}{5}$**

c. Write a proportion and label its means and its extremes. **Sample: $\underset{\text{mean}}{\overset{\text{extreme}}{\frac{a}{b}}} = \underset{\text{extreme}}{\overset{\text{mean}}{\frac{c}{d}}}$**

Skills Objective B: Use proportions to find missing parts in similar figures.

3. $\triangle AWD$ is the image of $\triangle UPO$ under a size change. Write three equal ratios involving the sides of these triangles. **$\frac{AW}{UP} = \frac{AD}{UO} = \frac{WD}{PO}$**

In 4 and 5, $\triangle MGT$ is the image of $\triangle VRS$ under a size change.

4. If $MG = 14$, $VR = 10$, and $MT = 21$, find VS. **15**

5. *Multiple choice.* Which equation is a proportion? **c**

   (a) $\frac{GT}{RS} = \frac{VS}{MT}$ (b) $\frac{MT}{GT} = \frac{VS}{VR}$

   (c) $\frac{GT}{RS} = \frac{MT}{VS}$ (d) $\frac{MT}{GT} = \frac{RS}{VR}$

189 ▶

Name _____

▶ **LESSON MASTER 12-4B** *page 2*

In 6 and 7, *UVWXYZ* is the image of *ABCDEF* under a size change.

6. If $XY = 20.4$, $FA = 42$, and $DE = 30.6$, find ZU. **$ZU = 28$**

7. If $WX = 30$, $VU = 44$, and $BA = 67.5$, what other segment length can you determine? Find that length. **CD; $CD \approx 46.0$**

Uses Objective E: Identify and determine proportional lengths and distances in real situations.

8. If 2.5 pounds of roast beef cost $9.98, what should 6 pounds of roast beef cost? **$23.95**

9. A computer printer prints 100 pages in 12 minutes. At that rate, how long would it take to print 750 pages? **90 min.**

10. If you read p pages in 10 hours, at that rate, how many pages can you read in s hours? **$\frac{ps}{10}$ pages**

11. A souvenir model of the Eiffel Tower in Paris is $\frac{1}{2000}$ the actual size. If the model is 15 cm tall, how many meters high is the Eiffel Tower? **300 meters**

12. The dilution rate for plant fertilizer is 1.5 oz of fertilizer to each 32 oz of water. How much water should be used for the full 24-oz bottle of fertilizer? **512 oz, or 4 gal**

Review Objective D, Lesson 4-5, and Objective A, Lesson 12-2

13. At the right draw $r_k \circ r_j (\triangle ABC)$. Label the image $\triangle DEF$. Then draw $S_2(\triangle DEF)$ with center O. Label the image $\triangle GHI$. How do the lengths of the sides of $\triangle GHI$ compare to the lengths of the sides of $\triangle ABC$? **They are 2 times as long.**

190

Name _____

LESSON MASTER 12-5 B

Questions on SPUR Objectives

Vocabulary

1. Define *similar figures*. **Two figures are similar if and only if there is a composite of size changes and reflections mapping one onto the other.**

2. What is a *similarity transformation*? **a composite of size changes and reflections**

3. What is a *ratio of similitude*? **the ratio of a length of an image to a corresponding length of a similar preimage**

Skills Objective B: Use proportions to find missing parts in similar figures.

4. $\triangle XYZ$ is the image of $\triangle DEF$ under a similarity transformation. Find each of the following.

   a. YZ **$10\frac{2}{3}$**

   b. DF **15**

   c. another angle measure **$m\angle D = 40$**

   d. a ratio of similitude **$\frac{4}{3}$**

5. $QTSR \sim POMN$. Find as many missing lengths as possible. **$NM = 3\frac{1}{3}$, $OM = 5\frac{1}{3}$, $QR = 27$**

191

Name _____

▶ **LESSON MASTER 12-5B** *page 2*

6. $\triangle GYT \sim \triangle UFZ$, with the ratio of similitude 4.5, $FZ = 31.5$, and $GT = 5$.

   a. Find as many other segment lengths as possible. **$YT = 7$, $UZ = 22.5$**

   b. If $m\angle Y = 62$ and $m\angle Z = 40$, find as many other angle measures as possible. **$m\angle F = 62$, $m\angle T = 40$, $m\angle G = m\angle U = 78$**

7. Parallelograms $ABCD$ and $DEFG$ are similar.

   a. Complete the following. The ratio of similitude is __?__ or __?__. **$\frac{7}{10}$ $\frac{10}{7}$**

   b. Find BC. **21**

   c. Find $m\angle A$. **105**

Uses Objective E: Identify and determine proportional lengths and distances in real situations.

8. A slide measures 35 mm by 23 mm. The full picture is projected on a screen and measures 120 cm long. What is the width of the picture on the screen? **≈ 79 cm**

9. Lucy is 5 ft 5 in. tall and her little sister Gwen is 4 ft 2 in. tall. In a photograph of the two sisters, Lucy is 6.25 in. tall. How tall is Gwen in the photograph? **≈ 4.81 in.**

10. A scale model of the solar system shows Mercury 24 inches from the sun. The actual distance is about 36 million miles. Earth is about 93 million miles from the sun. In the model, how far should Earth be from the sun? **≈ 62 in.**

11. On the 2-in.-by-2-in. photograph of a United States passport, the size of a person's face from the chin to the top of the head must not be less than 1 in. nor greater than $1\frac{3}{8}$ in. If a person's face measures 3.5 in. in a photograph, by what range of scale factors must the photograph be reduced for use on a passport? **$\frac{2}{7}$ to $\frac{11}{28}$, or $\approx .29$ to $\approx .39$**

192

278

LESSON MASTER 12-6 B

Questions on SPUR Objectives

Properties Objective D: Use the Fundamental Theorem of Similarity to find lengths, perimeters, areas, and volumes in similar figures.

1. At the right, $ABCD \sim UVWX$.
   a. What is the ratio of similitude? $\dfrac{2}{3}$ or $\dfrac{3}{2}$
   b. What is the ratio of their perimeters? $\dfrac{2}{3}$ or $\dfrac{3}{2}$
   c. What is the ratio of their areas? $\dfrac{4}{9}$ or $\dfrac{9}{4}$

2. $EFGHIJ \sim ONMLKJ$ with a ratio of similitude of $\dfrac{2}{5}$. The area of $EFGHIJ$ is 32 square units and the perimeter of $OMNLKJ$ is 14 units.
   a. What is the area of $OMNLKJ$? **11.52 units²**
   b. What is the perimeter of $EFGHIJ$? $23\dfrac{1}{3}$ **units**

3. Two figures are similar with a ratio of similitude of 4.2.
   a. What is the ratio of corresponding lengths? $\dfrac{4.2}{1}$
   b. What is the ratio of their perimeters? $\dfrac{4.2}{1}$
   c. What is the ratio of their areas? $\dfrac{17.64}{1}$
   d. What is the ratio of their volumes? $\dfrac{74.088}{1}$
   e. What is the ratio of corresponding angle measures? $\dfrac{1}{1}$

193 ▶

▶ **LESSON MASTER 12-6B** page 2

4. Two quadrilaterals are similar and have perimeters of 33 cm and 13.2 cm. If the area of the larger quadrilateral is 61.5 cm², find the area of the smaller. **9.84 units²**

5. Two rectangles are similar. The width of the smaller one is 8 ft and the width of the larger is 10 ft. If the area of the larger rectangle is 660 ft², what is the length of the smaller rectangle? **52.8 ft**

6. Two right triangles are similar and have areas of 36 m² and 144 m². If the hypotenuse of the larger triangle is 30 m long, what is the length of the hypotenuse of the smaller triangle? **15 m**

Uses Objective F: Apply the Fundamental Theorem of Similarity in real situations.

7. A drawing was enlarged 250% on a copy machine. What is the ratio of the areas of the two drawings? $\dfrac{6.25}{1}$

8. A toy train set is 1.5% the size of the actual train. If the volume of the toy boxcar is about 12.3 in³, what is the volume of the actual boxcar? **≈ 3.6 million in³, or ≈ 2100 ft³**

9. Two solid busts of Beethoven are similar and made out of the same material. Their heights are 22 cm and 38 cm. If the smaller bust weighs 14 kg, what is the weight of the larger? **≈ 72 kg**

10. A parade featured a 7-meter-tall balloon of Perky Penguin. Plastic souvenirs, similar to the balloon, were 12 cm tall. If the surface area of the souvenir is 600 cm², what is the surface area of the large balloon? **≈ 2 million cm², or ≈ 200 m²**

11. The kites at the right are similar. Their areas are 1900 in² and 1372.75 in². If the longer brace of the larger kite is 4 ft 2 in. long, what is the length of the longer brace of the smaller kite? $42\dfrac{1}{2}$ **in. or 3 ft 6.5 in.**

194

LESSON MASTER 12-7 B

Questions on SPUR Objectives

Uses Objective F: Apply the Fundamental Theorem of Similarity in real situations.

In 1 and 2, consider Alice's assortment of size-changing pills from *Alice in Wonderland*. Suppose Alice is 5 ft tall, weighs 100 pounds, and drinks an 8-ounce glass of orange juice every day.

1. If Alice takes a pill that makes her 6 times as large,
   a. how tall would Alice be? **30 ft**
   b. how much would Alice weigh? **21,600 lb**
   c. how much orange juice would she drink every day? Give your answer to the nearest *gallon*. **13.5 gal**

2. If Alice takes a pill that makes her $\dfrac{1}{6}$ as large,
   a. how tall would Alice be? **10 in.**
   b. how much would Alice weigh? **≈ .46 lb, or 7.4 oz**
   c. how much orange juice would she drink every day? **≈ .04 oz**

3. Two similar American flags are 2 ft long and 6 ft long. If the area of the red fabric on the smaller flag is 124 in², what is the area of the red fabric on the larger one? **1116 in²**

4. If a 16-inch pizza costs $13.50, about how much should a 10-inch pizza cost? **$5.27**

5. If an 8-inch pizza serves 2 people, how many people can be served from a 16-inch pizza? **8 people**

6. Two similar storage sheds are 3.8 m and 5.6 m tall.
   a. If the materials for a new roof on the smaller one cost $850, what would the materials for a new roof on the larger one cost? **$1845.98**
   b. The exhaust fan for the larger one moves twice as much air per minute as the fan for the smaller one. Will it do as good a job ventilating the shed? Explain your answer.
   No; the volume of the larger shed is ≈ 3.2 times that of the smaller, so the fan should move ≈ 3.2 times as much air.

195 ▶

▶ **LESSON MASTER 12-7B** page 2

7. Gilberto made a solid model of a volcano out of papier-mâché. He used 8 sheets of newspaper for the papier-mâché. Now he wants to make a similar volcano twice as tall.
   a. How many sheets of newspaper will he need? **64 sheets**
   b. How will the area of the bases of the two volcanoes compare?
   Area of larger will be 4 times area of smaller.

8. Mr. Crane picked two pumpkins from his garden. They appeared to be similar in shape. The larger one weighed 16 pounds and the smaller weighed 2 pounds. What was the ratio of their diameters? **≈ $\dfrac{2}{1}$ or ≈ $\dfrac{1}{2}$**

9. Two aluminum cans are similar. The larger uses 1.8 times the aluminum as the smaller. If the larger holds 48 ounces, what is the capacity of the smaller? **≈ 19.9 oz**

10. The areas of two similar ice skating rinks are 1200 ft² and 1728 ft². The fence surrounding each is the same height. If it takes 9 gallons of paint to paint the fence around the smaller rink, how much paint is needed for the fence around the larger rink? **10.8 gal**

11. If it takes 1200 gallons to fill a cylindrical swimming pool, how much would it take to fill a similar swimming pool with double the radius? **9600 gal**

12. A wooden crate has a volume of 2 m³. By what factor should each dimension be multiplied to make a similar crate with a volume of 54 m³? **3**

Review Objective B, Lesson 12-5

13. $\triangle SDM \sim \triangle TGK$
   a. Write three equal ratios involving the sides of these triangles.
   $$\dfrac{SD}{TG} = \dfrac{DM}{GK} = \dfrac{SM}{TK}$$
   b. Write three equations involving angle measures.
   $m\angle S = m\angle T$ $m\angle D = m\angle G$ $m\angle M = m\angle K$

196

LESSON MASTER 13-1 B — Questions on SPUR Objectives

Vocabulary

1. State the *SSS Similarity Theorem*.

If three sides of one triangle are proportional to three sides of a second triangle, then the triangles are similar.

Properties Objective F: Determine whether or not triangles are similar using the SSS Similarity Theorem.

In 2–5, *true or false*.

2. Triangles with sides measuring 3, 5, and 7 and 6, 10, and 14 are similar. — **true**

3. Triangles with sides measuring 1.5, 1.5, and 3.5 and 6, 10, and 12 are similar. — **false**

4. Triangles with sides measuring 5 ft, 6 ft, and 7 ft and 6 ft, 5 ft, and 7 ft are similar. — **true**

5. Triangles with sides measuring 3 cm, 4 cm, and 5 cm and 6 m, 8 m, and 10 m are similar. — **true**

In 6–13, determine whether or not the triangles in each pair are similar. If so, write a similarity statement using the correct order of vertices. Justify your answer. **Samples are given.**

6.

$\triangle ABC \sim \triangle FDE$;
$\frac{2.4}{3.6} = \frac{1.8}{2.7} = \frac{2}{3}$

7.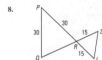

$\triangle XYZ \not\sim \triangle VZU$;
$\frac{6}{12} = \frac{4}{8} = \frac{1}{2}, \frac{4}{12} = \frac{1}{3} \neq \frac{1}{2}$

▶ LESSON MASTER 13-1B *page 2*

8.

$\triangle JKL \dotplus \triangle GKH$;
$\frac{4}{2} = \frac{3}{1.5} = \frac{2}{1}, \frac{2.1}{1.5} = \frac{7}{5} \neq \frac{2}{1}$

9.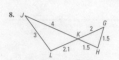

$\triangle PTR \sim \triangle PRA$;
$\frac{36}{27} = \frac{48}{36} = \frac{4}{3}$

10.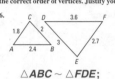

$\triangle NMO \sim \triangle QMP$;
$\frac{4}{8} = \frac{6}{12} = \frac{6.5}{13} = \frac{1}{2}$

11.

$\triangle OPQ \dotplus \triangle TSR$;
$\frac{21}{15} = \frac{35}{25} = \frac{7}{5}, \frac{26}{19} \neq \frac{7}{5}$

12.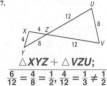

$\triangle EAD \sim \triangle CAB$;
$\frac{18}{36} = \frac{12}{24} = \frac{20}{40} = \frac{1}{2}$

13.

$\triangle FDE \sim \triangle FGH$;
$\frac{12}{8} = \frac{24}{16} = \frac{3x}{2x} = \frac{3}{2}$

Review Previous Course and Objective B, Lesson 12-4

14. Consider the proportion $\frac{12}{18} = \frac{72}{108}$.

a. Name the means. **18, 72**
b. Name the extremes. **12, 108**
c. Write three other proportions using these numbers. $\frac{18}{12} = \frac{108}{72}, \frac{108}{18} = \frac{72}{12}, \frac{12}{72} = \frac{18}{108}$

15. If $\frac{a}{b} = \frac{c}{d}$, give an instance of each case.

a. $\frac{a-b}{b} = \frac{c-d}{d}$ $\frac{1-8}{8} = \frac{24-16}{16} = \frac{1}{2}$
b. $\frac{a+b}{b} = \frac{c+d}{d}$ $\frac{12+8}{8} = \frac{24+16}{16} = \frac{5}{2}$

LESSON MASTER 13-2 B — Questions on SPUR Objectives

Vocabulary

1. State the *AA Similarity Theorem*. **If two angles of one triangle are congruent to two angles of another, then the triangles are similar.**

2. State the *SAS Similarity Theorem*. **If, in two triangles the ratios of two pairs of corresponding sides are equal and the included angles are congruent, then the triangles are similar.**

3. Explain why there is no ASA Similarity Theorem. **Sample: The AA Similarity Thm. renders side lengths irrelevant.**

Properties Objective F: Determine whether or not triangles are similar using the AA and SAS Similarity Theorems.

In 4–9, determine whether or not the triangles in each pair are similar. If so, write a similarity statement using the correct order of vertices. Justify your answer. **Samples are given.**

4.

$\triangle ABC \sim \triangle FED$; AA;
$\frac{CA}{DF} = \frac{CB}{DE}$, $m\angle C = m\angle D$, $m\angle F = m\angle A$

5.

$\triangle XYZ \dotplus \triangle UZV$; no AA, no SAS, no SSS

6.

$\triangle RSQ \sim \triangle PQR$; SAS;
$\frac{8}{20} = \frac{20}{50}$, $\angle PRQ \cong \angle RQS$

7.

$\triangle OLM \sim \triangle NMO$; AA;
$\angle LOM \cong \angle MNO$,
$\angle LMO \cong \angle MON$

▶ LESSON MASTER 13-2B *page 2*

8.

$\triangle QPR \dotplus \triangle STR$;
no AA, no SAS, no SSS

9.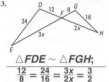

$\triangle ABC \sim \triangle ACD$; SAS;
$\frac{4}{8} = \frac{8}{16} = \frac{1}{2}$, $\angle BAC \cong \angle CAD$

10. At a ground distance of 1.5 miles from takeoff, a plane's altitude is 1000 yards. Assuming a constant angle of ascent, find the plane's altitude 5 miles from takeoff. **≈ 3333 yd**

11. Use the information in the diagram to find the width of the river. **80 m**
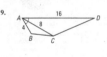

12. A man standing 5 meters from a 6-meter pole casts a 2.5-meter shadow, the tip of which aligns with the tip of the pole's shadow. How tall is the man? **2 m**

13. The diagram shows how an archaeologist can find the original height of a pyramid, even though its top has worn away. Find the original height of the pyramid. **160 m**

14. A tourist on the observation deck of an 800-foot building looks toward a 600-foot building which is one block away. Her car is parked two blocks beyond the shorter building. If no other building intervenes, can she see her car? **no**

15. The foot of a ladder is 1.2 m from a 1.8-m-high fence. The ladder touches the fence and rests against a building 1.8 m behind the fence.

a. Draw a diagram of the situation.
b. Determine how far up the building the top of the ladder can reach. **4.5 m**
c. How long is the ladder? **≈ 5.4 m**

LESSON MASTER 13-3 B

Questions on SPUR Objectives

Vocabulary

In 1 and 2, complete the *Side-Splitting Theorem* and its converse.

1. If a line is __?__ to a side of a triangle and intersects the other two sides in distinct points, it splits these sides into __?__ segments.

parallel   **proportional**

2. If a line intersects $\overline{OP}$ and $\overline{OQ}$ in distinct points X and Y so that $\frac{OX}{XP} = \frac{OY}{YQ}$, then $\overline{XY}$ is **parallel** to $\overline{PQ}$.

Sample:

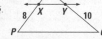

3. At the right, draw a picture of the situation in Question 2.

Skills Objective A: Find lengths in figures by applying the Side-Splitting Theorem and the Side-Splitting Converse Theorem.

4. Given $\triangle XYZ$ at the right, in which $RS \parallel YZ$, find each missing length.

   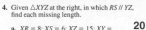

   a. $XR = 8; XS = 6; XZ = 15; XY =$ **20**

   b. $XS = 6; XR = 9; XY = 15; XZ =$ **10**

   c. $XS = 6; SZ = 4; XR = 8; RY =$ **$5\frac{1}{3}$**

   d. $XR = 6n; RY = 2n; XS = 9; SZ =$ **3**

5. In the diagram at the right, $h \parallel j \parallel k$. Find each missing length.

   a. $AC = 9; BC = 6; DF = 15; EF =$ **10**

   b. $AB = 4; BC = 13; EF = 39; DE =$ **12**

   c. $AB = 5y; DE = 2y; EF = 12; BC =$ **30**

6. Given $\triangle ADM$ at the right, in which $OP \parallel AD$, tell whether each statement is true.

   a. $\frac{x}{y} = \frac{z}{w}$ **yes**

   b. $\frac{x+y}{y} = \frac{z+w}{z}$ **no**

201 ▶

---

7. Name all pairs of parallel lines in the figure at the right.

$\overleftrightarrow{MP} \parallel \overleftrightarrow{LQ}, \overleftrightarrow{RN} \parallel \overleftrightarrow{QO}$

Uses Objective H: Use the Side-Splitting Theorem to find lengths and distances in real situations.

8. A half-mile ramp begins 2596 ft from a bridge. There is a support under a toll plaza which is located 1500 ft up the ramp.

   a. How far is the base of the support from the lower end of the ramp? **1475 ft**

   b. How high is the support? **≈ 273 ft**

9. Residents are to pay for new curbs in proportion to the footage their lots have on Latrobe. What part of the total cost must be paid by each resident?

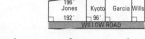

   Jones **$\frac{2}{5}$**   Kyoto **$\frac{1}{5}$**   Garcia **$\frac{3}{10}$**   Wills **$\frac{1}{10}$**

10. In the street map at the right, River Street is parallel to Lake Street and Pond Street. The intersection of River and State is 1200 ft from the intersection of Lake and State, and the intersection of Pond and State is another 800 ft. The intersection of Foster and Pond is 1000 ft from Foster and Lake. How far is it from Foster and Lake to the intersection of Foster and River?

   1500 ft

202

LESSON MASTER 13-4 B

Questions on SPUR Objectives

Vocabulary

In 1 and 2, given the positive numbers a and b,

1. define the *geometric mean*. **$g > 0$ such that $\frac{a}{g} = \frac{g}{b}$**

2. define the *arithmetic mean*. **$\frac{a+b}{2}$**

3. For the set $\{4, 9\}$, find the

   a. arithmetic mean. **6.5**   b. the geometric mean. **6**

4. State the *Right-Triangle Altitude Theorem*. **In a right $\triangle$, the altitude to the hypotenuse is the geometric mean of the segments into which it divides the hypotenuse, and each leg is the geometric mean of the hypotenuse and the segment of the hypotenuse adjacent to the leg.**

Skills Objective B: Calculate lengths using the Right-Triangle Altitude Theorem.

5. Given $\triangle MOP$ at the right, find each length.

   a. $MP = 3; MN = 12; MO =$ **6**

   b. $PN = 4; MN = 9; ON =$ **6**

   c. $PN = 28; PM = 7; OP =$ **14**

   d. $OP = 8; MP = NP; MN =$ **16**

6. Given the diagram at the right, find each length.

   a. $a = 30; c = 50; h =$ **24**

   b. $h = 12; m = 9; b =$ **20**

   c. $a = 24; m = 4; b =$ **≈ 142.0**

   d. $b = 8; m = 12; c =$ **16**

7. Find d in the diagram at the right.

   $d = 6\frac{2}{3}$

203 ▶

---

8. Use the diagram at the right to find each length.

   a. $a = 7\sqrt{5}; h = 14; c =$ **35** $; n =$ **28**

   b. $a = 6\sqrt{5}; b = 3\sqrt{5}; m =$ **12** $; n =$ **3**

Review Objective D, Lesson 5-7, and Objective D, Lesson 8-6

9. Find the sum of the measures of the angles in a 15-sided polygon. **2340**

10. Polygon $PQRSTU$ at the right is a regular hexagon. Give the measure of each angle.

   a. $m\angle OPQ$ **60**

   b. $m\angle ROT$ **120**

11. Polygon $ABCDEFGH$ at the right is a regular octagon. Give the measure of each angle.

   a. $m\angle ODE$ **67.5**

   b. $m\angle DOC$ **45**

In 12–15, find the missing length.

12.

   $8\sqrt{2} \approx 11.3$

13.

   12

14.

   10

15.

   4

204

281

LESSON MASTER 13-5 B
Questions on SPUR Objectives

Vocabulary

1. In the diagram at the right, **pentagon *ABCDE***
   is *inscribed* in ___**circle *O***___

In 2 and 3, complete the theorems.

2. According to the *Isosceles Right Triangle Theorem*, in an isosceles right triangle,
   if a leg is *x* then the hypotenuse is *x*√2.

3. The *30-60-90 Triangle Theorem* states that in a 30-60-90 triangle,
   if the shorter leg is *x* then the longer
   leg is *x*√3 and the hypotenuse is 2*x*.

Skills Objective C: Calculate lengths of sides in isosceles right triangles and in 30-60-90 triangles.

In 4–9, find the missing lengths.

4.

   $x = $ ___**12**___ ; $y = $ **12√3**

5.

   $x = $ **4√2** ; $y = $ **4√2**

6.

   $x = $ **3√3** ; $y = $ ___**6**___

7.

   $x = $ **2√3** ; $y = $ **2√6**

8.

   perimeter of square = ___**20**___

9.

   perimeter = **20 + 10√3**

▶ **LESSON MASTER 13-5B** *page 2*

9. A regular octagon's sides are extended to form a square as shown. Each side of the octagon is 3 units long. Find the length of a side of the square.
   3 + 3√2 units

10. How many 30-60-90 triangles can be drawn in a square with 6-cm sides, if the hypotenuse of each triangle is 6 cm? Draw a diagram to show how you would arrange the triangles.
    4 triangles   Samples:

Review Objective F and H, Lessons 13-1 and 13-2

In 11–14, tell whether or not the triangles are similar. If so, justify with a similarity theorem.

11.
    yes; SAS

12.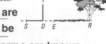
    yes; SAS or SSS

13. **no**

14. **yes; AA**

15. Explain how measuring the shadows $\overline{DS}$, cast by yardstick $\overline{YD}$, and $\overline{RE}$, cast by tree $\overline{TR}$, allows you to find the height of the tree.
    Sample:

    Assuming the sun's rays are
    parallel, $\frac{TR}{YD} = \frac{ER}{SD}$; *TR* can be
    determined as the other terms are known.

16. What measures are needed to find the distance from *A* to *B* across the lake?
    m∠COD, m∠BOA, CO, CD,
    BO

LESSON MASTER 13-6 B
Questions on SPUR Objectives

Skills

In 1–3, use the figure at the right.

1. Which side is adjacent to ∠*C*?   **$\overline{AC}$ or $\overline{BC}$**

2. Which side is opposite ∠*B*?   **$\overline{AC}$**

3. Which angle is opposite $\overline{AB}$?   **∠*C***

4. *Trigonometry* literally means   **angle measure**

Skills Objective D: Determine tangents of angles.

5. Consider △*ABC* at the right.

   a. Give tan *B*.   **$\frac{8}{12} = \frac{2}{3}$**

   b. Give tan *A*.   **$\frac{12}{8} = \frac{3}{2}$**

   c. From tan *B*, estimate m∠*B*.   **≈ 33.7**

   d. From tan *A*, estimate m∠*A*.   **≈ 56.3**

Skills Objective E: Estimate or determine exact values of the tangent ratio.

In 6–8, give exact values.

6. tan 30°   **$\frac{\sqrt{3}}{3}$**

7. tan 45°   **1**

8. tan 60°   **√3**

In 9–14, estimate to the nearest thousandth.

9. tan 40°   **.839**

10. tan 72°   **3.078**

11. tan 25°   **.466**

12. tan 58°   **1.600**

13. tan 33.24°   **.655**

14. tan 16.7°   **.300**

In 15 and 16, use △*KLM* at the right. a. Estimate the tangent of the given angle to the nearest hundredth.
b. Determine the measure of the angle.

15. a. tan *K*   **$\frac{1.75''}{2.5''}$**

    b. m∠*K*   **35**

16. a. tan *M*   **$\frac{2.5''}{1.75''}$**

    b. m∠*M*   **55**

▶ **LESSON MASTER 13-6B** *page 2*

Properties Objective G: Know the definition of tangent.

17. Use △*RST* at the right. Do *not* measure.

    a. Give the tangent of ∠*R*.   **$\frac{TS}{RS}$**

    b. $\frac{RS}{TS}$ is the tangent of which angle?   **∠*T***

    c. How is tan *R* affected if m∠*R* increases?   **tan *R* increases.**

Skills Objective I: Use tangents to determine unknown lengths in real situations.

18. How tall is Chicago's *Bat Column*, a sculpture by Claes Oldenburg, pictured at the right?
    ≈ 98 ft

19. How tall is the San Jacinto Monument, shown at the right?
    ≈ 407 ft

20. How tall is the Leaning Tower of Pisa, shown at the right?
    ≈ 61.5 m

21. How wide is the river below?
    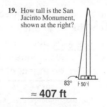
    ≈ 28.6 m

22. The angles of depression to the near and far banks of a river measure 49 and 11, respectively.

    a. Draw a picture of this situation.

    b. If the observer's eyes are 1.8m above the ground, how wide is the river?
    ≈ 7.7 m

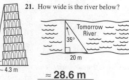
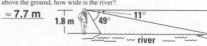

LESSON MASTER 13-7 B — Questions on SPUR Objectives

Skills Objective D: Determine sines and cosines of angles.

1. Use △ABC at the right.

a. Find BC. **10**

b. Find sin B. $\dfrac{3\sqrt{34}}{34}$

c. Find sin A. $\dfrac{5\sqrt{34}}{34}$

d. Find cos B. $\dfrac{5\sqrt{34}}{34}$ e. Find cos A. $\dfrac{3\sqrt{34}}{34}$

f. Estimate m∠B. **≈ 31**   g. Estimate m∠A. **≈ 59**

Skills Objective E: Estimate or determine exact values of sine and cosine ratios.

In 2–7, give exact values.

2. sin 30° $\dfrac{1}{2}$ 3. sin 45° $\dfrac{\sqrt{2}}{2}$ 4. sin 60° $\dfrac{\sqrt{3}}{2}$

5. cos 30° $\dfrac{\sqrt{3}}{2}$ 6. cos 45° $\dfrac{\sqrt{2}}{2}$ 7. cos 60° $\dfrac{1}{2}$

In 8–15, estimate to the nearest thousandth.

8. sin 40° **.643**   9. cos 40° **.766**

10. cos 65° **.423**   11. sin 83° **.993**

12. sin 47.8° **.741**   13. cos 56.1° **.558**

14. sin 70.5° **.943**   15. cos 29.6° **.869**

In 16–18, use △DEF at the right. Do *not* use a protractor.

16. Determine the approximate measure of each angle.

a. m∠D **40**   b. m∠F **50**

17. Calculate each sine to the nearest hundredth.

a. sin D **≈ .64**   b. sin F **≈ .76**

18. Calculate each cosine to the nearest hundredth.

a. cos D **≈ .76**   b. cos F **≈ .64**

▶ **LESSON MASTER 13-7B** *page 2*

Properties Objective G: Know the definitions of sine and cosine.

19. Define sin A.

Sample: Sin A is the ratio of the side opposite ∠A to the hypotenuse.

In 20–23, use △RST at the right.

20. Write a ratio for each function.

a. sin R $\dfrac{ST}{RT}$ b. cos R $\dfrac{RS}{RT}$

21. $\dfrac{RS}{RT}$ is the sine of which angle? **∠T**

22. $\dfrac{TS}{RT}$ is the cosine of which angle? **∠T**

23. How is sin R affected if m∠R increases? **s in R increases.**

Uses Objective I: Use sines and cosines to determine unknown lengths in real situations.

24. From a point at the foot of a hill, the angle of elevation of the top is 15°. The distance from the foot of the hill to the top is 150 meters. Find the height of the hill. **≈ 38.8 m**

25. A 30-foot ladder leans against a building making an angle of 72° with the ground.

a. How high on the building does the ladder reach? **≈ 28.5 ft**

b. How far from the building is the end of the ladder? **≈ 9.3 ft**

26. The tailgate of a tractor-trailer rig is 1 m off the ground. The greatest incline for efficiently loading the truck is 10°. How long should the ramp be for a 10° incline? **≈ 5.7 m**

27. A plane takes off at an angle of 24° with the ground.

a. How far has it traveled in a horizontal distance after it has traveled 3 miles? **≈ 2.74 mi**

b. How high, in feet, is the plane after it has traveled 3 miles? **≈ 6442 ft**

28. A biker pedaled up a slope of 6° for 150 meters and then another 100 meters at a slope of 9°.

a. How far did the biker travel in a horizontal distance? **≈ 248 m**

b. How far did the biker climb vertically? **≈ 31 m**

LESSON MASTER 13-8 B — Questions on SPUR Objectives

Skills Objective D: Use the SAS area formula.

In 1–4, find the area of the triangle.

1.   **≈ 6.52 units²**

2.  **.715 units²**

3. 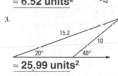 **≈ 25.99 units²**

4.  **≈ 65.96 units²**

5. Find the area of a regular pentagon with sides 8 centimeters long. **≈ 110 cm²**

6. Find the area of a regular decagon with sides 8 centimeters long. **≈ 492 cm²**

Uses Objective J: Determine components of vectors in real situations.

7. A hurricane is moving 30 mph in a direction 23° west of north. Find the components of its velocity. **W: 11.7 mph N: 27.6 mph**

8. An oil tanker traveled 32 knots (nautical miles) per hour on a course 38° north of west. Find the components of its velocity. **W: 25.2 kph N: 19.7 kph**

9. The Fox River flows at a rate of 5 kilometers per hour in a direction 80° south of east. Find components of the river's velocity. **E: .9 km/h S: 4.9 km/h**

10. A helicopter pilot wants to reach a point 3 km south and 6 km east of the takeoff location.

a. In which direction should the helicopter take off? **≈ 27° S of E or ≈ 63° E of S**

b. How far will the helicopter travel? **≈ 6.7 km**

▶ **LESSON MASTER 13-8B** *page 2*

11. A sailboat traveled 45 miles on a course 35° north of east and then traveled 60 miles on a course 75° north of east before the wind died down. Find the actual distance from its starting point that the boat lost its wind power. **≈ 99 mi**

Review Objectives D and I, Lesson 13-6 and 13-7

In 12–14, use △FGH at the right.

12. Find each trigonometric ratio.

a. tan F $\dfrac{GH}{FG}$ b. sin H $\dfrac{FG}{FH}$

c. cos H $\dfrac{GH}{FH}$ d. sin F $\dfrac{GH}{FH}$

13. How are sin H and cos F related? **sin H = cos F**

14. How is cos F affected if m∠F increases? **cos F decreases.**

15. The string of a kite forms an angle of 68° with the ground. If 250 m of string have been let out, how high is the kite? **≈ 232 ft**

16. A mine shaft forms a 15° angle with the ground and reaches a point 150 feet below the surface. How long is the shaft? **≈ 580 ft**

17. If the sun's rays make an angle of 70° with the ground, how long is the shadow of a person who is 180 cm tall? **≈ 65.5 cm**

18. From the top of a 100-foot lookout tower, a forest ranger spotted a fire at a 25° angle of depression. How far was the fire from the base of the lookout tower? **≈ 214 ft**

19. The angle of elevation from an observer on the roof of the Grande Hotel to the roof of the Rio Stock Exchange is a 10° angle. The buildings are 300 meters apart. How much taller is the Rio Stock Exchange than the Grande Hotel? **≈ 53 m**

20. A 90-foot escalator makes an angle of 18° with the lower level of a parking garage. How high does the escalator rise vertically? **≈ 28 ft**

21. A ladder mounted on a fire truck is 6 ft above the ground. If the maximum length of the ladder is 120 ft and the measure of the largest safe angle the ladder can make with the truck is 75°, how high will the ladder reach? **≈ 122 ft**

LESSON MASTER 14-1 B
Questions on SPUR Objectives

Vocabulary

1. Give the measure or range of measures for each arc.
   a. minor arc — between 0° and 180°
   b. major arc — between 180° and 360°
   c. semicircle — 180°

2. In the circle at the right, draw each of the following. **Samples are given.**
   a. an angle that intercepts JK
   b. the chord of JK

3. a. What is an *inscribed polygon*?
   a polygon whose vertices lie on a given circle

   b. Draw an inscribed pentagon in the circle at the right. **Sample:**

Skills Objective A: Calculate lengths of chords and arcs.

In 4–6, refer to ⊙U at the right. Find the indicated measure.

4. mDE   152°
5. UE   8.4 m
6. DE   ≈ 16.3 m

213 ►

In 7–11, use ⊙O at the right. a. Find the length of the chord of the indicated arc. b. Find the length of the indicated arc.

7. a 60° arc   a. 12′   b. 4π ≈ 12.6′
8. a 90° arc   a. ≈ 17.0′   b. 6π ≈ 18.8′
9. a 120° arc a. ≈ 20.8′   b. 8π ≈ 25.1′
10. a 42° arc a. ≈ 8.6′   b. 2.8π ≈ 8.8′
11. a 165° arc a. ≈ 23.8′   b. 11π ≈ 34.6′

12. Regular octagon ABCDEFGH is inscribed in circle Q, whose radius is 10 in. What is the perimeter of ABCDEFGH?
    ≈ 61.2 in.

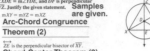

Properties Objective F: Make deductions from properties of radii and chords, and know sufficient conditions for radii to be perpendicular to them.

In 13–16, equilateral triangle XYZ is inscribed in ⊙D, m∠XDE = m∠YDE, and DF is perpendicular to YZ. Justify the given statement. **Samples are given.**

13. mXY = mYZ = mXZ
    Arc-Chord Congruence Theorem (2)

14. ZE is the perpendicular bisector of XY.
    Chord-Center Theorem (3)

15. YF = ZF
    Chord-Center Theorem (1)

16. XY ≅ YZ
    Arc-Chord Congruence Theorem (1)

214

LESSON MASTER 14-2 B
Questions on SPUR Objectives

Vocabulary

1. What is an *inscribed angle*?
   an angle whose vertex is on a circle and whose sides intersect the circle at points other than the vertex

Skills Objective B: Calculate measures of inscribed angles from measures of intercepted arcs and vice versa.
Objective C: Calculate measures of angles between chords from measures of intercepted arcs, and vice versa.

In 2–10, find the indicated measure.

2. m∠1 56
3. mUV 68°
4. m∠2 74

5. m∠3 90
6. m∠4 54
7. m∠5 40

8. mTQ 62°
9. mEF 102°
10. m∠6 45

215 ►

---

11. Find the measures of as many arcs and angles of the figure as you can.
    m∠SCO = m∠CSO = 31; m∠COM = 62; m∠MCO = m∠CMO = 59; m∠SCM = 90; mCS = 118°; mCM = 62°; mMCS = mMGS = 180°

12. Find the measures of the following arcs and angles of ⊙C.
    a. HR   114°
    b. m∠H   33
    c. m∠HCR   114
    d. JH   180°

Properties Objective G: Make deductions from properties of angles formed by chords.

13. Refer to the circle at the right.
    a. Find m∠R. n
    b. Justify your answer to Part a.
    Sample: By the Inscribed Angle Thm., m∠S = ½mPQ and m∠R = ½mPQ, so m∠R = m∠S = n.

14. The diagonals of quadrilateral ABCD are diameters of ⊙O. Explain why ABCD is a rectangle.
    Sample: Since the angles of ABCD are all inscribed in a semicircle, they are all right angles. By definition, ABCD is a rectangle.

216

LESSON MASTER 14-3 B
Questions on SPUR Objectives

Skills Objective D: Locate the center of a circle given sufficient information.

In 1 and 2, use the right-angle method to find the center O of the circle. **Samples are given.**

1.
2.

3. Use the perpendicular bisector method to find the center of the circle. **Sample:**

4. Use the perpendicular bisector method to find the center of the circle that contains this arc.
   Sample:

In 5 and 6, draw a circle through the three given points. **Samples are given.**

5.
6.

217 ►

In 7 and 8, draw a circle through the three vertices of the triangle.

7.
8.

Uses Objective I: Given the angle width of a lens and the width of an object, determine the set of points from which the object just fits in the picture.

9. A stage is 65 feet wide. A photographer, using a camera with a picture angle of 53°, wants to just fit the stage in a picture. How far back from the center of the front of the stage would the photographer need to stand?
   ≈ 65.2 ft

In 10–12, the top view of a ship, 1050 feet long, is shown. A photographer at sea wants to take a picture of this using a camera with an 84° field of vision.

10. Locate all points where the photographer's boat could be located to fit the ship exactly in the picture.

11. a. If the photographer wants to be directly in front of the middle of the ship, point M, how far from this point will the photographer need to be?
    ≈ 583 ft

    b. Locate this point P on the diagram. **Sample is given.**

12. Because of various obstacles, suppose the photographer can maneuver the boat no farther than 500 feet from the middle of the ship. The photographer has a variety of camera lenses. To fit the ship, what is the minimum size for the angle of vision on the lens?
    ≈ 93°

218

LESSON MASTER 14-4 B — Questions on SPUR Objectives

Vocabulary

1. What is a *secant*? **a line that intersects a circle in two points**

Skills Objective C: Calculate measures of angles between chords or secants from measures of intercepted arcs, and vice versa.

In 2–10, find the indicated measure.

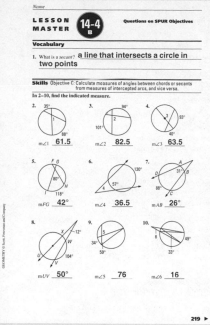

2. m∠1 **61.5**

3. m∠2 **82.5**

4. m∠3 **63.5**

5. mFG **42°**

6. m∠4 **36.5**

7. mAB **26°**

8. mUV **50°**

9. m∠5 **76**

10. m∠6 **16**

219 ▶

▶ **LESSON MASTER 14-4B** page 2

11. Find the measure of the indicated angle in the diagram at the right.

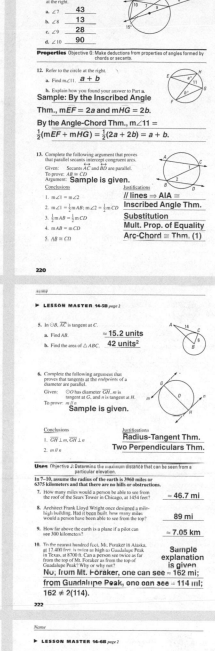

 a. ∠7 **43**
 b. ∠8 **13**
 c. ∠9 **28**
 d. ∠10 **90**

Properties Objective G: Make deductions from properties of angles formed by chords or secants.

12. Refer to the circle at the right.
 a. Find m∠11. **a + b**
 b. Explain how you found your answer to Part a.
 Sample: **By the Inscribed Angle Thm., mEF = 2a and mHG = 2b.**
 By the Angle-Chord Thm., m∠11 =
 $\frac{1}{2}(mEF + mHG) = \frac{1}{2}(2a + 2b) = a + b.$

13. Complete the following argument that proves that parallel secants intercept congruent arcs.
 Given: Secants $\overleftrightarrow{AC}$ and $\overleftrightarrow{BD}$ are parallel.
 To prove: $AB \cong CD$
 Argument: **Sample is given.**

Conclusions	Justifications
1. m∠1 = m∠2	**// lines ⇒ AIA ≅**
2. m∠1 = $\frac{1}{2}$m AB; m∠2 = $\frac{1}{2}$m CD	**Inscribed Angle Thm.**
3. $\frac{1}{2}$m AB = $\frac{1}{2}$m CD	**Substitution**
4. m AB = m CD	**Mult. Prop. of Equality**
5. AB ≅ CD	**Arc-Chord ≅ Thm. (1)**

220

LESSON MASTER 14-5 B — Questions on SPUR Objectives

Vocabulary

1. a. Define *tangent to a circle*. **a line in the circle's plane which intersects the circle in exactly one point**

 b. Define *tangent to a sphere*. **a line or a plane which intersects the sphere in exactly one point**

Properties Objective F: Make deductions from properties of radii and tangents, and know sufficient conditions for radii to be perpendicular to them.

In 2 and 3, complete the statement using the diagram at the right.

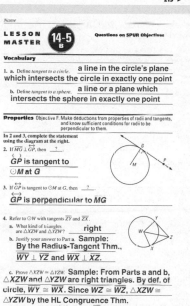

2. If $\overleftrightarrow{MG} \perp \overleftrightarrow{GP}$, then ___.
 GP is tangent to ⊙M at G

3. If $\overleftrightarrow{GP}$ is tangent to ⊙M at G, then ___.
 GP is perpendicular to MG

4. Refer to ⊙W with tangents $\overline{ZY}$ and $\overline{ZX}$.
 a. What kind of triangles are △XZW and △YZW? **right**
 b. Justify your answer to Part a. Sample:
 By the Radius-Tangent Thm., $\overline{WY} \perp \overline{YZ}$ and $\overline{WX} \perp \overline{XZ}$.

 c. Prove △XZW ≅ △YZW. **Sample: From Parts a and b, △XZW and △YZW are right triangles. By def. of circle, $\overline{WY} \cong \overline{WX}$. Since $\overline{WZ} \cong \overline{WZ}$, △XZW ≅ △YZW by the HL Congruence Thm.**

 d. What does Part c imply about $\overline{ZY}$ and $\overline{ZX}$? Why?
 Sample: $\overline{ZY} \cong \overline{ZX}$ because CPCFC.

221 ▶

▶ **LESSON MASTER 14-5B** page 2

5. In ⊙B, $\overline{AC}$ is tangent at C.
 a. Find AB. **≈ 15.2 units**
 b. Find the area of △ABC. **42 units²**

6. Complete the following argument that proves that tangents at the endpoints of a diameter are parallel.
 Given: ⊙O has diameter $\overline{GH}$, m is tangent at G, and n is tangent at H.
 To prove: m ∥ n
 Sample is given.

Conclusions	Justifications
1. $\overline{GH} \perp m$, $\overline{GH} \perp n$	**Radius-Tangent Thm.**
2. m ∥ n	**Two Perpendiculars Thm.**

Uses Objective J: Determine the maximum distance that can be seen from a particular elevation.

In 7–10, assume the radius of the earth is 3960 miles or 6375 kilometers and that there are no hills or obstructions.

7. How many miles would a person be able to see from the roof of the Sears Tower in Chicago, at 1454 feet? **≈ 46.7 mi**

8. Architect Frank Lloyd Wright once designed a mile-high building. Had it been built, how many miles would a person have been able to see from the top? **89 mi**

9. How far above the earth is a plane if a pilot can see 300 kilometers? **≈ 7.05 km**

10. To the nearest hundred feet, Mt. Foraker in Alaska, at 17,400 feet, is twice as high as Guadalupe Peak in Texas, at 8700 ft. Can a person see twice as far from the top of Mt. Foraker as from the top of Guadalupe Peak? Why or why not?
 Sample explanation is given. No; from Mt. Foraker, one can see ≈ 162 mi; from Guadalupe Peak, one can see ≈ 114 mi; 162 ≠ 2(114).

222

LESSON MASTER 14-6 B — Questions on SPUR Objectives

Skills Objective C: Calculate measures of angles between chords, secants, or tangents from measures of intercepted arcs, and vice versa.

In 1–9, find the indicated measure. You may assume tangents from the diagrams.

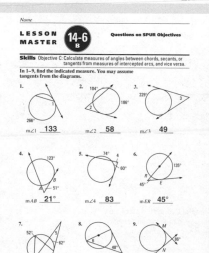

1. m∠1 **133**
2. m∠2 **58**
3. m∠3 **49**
4. mAB **21°**
5. m∠4 **83**
6. mER **45°**
7. m∠5 **21**
8. m∠6 **42**
9. mMN **94°**

223 ▶

▶ **LESSON MASTER 14-6B** page 2

In 10–19, refer to ⊙O at the right. $\overline{HS}$ and $\overline{HK}$ are tangents. Find the indicated measure.

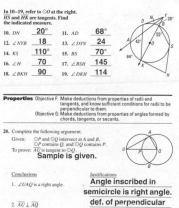

10. DN **20°**
11. AD **68°**
12. ∠NYB **18**
13. ∠DYN **24**
14. KS **110°**
15. BS **70°**
16. ∠H **70**
17. ∠BSH **145**
18. ∠BKH **90**
19. ∠DKH **114**

Properties Objective F: Make deductions from properties of radii and tangents, and know sufficient conditions for radii to be perpendicular to them.
Objective G: Make deductions from properties of angles formed by chords, tangents, or secants.

20. Complete the following argument.
 Given: ⊙P and ⊙Q intersect at A and B. ⊙P contains Q, and ⊙Q contains P.
 To prove: $\overline{AU}$ is tangent to ⊙Q.
 Sample is given.

Conclusions	Justifications
1. ∠UAQ is a right angle.	**Angle inscribed in semicircle is right angle.**
2. $\overline{AU} \perp \overline{AQ}$	**def. of perpendicular**
3. $\overline{AU}$ is tangent to ⊙Q.	**Radius-Tangent Thm.**

224

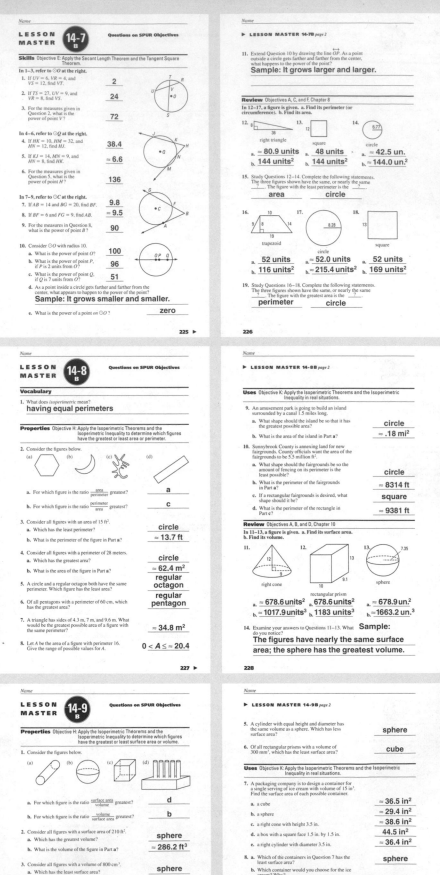

LESSON MASTER 14-7 B

Questions on SPUR Objectives

Skills Objective E: Apply the Secant Length Theorem and the Tangent Square Theorem.

In 1–3, refer to ⊙O at the right.

1. If $UV = 6$, $VR = 4$, and $VS = 12$, find VT. — **2**

2. If $TS = 27$, $UV = 9$, and $VR = 8$, find VS. — **24**

3. For the measures given in Question 2, what is the power of point V? — **72**

In 4–6, refer to ⊙Q at the right.

4. If $HK = 10$, $HM = 32$, and $HN = 12$, find HJ. — **38.4**

5. If $KJ = 14$, $MN = 9$, and $HN = 8$, find HK. — **≈ 6.6**

6. For the measures given in Question 5, what is the power of point H? — **136**

In 7–9, refer to ⊙C at the right.

7. If $AB = 14$ and $BG = 20$, find BF. — **9.8**

8. If $BF = 6$ and $FG = 9$, find AB. — **≈ 9.5**

9. For the measures in Question 8, what is the power of point B? — **90**

10. Consider ⊙O with radius 10.
    a. What is the power of point O? — **100**
    b. What is the power of point P, if P is 2 units from O? — **96**
    c. What is the power of point Q, if Q is 7 units from O? — **51**
    d. As a point inside a circle gets farther and farther from the center, what appears to happen to the power of the point?
    Sample: It grows smaller and smaller.
    e. What is the power of a point on ⊙O? — **zero**

225 ▶

▶ **LESSON MASTER 14-7B** page 2

11. Extend Question 10 by drawing the line $\overleftrightarrow{OP}$. As a point outside a circle gets farther and farther from the center, what happens to the power of the point?
Sample: It grows larger and larger.

Review Objectives A, C, and F, Chapter 8

In 12–17, a figure is given. a. Find its perimeter (or circumference). b. Find its area.

12. right triangle
    a. **≈ 80.9 units**
    b. **144 units²**

13. square
    a. **48 units**
    b. **144 units²**

14. circle
    a. **≈ 42.5 un.**
    b. **≈ 144.0 un.²**

15. Study Questions 12–14. Complete the following statements. The three figures shown have the same, or nearly the same ___?___. The figure with the least perimeter is the ___?___.
    area   **circle**

16. trapezoid
    a. **52 units**
    b. **116 units²**

17. circle
    a. **≈ 52.0 units**
    b. **≈ 215.4 units²**

18. square
    a. **52 units**
    b. **169 units²**

19. Study Questions 16–18. Complete the following statements. The three figures shown have the same, or nearly the same ___?___. The figure with the greatest area is the ___?___.
    perimeter   **circle**

226

LESSON MASTER 14-8 B

Questions on SPUR Objectives

Vocabulary

1. What does *isoperimetric* mean?
   having equal perimeters

Properties Objective H: Apply the Isoperimetric Theorems and the Isoperimetric Inequality to determine which figures have the greatest or least area or perimeter.

2. Consider the figures below.
   (a) (b) (c) (d)
   a. For which figure is the ratio $\frac{\text{area}}{\text{perimeter}}$ greatest? — **a**
   b. For which figure is the ratio $\frac{\text{perimeter}}{\text{area}}$ greatest? — **c**

3. Consider all figures with an area of 15 ft².
   a. Which has the least perimeter? — **circle**
   b. What is the perimeter of the figure in Part a? — **≈ 13.7 ft**

4. Consider all figures with a perimeter of 28 meters.
   a. Which has the greatest area? — **circle**
   b. What is the area of the figure in Part a? — **≈ 62.4 m²**

5. A circle and a regular octagon both have the same perimeter. Which figure has the least area? — **regular octagon**

6. Of all pentagons with a perimeter of 60 cm, which has the greatest area? — **regular pentagon**

7. A triangle has sides of 4.3 m, 7 m, and 9.6 m. What would be the greatest possible area of a figure with the same perimeter? — **≈ 34.8 m²**

8. Let A be the area of a figure with perimeter 16. Give the range of possible values for A. — **$0 < A \le ≈ 20.4$**

227 ▶

▶ **LESSON MASTER 14-8B** page 2

Uses Objective K: Apply the Isoperimetric Theorems and the Isoperimetric Inequality in real situations.

9. An amusement park is going to build an island surrounded by a canal 1.5 miles long.
   a. What shape should the island be so that it has the greatest possible area? — **circle**
   b. What is the area of the island in Part a? — **≈ .18 mi²**

10. Sunnybrook County is annexing land for new fairgrounds. County officials want the area of the fairgrounds to be 5.5 million ft².
   a. What shape should the fairgrounds be so the amount of fencing on its perimeter is the least possible? — **circle**
   b. What is the perimeter of the fairgrounds in Part a? — **≈ 8314 ft**
   c. If a rectangular fairgrounds is desired, what shape should it be? — **square**
   d. What is the perimeter of the rectangle in Part c? — **≈ 9381 ft**

Review Objectives A, B, and D, Chapter 10

In 11–13, a figure is given. a. Find its surface area. b. Find its volume.

11. right cone
    a. **≈ 678.6 units²**
    b. **≈ 1017.9 units³**

12. rectangular prism
    a. **≈ 678.6 units²**
    b. **1183 units³**

13. sphere
    a. **≈ 678.9 un.²**
    b. **≈ 1663.2 un.³**

14. Examine your answers to Questions 11–13. What do you notice? **Sample:**
The figures have nearly the same surface area; the sphere has the greatest volume.

228

LESSON MASTER 14-9 B

Questions on SPUR Objectives

Properties Objective H: Apply the Isoperimetric Theorems and the Isoperimetric Inequality to determine which figures have the greatest or least surface area or volume.

1. Consider the figures below.
   (a) (b) (c) (d)
   a. For which figure is the ratio $\frac{\text{surface area}}{\text{volume}}$ greatest? — **d**
   b. For which figure is the ratio $\frac{\text{volume}}{\text{surface area}}$ greatest? — **b**

2. Consider all figures with a surface area of 210 ft².
   a. Which has the greatest volume? — **sphere**
   b. What is the volume of the figure in Part a? — **≈ 286.2 ft³**

3. Consider all figures with a volume of 800 cm³.
   a. Which has the least surface area? — **sphere**
   b. What is the surface area of the figure in Part a? — **≈ 416.8 cm²**

4. a. What is the volume of the right square pyramid at the right? — **400 units³**
   b. What figure with the same volume has the least surface area? — **sphere**
   c. Find the surface area of the figure in Part b. — **≈ 262.5 units²**
   d. What is the surface area of the right square pyramid? — **360 units²**
   e. What figure with the same surface area has the greatest volume? — **sphere**
   f. Find the volume of the figure in Part e? — **≈ 642.3 units³**

229 ▶

▶ **LESSON MASTER 14-9B** page 2

5. A cylinder with equal height and diameter has the same volume as a sphere. Which has less surface area? — **sphere**

6. Of all rectangular prisms with a volume of 300 mm³, which has the least surface area? — **cube**

Uses Objective K: Apply the Isoperimetric Theorems and the Isoperimetric Inequality in real situations.

7. A packaging company is to design a container for a single serving of ice cream with volume of 15 in³. Find the surface area of each possible container.
   a. a cube — **≈ 36.5 in²**
   b. a sphere — **≈ 29.4 in²**
   c. a right cone with height 3.5 in. — **≈ 38.6 in²**
   d. a box with a square face 1.5 in. by 1.5 in. — **44.5 in²**
   e. a right cylinder with diameter 3.5 in. — **≈ 36.4 in²**

8. a. Which of the containers in Question 7 has the least surface area? — **sphere**
   b. Which container would you choose for the ice cream? Why?
   Sample: Cylinder; it stacks easily, is easily labeled, has small surface area, can be scooped from efficiently.

9. After completing a big project, a jewelry designer has enough gold plating left to cover a surface area of 35 mm² with a particular thickness of gold.
   a. What is the shape of the object with the greatest volume that could be plated? — **sphere**
   b. What is the volume of the shape in Part a? — **≈ 19.5 mm³**
   c. What would be the volume of the largest cube possible that could be plated with gold? — **≈ 14.1 mm³**
   d. Why might a jeweler be interested in the volume of the object to be plated?
   Sample: The volume determines worth.

230